Global Platform Work

Work and Everyday Life

Ethnographic Studies on Work Cultures

Series of the Commission "Working Cultures" in the Deutsche Gesellschaft für Empirische Kulturwissenschaft (German Society for European Ethnology and Folklore)

Edited by Irene Götz, Gertraud Koch, Klaus Schönberger and Manfred Seifert

Volume 25

Anna Oechslen works as a research associate at the Leibniz Institute for Spatial Social Research in Erkner. She holds a PhD in cultural anthropology from the University of Hamburg.

Anna Oechslen

Global Platform Work

Negotiating Relations in a Translocal Assemblage

Campus Verlag
Frankfurt/New York

This book has been published open-access with financial support from the open access publication fund of the Leibniz Association and the Leibniz Institute for Research on Society and Space.

Revised version of the dissertation "Global Platform Work. Negotiating Relations in a Translocal Assemblage", submitted at the University of Hamburg in 2022.

The work, including all its parts, is subject to copyright protection. The text of this publication is published under the "Creative Commons Attribution 4.0 International" (CC BY 4.0) licence.
The full licence text can be found at:
https://creativecommons.org/licenses/by/4.0/deed.en

Any use that exceeds the scope of the CC BY 4.0 licence is not permitted without the publisher's consent.
The images and other third-party material contained in this work are also subject to the aforementioned Creative Commons licence, unless otherwise stated under references / illustration index. Insofar as the material in question is not subject to the aforementioned Creative Commons licence and the usage in question is not permitted under statutory provisions, the consent of the respective rightsholder must be obtained.

ISBN 978-3-593-51807-7 Print
ISBN 978-3-593-45567-9 E-Book (PDF)
DOI 10.12907/978-3-593-45567-9

Copyright © 2023 Campus Verlag GmbH, Frankfurt/Main
Cover design: Campus Verlag GmbH, Frankfurt/Main
Typesetting: le-tex xerif, Typesetting-Font: Alegreya

Printed in the United States of America

www.campus.de
www.press.uchicago.edu

Contents

1. Introduction 7
   1.1 Background and context 8
   1.2 Research problem 11
   1.3 Research questions 14
   1.4 Conceptual framework: Assembling volatile connections 16
   1.5 Methodology 17
   1.6 Argument and structure of the dissertation 18
2. Literature Review: Lines of Transformation in the Gig Economy ... 21
   2.1 Overview: Dimensions of platform work 22
   2.2 Online platforms and the transformation of work 24
   2.3 Gaps and blind spots in the literature on platform work 37
3. Conceptual Framework: Work as Practices of Assembling 41
   3.1 De-centring economic productivity: Work beyond paid employment 41
   3.2 Platform-mediated work from a global assemblage perspective 51
   3.3 Working definition of practices of assembling 56
4. Research Approach and Methodological Perspectives 59
   4.1 Co-construction of research, researcher, and field 59
   4.2 The lens of digital ethnography 61
   4.3 Research process 62
   4.4 Concluding reflections on methodology 77

5. Negotiating Value 81
   5.1 What is the value of a logo? Negotiating fair rates 83
   5.2 Investing in subjective value: Trade-offs and long shots 89
   5.3 Process matters: Being valued as a creative professional 98
   5.4 Synthesis: Heterarchical negotiations of value in platform work 101

6. Managing Emotions 105
   6.1 Between thrill and frustration: Managing one's own emotions . 106
   6.2 Emotional relations 112
   6.3 "Finding you a designer you'll love": How platforms mediate emotions 123
   6.4 Synthesis: Limited knowledge and volatile trust 128

7. Aligning Relations 133
   7.1 Assembling the life-work continuum 134
   7.2 Everyday practices of aligning relations in platform work 145
   7.3 Synthesis: Ambiguous alignment 157

8. Synthesis: Negotiating Relations – Assembling Global Platform Work 163
   8.1 Summary of findings and answers to research questions 163
   8.2 Practices of assembling 168
   8.3 Work in a volatile, complex, and opaque environment 180

9. Conclusion 183
   9.1 Main contributions 184
   9.2 Significance and implications 187
   9.3 Limitations and directions for further research 189

List of Figures 191

Works Cited 193

Acknowledgements 203

1. Introduction

This study seeks to explore and theorise remote gig workers' everyday work practices of making and sustaining global connections mediated by online platforms. By shedding light on an aspect of work that is usually unpaid and often overlooked, the insights generated from this study are anticipated to contribute to debates about how work can be organised, managed, and allocated more fairly. Moreover, with the notion of 'practices of assembling', concepts of work are extended to better reflect everyday experiences of work in the gig economy. The study focuses on everyday practices by freelance designers based in India, who connect to overseas clients via online platforms. With online observations, in-depth semi-structured interviews, and digital photo diaries, I compiled key elements of a global assemblage of platform work and related them to each other.

This chapter begins with a short vignette of how Ankit,[1] one of the research participants of the study, organises his everyday work. This is followed by an outline of transformations in the world of work brought about by the growing influence of online platforms, and prevalent academic perspectives on platform work. Building on this, I present the conceptual framework, the purpose of the study, and the research questions guiding analysis. Subsequently, the research design and methodology are outlined. The chapter concludes with an outline of how the thesis is structured.

---

[1] All research participants' names have been pseudonymised to ensure the protection of their personal data.

1.1 Background and context

Ankit usually starts his workday in the early afternoon, Indian Standard Time. Most of his clients are based in the US or Europe, so it is still night or early morning for them when he sits down at his desk. He lives in Pune, a university town in India, not very far from Mumbai but not exactly in the centre of the creative industries, either. At the time of our interview in March 2020, he works as a freelance graphic designer, combining local jobs, which he gets mainly through recommendations, with remote gigs mediated by the online freelance platform 99designs.

On 99designs, he regularly participates in design contests like this one:[2] Manuela Altenhagen, a coach for personal development based in Germany, wants a new logo for her business, which should include her name and her slogan, "personal coach with heart". On the website, she provides a brief description of her business in German and English, using keywords like inner satisfaction, recognising one's strengths, and achieving harmony. Moreover, she has selected colours for designers to choose from and located the design she is envisioning with sliders along the lines of several pre-set categories, between classic and modern, grown-up and youthful, feminine and masculine, playful and sophisticated, economic and luxurious, geometric and organic, and between abstract and specific. In addition, she has attached a pdf document with exemplary designs that transport her ideas, including the font she likes, and specified that the logo should contain a heart to reflect her slogan.

What is more, Ankit can see what files he is supposed to deliver if he wins the contest and how much the winner will be paid: 190 US dollars, in this case, for a bronze contest. If Ankit decides to participate, he creates a logo to match Manuela's brief and hopes to hit the nerve of what she was looking for. With the information he gets from a contest brief, he often finds it challenging to grasp a client's vision – quite often, he finds that the information only equips him for "making a design based on an educated guess of what they would like" (Interview with Ankit, 01–03-20). If Ankit manages to win the contest, he will hand over the design that he has created in the file formats that were specified in the brief and sign the rights to the design over to Manuela Altenhagen. Afterwards, she will have five days to review his design

---

2 This fictional contest brief is based on an aggregation of different contest briefs; names and details have been altered to ensure anonymity.

and request minor changes until the payment is released to Ankit. If someone else's design is chosen, Ankit will not earn any money for the design that he has created.

Ankit originally studied animation, but he found that the Indian animation scene did not offer him many job opportunities. As an alternative source of income, he transitioned to graphic design, starting with small jobs for friends. Quite early on, he started using online platforms to get design jobs, attracted by ads he saw online and recommendations from friends. When he started venturing into platform work, he tried out different platforms, struggling to win any competitions at first as a young and rather inexperienced designer. By taking part in different contests, he gradually found out how to create designs that appeal to clients, and he took breaks in between to study design principles in depth via online courses and lectures that he found on YouTube. Now, he predominantly uses 99designs and he has advanced to the level of a platinum designer there. Like all designers who register on the platform, he had to verify his identity first by uploading his ID and started as an entry-level designer. This means that he could only participate in a limited number of contests in the beginning, and only bronze briefs like Manuela's were open to him. After around a month, he contacted the 99designs team to ask for his designs to be reviewed and proceeded to the next level after this. Over the course of a year, he made his way up to the highest level, platinum designer, which allows him to participate in all briefs from bronze to platinum. While bronze briefs start at roughly 200 US dollars, he can get up to 1400 US dollars for winning a platinum contest. The design levels are not necessarily a measure of the complexity of a task but rather reflect the stratification of designers: if a client submits a platinum-level brief, 99designs promises them submissions from their best designers.

Having access to all levels of design briefs means that Ankit can earn much more money on 99designs, of course, but it also makes his work there more complex. When he chooses which one of the many contests to participate in, he weighs the risks and rewards associated with each design level: if he chooses a lower-paying brief, his chances of winning are quite good, but he also will not be paid very much for his design. If he chooses a platinum brief, by contrast, he can earn a lot of money, but competition is fierce and his risk of losing and thus having worked in vain is high. To mitigate this risk and to make the decision on a brief a bit less complex, he has created a structure for himself where he switches between levels of briefs daily: he looks only at silver briefs on Monday, at gold briefs on Tuesday, and at platinum briefs on Wednesday, for example. This way, he spreads the risk and reduces the complexity of briefs on offer to some extent. He worries that if he did not do this, he may spend the whole day getting lost in different opportunities, never getting to the point of deciding which brief to apply for: "because, see, there are like a thousand briefs on 99designs and it's really hard to go through all of them, obviously, because there are a thousand briefs and, me personally, just my personality, I'm quite indecisive" (Interview with Ankit, 01–03-20). Once he has chosen what briefs he wants to work on during the day, he tries to finish them as efficiently as possible – as he puts it: "online, I have to dish out designs pretty fast, and I cannot spend a lot of time designing online, because, as I said, it can get rejected instantly, so, I have to just give them the gist of the design" (Interview with Ankit, 01–03-20). This phase of creating designs for design contests varies – sometimes, he gets stuck on a brief for the entire day, other times, he completes two or three in an afternoon if he does not have any local jobs to complete. Afterwards, he usually goes out to meet friends for a couple of hours and often fits in another shift after midnight until about 3 or 4 am to interact with clients who are online or to incorporate feedback that he got in the meantime.

Just like his remote clients, I have never met Ankit in person. I found his account through the "Indian designers" subgroup of the 99designs designers' forum. Later, I found out that he is mainly active there to catch the 99designs team's attention, hoping to be featured on their website and thus to increase his chances to be approached by prospective clients to work together without going through a design contest first. We talked on Skype in early March 2020, about two weeks before face-to-face interviews became a thing of the past for the remainder of my thesis due to the outbreak of the COVID-19 pandemic. At that time, the medium of communication was more a matter of convenience, to bridge the roughly 850 kilometres between Bengaluru, where I was based during my field stay, and Pune, where he lives and works. As an active user of the online platform 99designs, Ankit is one of millions of workers in the rapidly growing global gig economy.

Online platforms have come to mediate a wide range of different jobs, from location-based services, such as driving a taxi or delivering meals, to web-based services, including graphic design or translation but also medical consultations, for example (cf. ILO, 2021, p. 43). As the vignette above illustrates, continuously forming new work connections, navigating these multiple connections, and interacting with the mechanisms of the online platform, takes a lot of work. Gig workers who connect to clients remotely through online platforms spend a lot of time and effort organising their work and preparing the ground for gigs – according to an ILO report, "[f]or every hour of paid tasks, workers spend about 23 minutes on freelance platforms and 20 minutes on microtask platforms doing unpaid work" (ILO, 2021, p. 166), such as searching for work, setting up and curating one's profile. Although they make up such a substantial portion of workers' time, these practices are usually unpaid and not counted within the category of work. In this thesis, I will focus primarily on practices of making and sustaining connections in an uncertain environment. I will draw on prevalent research perspectives on platform work to outline how the growing influence of online platforms on the organisation, allocation, and management of work is transforming the world of work.

1.2 Research problem

First, the gig economy organises work as loose and short-term relations, thus making workers' everyday practices very volatile. Most gig platforms have a drastic oversupply of workers: out of the 42781 freelancers registered on 99designs in September 2020, for example, only 37 percent had completed at least one project, and only 10 percent had completed more than ten. On Guru, another online web-based freelance platform, only 0.5 percent of over a million registered workers had earned more than one US dollar (ILO, 2021, p. 50). In the academic literature on the gig economy, the lack of stability and the shift of risk to workers is frequently associated with increasing precarity (cf. e.g. Kalleberg & Vallas, 2018; Sutherland et al., 2020; Wood & Lehdonvirta, 2021b).

Second, online platforms manage and mediate work processes. Technological processes are closely intertwined with economic interests here: the affordances and constraints, that is, the range of possible uses, that online platforms provide are based on their respective business models (van Dijck et al., 2018). In the literature on platform work, authors have come to different conclusions about the degree to which online platforms can control workers – while some define gig work by the absence of an employer (Friedman, 2014), others find that online platforms play an important role in structuring work processes with technological features (e.g. Aneesh, 2009) or rule sets (e.g. Jarrahi et al., 2020).

Third, work relations are spatially reconfigured by the rise of platform work, prompting Graham and Anwar (2019) to proclaim the emergence of a "planetary labour market" enabled by digital technologies. Unlike the classic business process outsourcing (BPO) industry, online platforms outsource jobs and services without a mediating formal organisation (Graham, Hjorth, & Lehdonvirta, 2017, p. 137), and work is spread globally in more dispersed ways. However, work relations in the remote gig economy are still predominantly formed between clients from high-income countries and workers from low-income countries (ILO, 2021, p. 53), and workers' location affects what they earn for a gig on average (Beerepoot & Lambregts, 2015), as well as whether clients will trust them with tasks that require special skills (Gerber & Krzywdzinski, 2019, p. 37). That is, not only technology affects the spatial reconfiguration of work through online platforms, but also various social, cultural, and economic factors. For workers, the planetary labour market also increases complexity and competition, as they sort through an almost unsurmountable number of briefs, hoping to be selected from a global crowd of workers. While the academic literature has made important contributions to understanding global platform work, it also misses some perspectives, which I will outline below.

First, while the literature on work experiences in the gig economy is growing, there is still a stronger focus on work regimes than on everyday practices and workers' perceptions. Against this backdrop, Gandini (2019) proposes "not to overstate the relevance of employment regimes [and instead] to expand our interest to these workers' experiences" (Gandini, 2019, p. 1052). What is more, online platforms as novel actors in work constellations call for a framework that leaves space for how different actors' roles are negotiated. Categorising work in a dichotomy between flexibility and stability misses important nuances of workers' practices and experiences (cf. Ivancheva & Keating, 2020). As Wittel (2004) argues, especially political economy approaches to digital labour reduce labour to an abstract category, neglecting subjective experiences and workers' agency (p. 17).

Second, existing approaches to platform work often neglect the heterogeneity and ambiguity of platform workers' experiences. When platform work is studied, especially in terms of its precarity, authors usually – implicitly or explicitly – take a Fordist model of standard employment, that is, full-time permanent employment (cf. ILO, 2016, p. 11), as a point of reference. Within this framework, the loose connections of gig work are classified as a departure from stable employment. However, this perspective neglects that standard employment relationships have historically and geographically been an exception rather than the norm (Neilson & Rossiter, 2008). Considering the global spread of work connections through platform work, it is important to depart from perspectives that only reflect the experiences of a small proportion of those who perform platform work. While a framework of exploitation by platform capitalism provides important insights into working conditions, it often leaves little space for the heterogeneity and ambiguity of workers' experiences, as well as their agency. Thus, categorising work in a dichotomy between flexibility and stability misses important nuances of workers' practices and experiences (cf. Ivancheva & Keating, 2020).

Third, a narrow view of work is often applied when studying platform work, focusing on activities that are considered directly economically productive. Connecting this point to the one made above, the unpaid work that is necessary to enable the standard employment relationship is often overlooked. Discourses on de-limitation of work (Gerber & Krzywdzinski, 2019; Gregg, 2011) or subjectification (Huber, 2013; Krohn, 2013), too, suppose a pre-existing clear distinction between work and non-work that is only recently eroding. As a result, practices beyond paid employment are often neglected within these perspectives. This includes care work, for example, but also the unpaid work done by platform workers, which I have described above. To grasp the scope of unpaid work done by gig workers to navigate the uncertain work environment of the platform, concepts of work that extend beyond the job descriptions on the platform are necessary. Moreover, across different perspectives, workers' integration in interdependent relationships is regularly overlooked (Ivancheva & Keating, 2020, p. 274).

As I have outlined above, online platforms contribute to a transformation of how work is organised, managed, and allocated. This development is reflected in a transformation of work practices: as actors in a work environment that is characterised by loose and short-term work connections, online platforms steering work processes, and an unevenly global labour market, remote freelancers perform a great deal of unpaid work to prepare the ground for paid gigs. While the literature on working conditions in the gig economy is growing, little is known yet about the everyday work practices of navigating this uncertain work environment. The emergence of these work practices, moreover, poses the question of how work can be conceptualised in a way that reflects the ambiguities and the heterogeneity of gig workers' experiences, and that accounts for the multiple dimensions of work beyond paid labour.

1.3 Research questions

To address the research problem outlined above, this study seeks to explore and theorise remote gig workers' everyday work practices as making and sustaining global connections mediated by online platforms. By approaching work from a relational angle, I aim to centre practices and experiences, transcend categories of paid or unpaid work, and foreground the interdependence of actors. The study focuses on the elements of remote platform work that are directly connected to managing the uncertain work environment, largely leaving further aspects of work in the gig economy aside. It can thus not provide a full picture of work but aims to contribute one element to a spectrum of work practices.

The research questions guiding this study start from the assumption that while online platforms provide the technological infrastructure to make global connections, it takes work to put these connections into practice and to stay connected over time. How gig workers relate to other human and nonhuman actors is influenced by technology, but also by explicit and implicit rules of conduct, by power asymmetries, and by their implication in interdependent relationships beyond platform work. Accordingly, throughout the analysis chapters, I will explore the work of making and sustaining connections. Reflecting the notion of a "life-work continuum" (Ivancheva & Keating, 2020), both relationships with clients and with platforms as nonhuman actors, and relationships beyond the realm of platform work are included in this exploration. Approaching this combination of elements from the perspective of everyday work practices, the overarching question of the study is:

How can platform work be conceptualised through the lens of making and sustaining connections?

The exploration of gig workers' practices of making and sustaining connections is embedded in the three critical lines of transformation that I have outlined above: the volatility of the gig economy, the management of work processes by online platforms, and the global reach of work connections. The research questions reflect these aspects:

How do gig workers navigate the volatility of work relations?

This question is directed at the freelancers' everyday work practices. It guides the exploration of how freelancers organise their work, as well as the strategies they develop to deal with the uncertainty of their work environment. Do they try to introduce stability, or do they embrace the flexibility of their work? How do they try to stand out to prospective clients, and what resources do they mobilise to be successful? This set of sub-questions addresses the heterogeneous experiences of platform work.

How do online platforms mediate work practices?

This question connects freelancers' work practices to their interaction with the online platforms that they use. It directs the exploration of platform work at how workers relate to the technological infrastructure of online platforms, as well as how they negotiate the rules set up by them. Through this guiding question, I aim to incorporate the ambiguities of worker agency and platform control into the analysis.

How do remote freelancers align global work relations with local, situated practices?

This final sub-question points to practices of relating to clients from different cultural and geographical backgrounds. I aim to explore the friction between the global form of platform work and situated work practices by asking how workers anticipate cultural stereotypes in the way they present themselves, as well as how they work on aligning different scales.

The three themes reflected in the research questions are interrelated and jointly contribute to the exploration of making and sustaining connections in remote gig work.

1.4 Conceptual framework: Assembling volatile connections

Taking the premise that work is a socially constructed category as a starting point, the conceptual background of this study is based on research approaches that critically examine and expand what counts as work, going beyond paid labour or occupation. As Star and Strauss (1999) argue, work as a category is not self-evident, but depends on how a situation is defined – and who has the power to define it. First, from an STS perspective, this includes invisible background work associated with technology (Star & Strauss, 1999; Vertesi, 2014). Second, I connect my research to feminist perspectives on work. Feminist scholars have sought to shed light on unpaid work, frequently performed by women, such as care work, by framing reproductive labour as work in its own right (cf. Mackenzie & Rose, 1983). Moreover, work has been expanded to an emotional (Hochschild, [1983] 2012) and affective (Hardt, 1999) domain. Third, taking it one step further from adding new aspects to a nevertheless relatively stable category of work, more recent perspectives propose to fundamentally rethink work and the productive domain to account for the embeddedness of economic actors in interdependent relationships (cf. Ivancheva & Keating, 2020).

In addition, I use the term "global assemblage" (Ong & Collier, 2005) as a sensitising concept to construct the field of research. The ontology of assemblage reflects the tension between the technological promise of a global labour market and the actual situated work practices and lived experiences of graphic designers using gig work platforms in India. The practices that constitute the field of platform work are constantly in flux and both the elements and how they relate to each other keep changing. As the phenomenon I study is highly dynamic, it cannot be grasped by ideas of a static and bounded field. I use the term volatility here to reflect how loose the connections that gig workers make are: volatility implies that there is no stable structure as an endpoint for gig workers. Instead, they continuously work on making and sustaining connections, thus contributing to the assemblage of platform work.

While the feminist perspectives outlined above provide the foundation for a broad understanding of work, including both paid and unpaid practices, and acknowledging their interdependence, the assemblage perspective provides a framework to grasp the work of making and sustaining connections. As Li (2007) argues, "[a]ssemblage flags agency, the hard work required to draw heterogeneous elements together, forge connections between them and sustain these connections in the face of tension" (p. 264). Connecting the deconstruction of the category of work with the assemblage concept, I tentatively frame work as the continuous effort of making and sustaining connections. This perspective also informs the research design of this study. Rather than building up a coherent image of work from constitutive elements, I feather out different practices and relate them to each other, focusing on the building process instead of its result.

1.5 Methodology

To address the research questions posed above, I have chosen a "non-digital-centric approach to the digital" (Pink et al., 2016, p. 7), that is, I have studied digital media through the everyday practices of their use (cf. also Hine, 2015, pp. 28–29). I have focused my research on the experiences of graphic designers in India: by choosing a creative type of work that requires specialised skills, I anticipated a higher level of personal interaction and a stronger need to stand out as the best one for a job than for more routine tasks. India as a geographical frame was chosen as one of the countries with the largest populations of freelancers on online platforms (ILO, 2021, p. 53). I switched between sampling, collecting, and analysing material in an iterative process, using coding techniques based on Grounded Theory (Strauss & Corbin, 2003).

At the beginning of the research process, I generated an overview of different online platforms from the literature and through online research. From the large field of different online platforms, I selected four for a closer investigation through theoretical sampling: 99designs, Upwork, Talenthouse, and Fiverr. I conducted online walkthroughs of these platforms to establish their "environment of expected use" (Light et al., 2017), and observed debates in the online forums that are part of the platforms (cf. Hine, 2015, pp. 157–180). Based on this exploration of the platform-mediated work environment, I conducted semi-structured interviews with creative professionals during a field stay in Bengaluru in February and March 2020. As the COVID-19 pandemic brought about travel and contact restrictions shortly after my field stay had started, the research design had to be adjusted: instead of shadowing remote freelancers at their places of work, I conducted follow-up interviews after a first round of selective and axial coding (Strauss & Corbin, 2003) to report back and to refine my hypotheses. To fill in the gaps in my material, I created photo prompts and short questionnaires, based on which research participants documented and reflected on their everyday work practices for seven days.

1.6 Argument and structure of the dissertation

The rationale of this study emanates from the need for an understanding of work that reflects the ambiguities and heterogeneity of gig workers' experiences, and that accounts for the multiple dimensions of work beyond paid employment. It starts from the observation that online platforms are transforming the world of work, leading to a complex, volatile, and dynamic work environment. Remote gig work is characterized by loose and short-term work connections on a global scale, and platforms have emerged as novel actors in work constellations. Navigating this work environment brings about work practices that current concepts of work cannot fully grasp. Using standard employment relationships as a reference and neglecting workers' integration in interdependent relationships, they capture only a part of the activities of platform work, while others remain not only unpaid but also unnoticed. By applying a global assemblage perspective to platform work, the focus of this thesis is directed at workers' everyday practices of making and sustaining connections, which I refer to as practices of assembling in this study. This focus on relational practices allows for an exploration beyond a dichotomy between flexibility and stability, incorporating affective relationships within and beyond platform work, as well as multiple spatial scales.

Throughout the study, different dimensions of practices of assembling are explored and related to each other, including affective dimensions, negotiations over value, and relationships beyond platform work. From this kaleidoscope of practices, I distil four characteristic features of practices of assembling: guessing and anticipating, adapting to constant change, producing relatable selves, and creating temporary alignment. These features reflect how freelancers interact with the platform-mediated work environment by continuously negotiating uncertain relations. From this vantage point, I compare my findings about work in an assemblage to existing accounts of work, focusing on flexibility and precarity, worker agency, and the subjectification of workers.

The results of this study are significant on several levels: First, by amplifying stories of everyday work experiences in the gig economy, unpaid and largely invisible aspects of gig work are elucidated. Shedding light on mostly invisible and unpaid aspects of work can contribute to the articulation of demands for fair working conditions. Second, the lens of global assemblages provides a perspective on work beyond dichotomies between flexibility and stability, or work and non-work. This allows for a more nuanced classification of what platform work entails. Understanding the everyday negotiations of gig workers' lives may "begin a longer conversation about the better workplaces we might imagine for the future" (Gregg, 2011, p. 18). This is relevant for various actors: gig workers, workers' initiatives and unions, platform operators, as well as policymakers seeking to adjust regulatory frameworks to changing work environments. Third, this study seeks to contribute to academic debates on the transformation of work in digitally mediated environments from a feminist perspective, expanding the notion of work to incorporate relationships and their various dimensions. The insights generated on practices of assembling can inform perspectives on work beyond remote platform work by providing a relational framework.

The study is organised as follows: In Chapter 2, I present a focused review of the literature on working conditions in the gig economy. I provide an overview of the research on platform work and outline the literature along three lines of transformation: volatile work connections in the gig economy, platforms as novel actors in work constellations, and spatial figurations of platform work. Based on this, I further elaborate on the gaps in the literature. In Chapter 3, I lay out the conceptual framework of this study. First, I outline research perspectives that have aimed to expand and deconstruct the category of work by foregrounding a variety of practices beyond economic productivity. Second, I elucidate the assemblage perspective that I use to construct the field. Building on these two elements, I develop a tentative understanding of work as practices of assembling. In Chapter 4, I present my methodology and reflect on the research process. I locate my study within a methodology of digital ethnography and outline the tools from Grounded Theory that I have used. Moreover, I describe how I iteratively gathered and analysed material through online analysis, interviews, and digital photo diaries. Finally, I reflect on instances of friction in the research process and ethical implications.

Subsequently, I present my findings, organised along three sets of practices. In Chapter 5, I explore how platform workers continuously negotiate the value of their work, how the value of their work is entangled with their value as workers, and how the process of negotiation is framed and structured by online platforms. In Chapter 6, I show how platform workers manage both their own and their clients' emotions, and how online platforms mediate emotions. In Chapter 7, I look beyond the realm of platform work to explore how remote freelancers align platform work with further elements of their lives. I describe how they are integrated into interdependent relationships and point out the specific challenges that platform work brings about for integrating it with life beyond the platform. In Chapter 8, I summarise my findings and synthesise them into four characteristic practices of assembling, which reflect the complexity, volatility, and opacity of the platform-mediated work environment. Finally, in Chapter 9, I point toward the contribution that this study makes to the study of work, as well as its significance and implications. Moreover, I reflect on the limitations of the study and ways in which further research can build on it.

2. Literature Review: Lines of Transformation in the Gig Economy

As I have elaborated in Chapter 1, this study seeks to explore and theorise remote gig workers' everyday work practices of making and sustaining global connections mediated by online platforms. The literature review provides a backdrop to the focus of the study on the invisible and unpaid work of organising one's everyday practices as a remote platform worker and the research gap that I am going to address with it. The literature review was developed throughout the study alongside an iterative process of collecting and analysing material. After an initial overview of the existing body of work to focus my research interest, I continuously used literature to probe preliminary hypotheses, compare and contrast, and guide theoretical sampling (cf. Strauss & Corbin, 2003). Research on platform work is developing as dynamically as the field itself: while academic literature on the gig economy was quite scarce a few years back, with grey literature or business advice dominating, research in this field has grown tremendously since and now includes more detailed and critical investigations. I focus on studies on the gig economy from social sciences and humanities in this literature review, leaving out the equally growing literature that deals with legal questions, such as the categorisation of gig workers.

In the first part of the chapter, I provide an overview of the gig economy and the range of work practices covered by the term. Against this backdrop, I then outline three central themes of the research on the gig economy: the organisation of work in the form of gigs, the management of work processes by online platforms, and the globally dispersed work relations of remote platform work. Based on a synthesis of this review, I finally point out the gaps in the literature on platform work that I aim to address with this study.

2.1 Overview: Dimensions of platform work

Broadly defined, online platforms are "a programmable digital architecture designed to organize interactions between users" (van Dijck et al., 2018, p. 4). The platform business model of creating two- or multi-sided markets to bring together diverse actors predates online platforms: Rochet and Tirole (2003) have used the example of shopping malls connecting retailers and consumers to illustrate how platforms operate. Over the past years, online platforms have come to play an important role in a broad range of different activities, causing scholars to proclaim the emergence of a "platform economy" (Kenney & Zysman, 2016, p. 61), "platform capitalism" (Langley & Leyshon, 2017; Srnicek, 2017), or "platform society" (van Dijck et al., 2018).[1] In this study, I focus on a specific form of social interaction: work. When I write about platform work here, I refer specifically to platform-mediated gig work, that is, workers connecting to clients via online platforms to perform single, clearly delineated tasks. I exclude both the work done by platform employees and the work of developing the technological infrastructure of online platforms.[2]

Woodcock and Graham (2020, pp. 42–45) divide the sections of the gig economy along spatial and temporal lines: They differentiate, first, between high or low degrees of geographic 'stickiness', that is, whether a job can be performed remotely. They refer to work that is bound to a specific location as 'geographically tethered work' and work that can be done remotely as 'cloudwork'.[3] Second, they differentiate between jobs by their temporality, leading to four types of work: they distinguish 'geographically tethered platform work', such as driving for Uber, performing domestic work via Helpling, or delivering food via Deliveroo, from traditional waged employment by temporality: while traditional employment would usually last over a longer time, one gig usually lasts a few hours at most. In the realm of cloudwork, the authors distinguish between the categories of microwork

---

[1] For a more detailed account of the development of online platforms, see Ibert et al. (2022, pp. 566–568).
[2] Gray and Suri (2019) argue that a lot of the developments attributed to automation and AI are based on 'ghost work', such as content moderation or transcription. There are some overlaps with platform-mediated work, but the background work of the digital economy goes beyond the scope of this thesis.
[3] Other authors have used 'crowdwork' to refer to remote platform work (e.g. Krzywdzinski and Gerber (2021); Wallis (2021)).

and online freelancing.[4] Microwork is often done directly via the interface of platforms such as Amazon Mechanical Turk, and work is often divided into minuscule tasks that may last only a few seconds. Online freelancing, by contrast, involves more complex tasks, which are usually completed outside the platform. Here, online platforms serve to connect workers and clients, often with both parties being able to bid and negotiate over rates.

The India-based graphic designers at the centre of interest in this study, who are connecting to worldwide clients via different online platforms, such as Upwork or 99designs, fall into the category of online freelancing. Ticona et al. (2018) refer to platforms mediating online freelance work as 'marketplace platforms' and argue that as these platforms manage and control the work process less, self-branding is much more important and standing out to clients as the best candidate for a job plays a bigger role. This differentiation is an important backdrop for the literature on platform work or the gig economy.[5] While there are some general characteristics of platform- mediated work, which will be outlined in more detail below, different forms of platform work also entail vastly different work experiences. So far, location-based platform work has attracted a large proportion of scholarly attention, especially studies on delivery riders (e.g. Barratt et al., 2020; Goods et al., 2019; Heiland, 2021; Tassinari & Maccarrone, 2020; Veen et al., 2020) or taxi services (e.g. Chan, 2019; Rosenblat & Stark, 2016; Wells et al., 2021; Zwick, 2018). While studies on remote platform work were originally focused on microwork, especially on Amazon Mechanical Turk (e.g. Bucher & Fieseler, 2017; Irani, 2013, 2015), there is now also a growing number of studies on freelance platforms (e.g. Anwar & Graham, 2021; D'Cruz & Noronha, 2016; Shevchuk et al., 2021; Sutherland et al., 2020). However, although design tasks make up a substantial portion of remote freelance work, studies specif-

---

4 Gerber and Krzywdzinski (2019) differentiate platform work along similar lines between micro and macro tasks.
5 In this study, I use the term 'platform work' to incorporate the organisation in the form of gigs and the management of work by digital platforms. I use 'gig work' in instances where I want to stress that a practice is specifically impacted by the volatility of work connections. Moreover, I follow the ILO (2021) in the use of the terms 'location-based platforms' and 'online web-based platforms' for geographically sticky and remote work, respectively. I focus on remote platform work in this study – in the analysis, I will only mention it specifically to highlight how the remoteness is relevant to the situation and otherwise just speak of platform work. The platform workers whom I have interviewed for this study predominantly referred to themselves as 'freelancers'. To reflect this, I also frequently use this term to refer to them in the analysis section.

ically on creative work or design are still scarce (with a few notable exceptions, see e.g. Demirel et al., 2021).

2.2 Online platforms and the transformation of work

After having outlined the dimensions of the gig economy, as a next step, I will review the academic literature on platform work along three themes: First, I outline how the literature on the gig economy frames volatile work connections. Second, I focus on the literature on how online platforms control work processes. Third, I outline how spatial constellations of platform work have been viewed in the literature so far. I argue that these three aspects of platform work are interconnected and bring about specific experiences and practices.

2.2.1 Freedom or precarity? Volatile work connections in the gig economy

One line of transformation regarding platform work that has received ample scholarly attention is the change of working conditions brought about by the organisation of work as gigs, that is, single, clearly delineated tasks (Friedman, 2014). Compared to a standard employment relationship, gig work is characterised by loose and short-term connections. While the high degree of flexibility of these work constellations is uncontested, its implications for working conditions and experiences are subject to controversial debates. Depending on research focus and perspective, scholars have come to different conclusions on the question of whether this entails freedom, precarity – or both. In the following subchapter, I will outline the central arguments in this debate.

Kalleberg and Vallas (2018) define precarious work as "work that is *uncertain, unstable,* and *insecure* and in which *employees bear the risks* of work (as opposed to businesses or the government) and *receive limited social benefits and statutory protections*" (p. 1). Precarity, then, implies a combination of volatile connections with vulnerability. To them, the digitalisation of work and its increasing organisation through online platforms are drivers of precarity (Kalleberg & Vallas, 2018, p. 5). Further authors researching the platform economy conclude that gig work is precarious, too, also arguing that risk is shifted to workers (Friedman, 2014; Ravenelle, 2019) and that workers often do not know whether they will have an income the next day (Altenried, 2021b, pp. 61–62). Moreover, they contend that workers have poor bargaining power and little chance to develop their skills on the job (Graham, Hjorth, & Lehdonvirta, 2017), that payment is usually low (Scholz, 2017; Wood et al., 2019a), and that working hours are often irregular (Wood et al., 2019a) and hard to predict (Schneider & Harknett, 2019; Wood, 2018). Looking at the implications of these working conditions for work practices and experiences, scholars have found that many platform workers suffer from social isolation, sleep deprivation and exhaustion (Wood et al., 2019a). What is more, workers have to perform additional unpaid work preparing the ground for gigs (Wood et al., 2019b). Adding an emotional dimension to the notion of precarity, Petriglieri et al. (2018) argue that as independent workers are less defined by belonging to an organisation, they face the task of creating and defining their work identities for themselves. This absence of a 'holding space' for their identity brings about emotional tension, as they contend based on a study of independent workers.

The loose and short-term work connections of the gig economy are not exclusively described as precarious: it is especially the promise of independently organising one's work and not answering to an employer, that is, to work with greater flexibility, that motivates many workers to sign up to work on a platform (Altenried, 2021b, p. 63). However, many authors agree that the flexibility of the gig economy benefits employers and platform companies much more than workers. According to Griesbach et al. (2019), for example, freedom often remains an illusion for workers: under constant pressure to make enough money, they are only flexible in theory. In practice, then, many gig workers are constantly available for clients, ready to grasp the next opportunity to get work (Altenried, 2021b, p. 63). What is more, the unpredictability of gig work comes with challenges for connecting paid work and care (Warren, 2021). Moreover, gig workers' ability to control their own work time is met with structural and cognitive-cultural constraints (Lehdonvirta, 2018) and control mechanisms put in place by online platforms further reduce workers' opportunities to flexibly manage their work time (Wood et al., 2019a).

While most authors who study work in the platform economy find that there is precarity in gig work, they differentiate this diagnosis to varying degrees and along the lines of different dimensions. Griesbach et al. (2019) find that while the food delivery riders at the centre of their study do work under precarious circumstances by standards of employment, their perspectives are much more ambivalent and also leave space for notions of freedom and independence. Similarly, Dunn (2020) finds that how working conditions are perceived differs between workers, as they approach platforms with different motivations, characteristics, and intentions. Based on similarly diverse work experiences reported to them, Myhill et al. (2021) argue that existing categories to assess what good work entails focus too much on traditional employment and cannot adequately grasp the diverse experiences of gig workers. Moreover, Schor et al. (2020) contend that gig work is not inherently precarious for everyone: their study of work in different location-based platforms finds that experiences of freedom or precarity depend on how platform work is integrated into a constellation of different sources of income. For those who do not depend on an income from the platform as much, platform work can be very flexible, while those who do depend on it experience precarity to a greater degree. Howcroft and Bergvall-Kåreborn (2019) differentiate working conditions and degrees of precarity along the lines of different types of crowdwork, thus contributing to the argument that considering all platform work as precarious would be an oversimplification. According to Sutherland et al. (2020), precarity in platform work is mitigated as workers develop 'gig literacies' over time, learning to use platforms more effectively and reducing their risk of being rejected for jobs.

Against this backdrop, some authors have created models of uncertainty in platform work that seek to grapple with the ambiguities of freedom and precarity. Wood and Lehdonvirta (2021b) take the ambivalence between precarity as a defining feature of platform work and the heterogeneity of workers' experiences as a starting point and find that the ranking and reputation systems of online platforms create a volatile working environment even for experienced gig workers. As they conclude, precarity in the sense of a lack of stability is inherent in platform work despite differences in everyday work practices and experiences. Caza et al. (2022) develop a conceptual framework along the lines of six challenges they have identified to be commonly faced by gig workers: viability, organisational, identity, relational, emotional, and career-path uncertainty. By doing so, they depart from the rather broad and loaded term precarity and replace it with a multi-dimensional understanding of uncertainty. Based on a study on remote gig work in several African countries, Anwar and Graham (2021) discuss flexibility, freedom, precarity, and vulnerability in their research participants' work, concluding that, in fact, all four terms can be applied and help carve out different dimensions. They argue that it is necessary to move beyond a development discourse on freedom and flexibility through platform work in low-income countries and to integrate both: their flexibility as something they value, as well as the vulnerability that comes with it.

Regarding precarisation as an overarching process, authors come to different conclusions about whether platform work is indicative of a larger trend of increasingly precarious working conditions, impacts, or even drives this process. Ruyter and Brown (2019) argue that precarity is not something new at all but rather has been predominant for most of the history of capitalist societies. Kalleberg (2018) embeds platform work within a larger trend of precarisation; similarly, Ravenelle (2019) perceives the shifting of risk and liability to workers as a symptom rather than the cause of the casualisation of labour. Building on Marxian concepts, Joyce (2020), too, argues that work in platform capitalism is not novel, but that platform workers' struggles and resistance can be understood as a continuation of historical worker struggles. While also embedding platform work in a present transformation of global capitalism, Altenried (2021b) argues that digital technology and the new role of data bring about new aspects for the study of precarious platform work. This perspective is shared by Griesbach et al. (2019), who perceive the gig worker as the ideal type of the precariat. Along similar lines, Tassinari and Maccarrone (2020) contend that gig work is a "new frontier of precarious work" (p. 36). The oversupply of labour on digital labour platforms is perceived to exacerbate precarity (Graham, Lehdonvirta, et al., 2017) and further authors argue that labour platforms create precarious working conditions (Dunn, 2020) or increase precarity (Cant, 2020; Sutherland et al., 2020). Taking on an intersectional perspective on exploitation in platform work, van Doorn (2017) embeds platform work within the historical context of exploitation along the lines of gender and race. He argues that inequality is an inbuilt feature of the on-demand economy, further contributing to the gendered and racialised exploitation of low-income workers.

To sum up, the volatility and risk associated with gig work are reflected in working conditions in diverse and sometimes ambivalent ways. Framing work as precarious sometimes glosses over the different dimensions and practices of loose work connections. To study their implications for work experiences in a meaningful way, it is important to be specific rather than producing broad statements about precarity. Paying attention to specific constellations of workers' perceptions, platform features, and contributing structural factors can offer more fine-grained analyses of the volatility of the platform-mediated work environment.

2.2.2 Agency or control? Platforms as novel actors in work constellations

While the focus of the previous subchapter was on how work is organised in the form of gigs and what that entails, this subchapter deals with how online platforms manage work processes. Friedman (2014) entitled his article on gig work in the US "workers without employers", which is true in a legal sense: in most cases, platform workers are not categorised as employees but as independent contractors. Moreover, workers often start platform work with an expectation of disintermediation, that is, of working independently (Gandini & Pais, 2020, p. 232). However, empirical research has established that platforms do manage and control work processes in various ways. Technological processes are closely intertwined with economic interests here: the affordances and constraints, that is, the range of possible uses, that online platforms provide are based on their respective business models (van Dijck et al., 2018). This subchapter, then, is based on the premise that online platforms manage work processes, exploring how they do so and what agency workers have in relation to platforms.

Referring not only to online platforms but more generally to work mediated by technology, Aneesh (2009) has introduced the term "algocratic management". What sets this form of governance apart from a hierarchical or market organisation is that

> "[a]ction is controlled neither by socializing workers into regulatory demands, nor by punishing workers for their failure, but by shaping an environment in which there are only programmed alternatives to performing the work. Thus, work involves a lower focus on the knowledge of regulations and a greater stress on the ability to use a software program" (Aneesh, 2009, p. 356).

In this view, there is relatively little space for negotiation: workers face a range of possibilities for action and can only act within it. While Aneesh based his analysis on the integration of workers in the software industry in a common framework spanning the US and India, online platforms use similar mechanisms to steer work processes, which are mainly referred to as algorithmic management (Krzywdzinski & Gerber, 2021) or algorithmic control (Prassl, 2018; Veen et al., 2020; Wood et al., 2019a). Also stressing the power of digital technologies to manage work processes, Moore (2018) speaks of "neo-Taylorism": she argues that in digitalised work environments, beyond just standardising tasks, workers are increasingly surveilled and quantified. Altenried (2022) applies a similar perspective specifically to online platforms mediating work with 'digital Taylorism'. He argues that the algorithmic architecture of online platforms allows for the integration of distributed and diverse workers in front of their computers or smartphones into standardised labour processes. Huws (2016) attributes a paradigm shift towards what she calls "logged labour" to the increasing importance of online platforms for various work processes:

"Workers are, therefore, 'logged' in several different senses: their work is chopped up into separate tasks just as trees are logged in a lumber yard; they are 'logged' in the sense of being monitored continuously by employers, clients or their intermediaries, and they are 'logged' on in the sense of being required to be connected to the Internet, ready to receive a summons to work at any time" (Huws, 2016, p. 22).

While these approaches provide important insights into aspects of the management of platform work, it is important to differentiate the argument of standardisation when applying it to complex tasks managed via online platforms. The theorisation of how work is managed by online platforms has so far been done overwhelmingly based on studies of microtasks. However, the management of work processes for macro tasks is more complex, less standardised, and requires more of a communication process (Jarrahi et al., 2020, p. 180). Moreover, matching clients and freelancers is more complex in knowledge work (Jarrahi et al., 2020, p. 181). What is more, technological structures are only one of several ways in which online platforms exert control.

Gandini (2019) suggests applying the Marxian concept of labour process theory to studying the role of online platforms in managing work processes, framing them as digital-based points of production. He argues that

"beyond their role of market intermediaries, platforms act as the milieu within which the capital-labour relation is enacted upon workers. Akin to a factory, or an office, the platform represents the place whereby the social processes of production are put under logics of managerialization and work organization within a single, clearly delimited environment" (Gandini, 2019, p. 1045).

Instead of an employer who controls work processes, then, he views platforms as corresponding to a factory, that is, the place where control happens. Altenried (2017, 2022), too, uses the image of a factory referring to platform work, albeit especially focusing on the standardisation of tasks in this respect. Moreover, several authors have taken up labour process theory for empirical studies on platform work: Heiland (2021), for example, investigates the contested production of spaces based on a study of food delivery platforms in Germany, using a framework of labour process theory to elucidate how online platforms control delivery riders' routes. Also using a framework of labour process theory, Veen et al. (2020) contend that online platforms control labour processes in various ways, going beyond algorithmic management, in their study on food delivery workers in Australia. They point out the extensive surveillance enabled by the technological infrastructure, information asymmetries, and opaque performance management as central instruments of control.

Based on an empirical study of Uber drivers' experiences, Rosenblat and Stark (2016), too, stress the important role of information asymmetries in how online platforms control workers. They find that the notion of algorithms and automated decisions is leveraged by the platform to obfuscate its managerial role. Similarly, Shapiro (2018) finds that platforms limit workers' ability to make informed decisions by keeping mechanisms in the dark, further contributing to the argument that the opacity of the platform-mediated work environment limits worker agency. Jarrahi et al. (2020) focus on the online freelancing platform Upwork in their study, also concluding that the platform manages work processes with a variety of functions. Platformic control, which they propose as an alternative to algorithmic control, encompasses a combination of algorithmic decision-making, technological features, and business rules. They identify six functions by which Upwork frames interaction: managing transactions, channelling communication, resolving conflicts, providing information, evaluating performance, and gatekeeping (Jarrahi et al., 2020, p. 169). This combination of features not only goes beyond technological aspects but also leaves more space for negotiations and worker agency: differently from the standardisation of tasks reflected in algorithmic control, platformic control considers both platform mechanisms and the process of negotiating their effects.

This leads to a further distinction of platform control mechanisms: direct or indirect control. Krzywdzinski and Gerber (2021) argue that labour control in crowdwork consists of two main forms: direct, automated control, and indirect control, that is, creating motivation and commitment through gamification. A central mechanism of indirect control, which is present on almost all gig work platforms, is the establishment of rankings and reputation mechanisms, which provide incentives to be continuously active on the platform (Gerber & Krzywdzinski, 2019, p. 29). Gandini (2019), too, argues that online platforms exert control through ranking and reputation mechanisms: he finds that they motivate workers to perform unpaid labour in the hopes of improving their position on the platform. Managing one's online reputation is part of personal branding, that is, curating the image that one portrays via the platform (Gandini & Pais, 2020). Ticona et al. (2018) argue that this practice plays a much more important role in marketplace platforms than in on-demand platforms. However, personal branding also plays a role there, as Chan (2019) finds in his study on Uber drivers who produce YouTube videos giving fellow drivers advice on how to succeed on the platform.

While the arguments outlined above focus on the framework that platforms provide, there is also an increasing number of studies considering the ambiguities of agency and control in everyday work practices of relating to these frameworks. Shapiro (2018) argues that workers do have agency in how they deal with the setup of the platform: he finds that workers reflect on the rationalities behind platform mechanisms and only go along with them as long as they are congruent with their interests. Several authors differentiate between collective and individual agency, stating that while workers can exercise agency on an individual level to some extent, there is hardly any chance for collective action. Veen et al. (2020), for example, find that surveillance, information asymmetries, and opaque performance metrics leave workers with close to no collective agency. Based on similar observations, Barratt et al. (2020) speak of 'entrepreneurial agency', that is, the individualised agency directed toward improving one's situation. This is reflected in workers' interaction with rankings and reputation systems, for example.

Wood and Lehdonvirta (2021a) do find evidence of collective agency by gig workers, which co-exists with their self-perception as self-employed freelancers. They conclude from their study of remote gig workers that platforms create 'subordinated agency': while workers act as entrepreneurs in relation to their clients, platforms' measures of control mean that they are not free agents. Building on the notion of algorithmic control outlined above, Vallas and Schor (2020) argue that online platforms selectively incorporate many features of markets, hierarchies, and networks, thus producing a distinct form of governance. They contend that

"platforms govern economic transactions not by expanding their control over participants but by relinquishing important dimensions of control and delegating them to the other two parties to the exchange. [...] The platform firm retains authority over important functions—the allocation of tasks, collection of data, pricing of services, and of course collection of revenues—but it cedes control over others, such as the specification of work methods, control over work schedules, and the labor of performance evaluation" (Vallas & Schor, 2020, p. 282).

In this context, it is not clear whether the room for manoeuvre that workers have is a sign of their agency or part of the platform's business model. It illustrates, however, that agency and control in platform work are multifaceted and contingent.

To sum up, online platforms manage work processes through a variety of different mechanisms, including but not limited to their technological features. The opacity of platform mechanisms is not simply a by-product of technological mediation, but information asymmetries serve to constrain workers' agency. Overall, there appears to be neither complete control by platforms nor complete worker agency. Instead, agency and control are negotiated in complex relationships between platforms and workers.

2.2.3 Unevenly dispersed: Spatial figurations of platform work

After having outlined prominent strands of research on the organisation and management of platform work, I deal with a third aspect in this subchapter: the reconfiguration of how work is spatially distributed with the emergence of platform work. While the research referred to above spanned location-based as well as remote work, the development outlined here is specific to remote platform work. With online platforms mediating connections, clients can hire someone anywhere in the world with an internet connection to create a logo or website for them, or an anonymous 'crowd' of people in different places can work together on a project that has been divided into minuscule tasks. Platform companies leverage this development to promote platform work as granting unlimited access to jobs and chances for success: the freelance design platform 99designs, for example, proclaims that "design doesn't do borders" and "every designer, from Sydney to Serbia, can be successful on our platform".[6] Research on translocal work connections mediated by online platforms remains relatively scarce, but existing studies suggest that the implications of platform work for access to work and work experiences are much more ambiguous than this proclamation of a compressed space without borders suggests. Platforms do provide opportunities for inclusion in previously more closed-off labour markets, but these labour markets are also stratified and there is discrimination (Graham, Hjorth, & Lehdonvirta, 2017). Below, I will outline central perspectives on how the spatial reconfiguration

---

6 http://99designs.com/about, last checked on 16/05/2022.

of work through online platforms is not only affected by technology but also by various social, cultural, and economic factors. Moreover, I will consider the implications of these factors for work practices.

Work relations being formed across large distances do not constitute a new development brought about by online platforms or even by digitalisation. Altenried et al. (2020), for example, use the term "platform mobilities" to describe how work is spread globally via online platforms. Building on Aneesh's (2006) concept of virtual migration, they argue that translocal work relations mediated by online platforms are a continuation of labour migration – with the difference that workers do not physically move to another country but share a technological infrastructure with their clients.[7] Embedding remote platform work in a history of business process outsourcing (BPO), Graham, Hjorth, and Lehdonvirta (2017) argue that the organisation through online platforms brings about a greater dispersion of work: differently from the BPO industry, through online platforms, jobs can be outsourced without a mediating formal organisation (Graham, Hjorth, & Lehdonvirta, 2017, p. 137). Moreover, online platforms do not need to operate in spatial proximity to workers but mediate work connections between multiple places on a global scale, which sets them apart from call centres, for example. This has prompted Graham and Anwar (2019) to state the emergence of a "planetary labour market" enabled by digital technologies. Differently from both labour migration and BPO work, remote gig workers often connect to clients based in various countries in parallel, which is reflected in their work time covering the business hours of different time zones (Shevchuk et al., 2021).

However, work relations in the remote gig economy are still predominantly formed between clients from high-income countries and workers from low-income countries (ILO, 2021, p. 53). What is more, differences in payment reflect this categorisation in high- or low-income countries (Beerepoot & Lambregts, 2015). That is, the physical location of workers impacts what they earn for a gig, which reflects that technological integration is not the only factor to be considered. At the same time, global competition for work seems to lead to lower overall wages (Beerepoot & Lambregts, 2015). Ettlinger (2017) points out the paradox of how the platform-mediated global labour market is technologically almost independent of physical lo-

---

7 There is also an emerging strand of literature studying location-based platform work from a migration perspective, cf. e.g. Altenried (2021a); van Doorn and Vijay (2021).

cation, but still spatially differentiated in practice. She finds that there are separate regional regimes targeting workers in 'developed' countries, "underpinned by assumptions among firm agents about an exclusive geography of talent" (p. 30), as well as a deterritorialised regime targeted at finding the lowest prices worldwide, and localised regimes targeted specifically at workers in very low-income countries, mediated by governments and social enterprises. She traces this differentiation back to

"ethnocentric assumptions that cast labour markets in underdeveloped countries as unsuited for cognitive piecework [...]. Such spatial discrimination echoes the socio-spatial dynamics of the post–World War II and earlier colonial international spatial divisions of labour whereby the so-called third world and former colonial territories respectively were conceptualised as a vast reservoir of cheap, unskilled labour, and high-skilled labour was presumed to be geographically fixed in the so-called first world" (Ettlinger 2017, p. 28).

Casilli (2017) comes to a similar conclusion, arguing that colonial discourses are reflected in the practice of globalised platform work. In their empirical study on freelance designers, Demirel et al. (2021) find that how their research participants' skills and identities are valued by clients and other designers depends to a large part on their congruence with cultural codes of the Global North. Using a Bourdieuian framework, they conceive of language as a form of cultural capital that is significant not just for getting information across – they find that "the use of English by freelancers in their online profiles and communications is closely monitored not only for its fluency but also for its articulation of Global North business etiquette and specific client-focused corporate practices" (Demirel et al., 2021, p. 926). The issue of language skills is one example of how a globalised labour market is structured by cultural aspects of working together. Moreover, it illustrates that the line between necessary skills and biases based on cultural differences is often blurry. This is in line with Gerber's and Krzywdzinksi's findings that clients, who are, as I have established above, disproportionately based in countries of the Global North, rather trust workers from the same region with tasks that require specialised skills (Gerber and Krzywdzinski 2019, p. 37). They, too, attribute these preferences to language to some degree but also suggest that cultural prejudice plays a role in who is hired (Gerber & Krzywdzinski, 2019, pp. 36–37).

By structuring interaction, online platforms can influence how the chances for success are globally distributed. Agrawal et al. (2016) argue that the rules and interfaces set up by online platforms can mitigate the disadvantage of one's physical location: in a quantitative analysis of oDesk (now Upwork), they found that applicants from 'less developed countries' are 60 percent less likely to be hired. However, information on their job experience on the platform and verified credentials disproportionately benefit these applicants. On the other hand, Irani (2015) has argued with regard to the microtask platform Amazon Mechanical Turk that workers are sorted along the lines of their geographical location by the platform, reinforcing the discrimination described above. Workers, too, interact with the infrastructure that the platform provides to mitigate disadvantages based on their location, for example by creating accounts in different countries via proxy servers (Graham, Lehdonvirta, et al., 2017) or sharing accounts with friends or relatives in countries that are associated with higher wages (Wallis, 2021). These practices reflect how stratified the 'planetary labour market' is, but also show that workers have some room for manoeuvre and that they can make use of gaps and loopholes in the platform-mediated work environment.

D'Cruz and Noronha (2016) focus on freelancers' perceptions in their empirical study of India-based freelancers working on Elance-oDesk, the predecessor of the online freelance platform Upwork. The article finds that most freelancers perceive their work on the platform predominantly in a positive way. However, they also point out that their research participants face racism in their everyday work:

"Aversive racism from clients and fellow freelancers, calling into question workers' competence, bid amounts and remuneration rates, accompanied by divergences linked to ethos, language and time, bring a negative tenor to work-related interactions and make it more difficult to complete tasks that are already complicated by their virtual and often asynchronous forms" (D'Cruz & Noronha, 2016, pp. 60–61).

These inequalities are continuously reproduced and challenged in relations between platforms, clients, and workers. While there is ample research on how inequality is mediated by digital technologies (cf. e.g. Amrute, 2016; Ash et al., 2018; Cirucci, 2017; Kolko et al., 2000; Matamoros-Fernández, 2017; Nakamura, 2012; Noble & Tynes, 2016), platform-mediated work has not played a big role in this strand of research so far. To sum up, work relations are spatially reconfigured in ambivalent ways. Research suggests that online platforms are far from rendering space irrelevant, but they also offer opportunities for inclusion into labour markets and (not always intentionally) spaces to negotiate workers' positions.

2.2.4 Synthesis: Ambiguous implications of a platform-mediated work environment

As the perspectives that I have outlined above suggest, online platforms have contributed to transformations of work on several levels. The organisation of work in the form of single, clearly delineated tasks has rendered work connections loose and volatile: as risk is simultaneously shifted to workers, they are often in a vulnerable position. While several authors assess online platforms as drivers of precarity, gig work is often seen as embedded within larger lines of transformation toward non-standard employment. However, existing research also shows that work experiences in the gig economy, including experiences of precarity, vary greatly depending on the form of gig work (Howcroft & Bergvall-Kåreborn, 2019), the role of gig work in larger work constellations (Schor et al., 2020), and workers' personal motivation (Dunn, 2020). Moreover, several scholars have questioned whether workers can enjoy the flexibility proclaimed especially by the platforms themselves, as they experience pressure to make enough money (Griesbach et al., 2019) and work processes are managed by online platforms. Working in the gig economy, then, implies a volatile work environment, with heterogeneous and ambiguous implications for workers.

The role that online platforms play in managing work processes includes technological features, often referred to as algorithmic control (Prassl, 2018; Veen et al., 2020; Wood et al., 2019a). Online platforms frame social interaction according to their business interests by setting up an environment of possible use (van Dijck et al., 2018). Moreover, "platformic management" (Jarrahi et al., 2020) also includes rules of conduct and further aspects of managing work beyond technological mediation. Online platforms also leverage information asymmetries as a means of worker control. While these mechanisms constrain workers' agency, workers also find ways to resist or bend the rules, and they can influence the larger system through their practices (Shapiro, 2018). With tasks being allocated in a translocally dispersed way, platforms contribute to a "planetary labour market" (Graham & Anwar, 2019) or increased "virtual migration" (Altenried et al., 2020; Aneesh, 2006). The research has also shown, however, that platform work does not render workers' location irrelevant by any means.

The existing research on platform work, then, paints the picture of a work environment that is highly volatile, opaque, and complex. The literature review suggests that the implications of the platform-mediated work environment are ambivalent, bringing about elements of freedom and precarity, autonomy and control, and providing access to a global labour market to more people while simultaneously reflecting or even consolidating discrimination. While the work cited above has made important contributions to understanding global platform work, the present literature also misses some perspectives, which I will outline below.

2.3 Gaps and blind spots in the literature on platform work

First, while the literature on platform work finds that both the field as a whole and work relations are highly dynamic and uncertain, the practices of navigating this uncertain work environment have received relatively little scholarly attention so far. This is, in part, because the research on platform work has focused strongly on work regimes rather than work practices and experiences. While there are already some studies on work practices and workers' perceptions, and the literature on these aspects of platform work is growing, studies on working conditions in the gig economy still predominantly focus on the structural aspects of how work is organised. Based on this observation, Gandini (2019) proposes "not to overstate the relevance of employment regimes [and instead] to expand our interest to these workers' experiences […] as well as on the social and cultural implications deriving from working in a context where relations of production are fluid and social relations at work are heavily transactionalized" (Gandini, 2019, p. 1052).

What is more, online platforms as novel actors in work constellations call for a framework that leaves space for negotiating different actors' roles. Overall, research on negotiations over agency between platforms and workers is still relatively scarce. Moreover, researchers studying the role of platforms managing work processes often categorise workers in existing concepts of actors in work relations. This involves likening or contrasting workers to employees or independent contractors, but also understandings of platforms as a point of production, in the tradition of a factory (Altenried, 2022; Gandini, 2019). Comparing online platforms to employers (Friedman, 2014) does not reflect the flexibility of working arrangements, but conceiving of workers as independent contractors, as especially many platform companies do, underestimates the level of influence that online platforms have as mediators of social interaction (van Dijck et al., 2018). Categorising work in a dichotomy between flexibility and stability misses important nuances of workers' practices and experiences (cf. Ivancheva & Keating, 2020). As Wittel (2004) argues, especially political economy approaches to digital labour reduce labour to an abstract category, neglecting subjective experiences and workers' agency (p. 17).

Second, both conceptual and empirical contributions to the literature on platform work have largely generalised work experiences in the Global North. Overall, there is little research on translocal work connections mediated by online platforms so far. The low number of publications dealing with translocal platform work reflects a focus on location-based gig work and an overall focus on Europe and North America in the literature. Perspectives on the structure of the platform economy, including exploitation and precarity as defining features, provide important insights into working conditions but often leave little space for the heterogeneity and ambiguity of workers' experiences. While some of the literature on platform work has differentiated how workers experience uncertainty, a lot of studies create the image of one general experience of platform work. However, as the literature on global work connections suggests, workers' location, for example, makes a big difference in how platform work is experienced. As D'Cruz and Noronha (2016) argue, platform work, too, has predominantly been theorised through a Western lens, generalising work experiences with little regard for diversity across labour markets. Since their paper was published, some notable works of research have contributed to addressing this gap: a large research project on 'platform work at the global margins' has gathered workers' accounts from several countries in Africa and Southeast Asia (cf. e.g. Graham & Anwar, 2019; Wood et al., 2019a), Wallis (e.g. 2021) has studied remote platform work between Germany and Romania, Shevchuk et al. (2021) in Russia, and Qadri (2021) has focused on location-based gig workers' experiences in Indonesia. By focusing on the work practices of remote freelancers based in India, I aim to contribute to this emerging strand of literature.

In this context, it is also important to challenge the frameworks within which work is studied. Considering the global spread of work connections through platform work, it is important to depart from perspectives that only reflect the experiences of a small proportion of those who perform platform work. Especially studies on precarity in platform work usually – implicitly or explicitly – take a Fordist model of standard employment, that is, full-time permanent employment (cf. ILO, 2016, p. 11), as a point of reference. Within this framework, the loose connections of gig work are classified as a departure from stable employment. However, this perspective neglects that standard employment relationships have historically and geographically been an exception rather than the norm (Neilson & Rossiter, 2008). Moreover, the discourse on precarity has been framed predominantly in androcentric and Eurocentric ways, focusing on work that is performed by male workers in the Global North (cf. Ivancheva & Keating, 2020). D'Cruz and Noronha (2016), for example, consider the term 'informal' more suitable to the Indian context than 'precarious' when describing their research participants' working conditions in platform work (p. 58).[8]

Third, a narrow view of work is often applied when studying platform work, focusing on activities that are considered directly economically productive. Woodcock and Graham (2020), for example, refer to paid work as "a relationship in which one person sells their time to another" (p. 11). This illustrates Wittel's (2017) observation that "[t]hroughout the last century, labour has been analysed in the western hemisphere as wage labour only" (p. 258). Feminist scholars have challenged the dominance of paid labour in concepts of work, arguing for a profound rethinking of work and the productive domain (cf. Ivancheva & Keating, 2020). When work is defined strictly by its economic productivity, the interdependence of paid and unpaid work is often overlooked. As a result, practices beyond paid employment are often neglected within these perspectives. This includes care work, for example, but also the unpaid work done by platform workers, which I have described above. Scholars have found that platform workers perform unpaid emotional labour trying to mitigate the uncertainty of the work environment by building rapport with their clients – both location-based gig workers (Rosenblat & Stark, 2016) and remote freelancers (Wood & Lehdonvirta, 2021b). However, so far, research lacks the language and concepts to grasp the unpaid work brought about by transaction-based work, as Jarrahi et al. argue (2020, p. 182). To grasp the scope of unpaid work done by gig workers to navigate an uncertain work environment, concepts of work are necessary that extend beyond the job descriptions on the platform, also taking relationships beyond paid work into account. In a similar vein, Ivancheva and Keating (2020) contend that both the Marxian proletarian and the neoliberal subject are conceived of as completely autonomous, neglecting their embeddedness in interdependent relationships of love, care, and solidarity (p. 274).

---

8 For a more detailed review of the debate on informality in the Global South, see e.g. Cooper et al. (2021).

To sum up, online platforms contribute to a transformation of how work is organised, allocated, and managed. This development is reflected in a transformation of work practices: as actors in a work environment that is characterised by loose and short-term work connections, an unevenly global labour market, and online platforms steering work processes, remote freelancers perform a great deal of unpaid work to prepare the ground for paid gigs. While the literature on working conditions in the gig economy is growing, little is known yet about the everyday work practices of navigating this uncertain work environment. Furthermore, the emergence of these work practices poses the question of how work can be conceptualised in a way that reflects the ambiguities and the heterogeneity of gig workers' experiences, and that accounts for the multiple dimensions of work beyond paid labour. To contribute to closing this gap, this study seeks to explore and theorise remote gig workers' everyday work practices from a broader perspective. By using a lens of everyday practices, I aim to produce a fine-grained image of the heterogeneous and ambivalent implications of the platform-mediated work environment. Moreover, I focus on unpaid aspects of platform work, defining work deliberately broadly as making and sustaining connections. I situate these connections in relation to the role of online platforms and their translocality. In the next chapter, I will lay out the conceptual framework I use to incorporate dynamic relationships beyond paid work into my analysis.

3. Conceptual Framework: Work as Practices of Assembling

To address the gaps outlined above, I propose to study platform work by combining feminist approaches that seek to extend the concept of work beyond paid labour with an assemblage perspective. In the first part of the chapter, I explore alternative perspectives to conceptualising work as paid employment. In the second part of the chapter, I outline assemblage as a sensitising concept to construct my field of research as made up of volatile connections. Finally, I bring both together to develop a tentative understanding of practices of assembling in remote platform work.

3.1 De-centring economic productivity: Work beyond paid employment

I have established above that the idea of work as selling one's time to someone else excludes practices that are not considered directly economically productive. While the literature on platform work mostly focuses on paid work, scholars from a range of different fields have conceptualised work in broader terms. I will outline some of these perspectives below as a foundation for my approach to studying work practices in this thesis. Empirical studies on platform work often do not specify what 'work' means but treat it as a self-evident category. However, in this study, I start from the assumption that "[w]hat will count as work does not depend *a priori* on any set of indicators, but rather on the definition of the situation" (Star & Strauss, 1999, p. 14). Star and Strauss (1999) contend that work is not per se visible or invisible, but that what counts as work is often a question of who is in power to define it. One of the examples they use to illustrate this is domestic service work: drawing on existing empirical studies, they show how both the work and the person doing the work are rendered invisible and how this invisibility is linked to a lack of power (pp. 16–18). This implies that the categorisation of work reflects power relations. Starting from this premise, I first introduce perspectives on invisible 'background' work in dealing with technology. Second, I outline approaches that consider emotional and affective dimensions of work. Third, I introduce feminist perspectives directed at expanding and deconstructing the category of work.

3.1.1 Invisible background work: Dealing with technology

From a Science and Technology Studies (STS) perspective, invisible work has been discussed in terms of covert processes that need to be considered when designing technological tools to support work. In this strand of research, working with technology and work practices mediated by technology have both been covered. Recognising that technology does not just make work easier, but also implies additional work, adds an important element to studying platform work. In their reflection on the invisibility of work referred to at the beginning of this chapter, Star and Strauss (1999) look into the context of computer-supported cooperative work. Thinking about features of visibility and invisibility serves them as a starting point for thinking about how relations between visible and invisible work can be incorporated into the design of infrastructure.

An important concept they include in their exploration is articulation work (cf. Strauss, 1985), that is, the effort that goes into dealing with unexpected situations and contingencies when interacting with technological systems (Star & Strauss, 1999, p. 10). But they also include what they call 'backstage work' into invisible work: the work that is done away from the public eye in preparation for the visible product of work – such as a dancer's hours of training or an ethnographer's stack of notebooks filled with messy fieldnotes. Here, too, they stress that what part of work becomes visible varies between different fields and often cannot be distinguished clearly (pp. 21–22). Therefore, the authors take a critical stance towards purely technological approaches to improving work processes mediated by technology. Especially in a context of inequality, they argue that "if the system does not account for the matrix of visible and invisible work and its questions of equity, those at the bottom will suffer" (Star & Strauss, 1999, p. 25).

Focusing on the users' rather than the designers' perspective, Vertesi (2014) looks into work practices in the context of multiple infrastructures. She stresses that it takes work to create copresence through heterogeneous infrastructures that work according to different logics. The product of this work is a "seamful interactional space" (Vertesi, 2014, p. 273). She argues that the image of seams is more useful to grasp the messy overlap between the standards of use and interactional possibilities tied to each infrastructure than thinking of them as layers or boundaries. These messy overlaps do not imply that actors are incapacitated by dealing with different logics. Instead, they align different infrastructures in practice – not producing a stable balance, but rather fleeting moments of alignment. Moreover, Vertesi makes a case for studying actors' observable activities wrestling with the limitations of infrastructures and using opportunities for moments of alignment instead of zooming out to a meta-infrastructural analysis. She argues that it is not necessary to look at international agreements or global maps to observe global entanglements, as these are present in micro-practices (Vertesi, 2014, p. 268). Vertesi applies this notion to socio-technical practices, such as connecting hardware with different regionally specific plugs to the same computer.

These approaches underline that technology does not simply make work easier – very often, technological advances rather rely on outsourcing work out of sight. The authors point to several ways in which unpaid and unrecognised work is performed as a foundation for paid work. Moreover, they point to the challenges of integrating different systems into work practices. Below, I will outline how scholars from different fields have introduced an emotional and affective dimension to work.

3.1.2 Incorporating the realm of emotions

With her concepts of emotion work and emotional labour, Hochschild [1983] 2012) was a pioneer in expanding the focus of work to an emotional domain. The sociologist points out that a lot of jobs do not only include physical and mental strain, but also emotional strain. With the concept of 'emotion work', she describes the everyday management of emotions on an individual level, while 'emotional labour' signifies managing one's own emotions in the context of paid work. While Hochschild developed these concepts to better grasp the work especially done by women in the service sector, they have been adapted to many contexts within and beyond the spheres of work studies since (cf. Koch & Buchanan, 2013). They also offer fruitful connections to the study of platform workers' practices: emotion work comes into play when freelancers deal with the disappointment of being rejected by a client, for example. When they strive to build trust with prospective clients by being approachable and likeable, they perform emotional labour. Hochschild refers to the social aspect of emotion work as 'feeling rules' (cf. Koch, 2013 for the application to work culture studies).

In a similar vein, albeit within a Marxian framework, Hardt (1999) has introduced the concept of 'affective labour', which also relates to the management of emotions. While the concept of emotion work rather refers to regulating one's own emotions or performance, affective labour is directed toward producing and manipulating affect in others (Hardt & Negri, 2000, p. 293). Going beyond face-to-face interaction, affective labour also refers to mediated interaction, such as advertising (Hardt, 1999, p. 91). Hardt defines affective labour as a kind of immaterial labour (cf. Lazzarato, 1996): this implies that the product of labour is immaterial, but also that it is often not recognised as labour. Marxist feminists have taken up this notion to foreground the labour predominantly performed by women (e.g. Weeks, 2007), and carved out different dimensions of affective labour, such as commercial and non-commercial care work, as well as the production of affect in service professions, which is especially relevant for this study (Oksala, 2016). Research from a Marxian perspective generally looks at work as part of the interplay between capital and labour. Consequently, work practices are always put in the context of the capitalist exploitation of labour – in the case of gig workers, this means looking at how they contribute to the platform's profit in various ways, for example. Accordingly, affective labour, too, is categorised by how it contributes to the production of a value surplus.

Focusing on how the neoliberal system and digital technologies interact and reinforce each other, Terranova (2000) has introduced the notion of 'free labour' to grasp how the digital economy exploits users' unpaid practices, also classifying it as cultural or affective labour. When she speaks of 'digital labor', she refers to the work that goes into producing digital content – this includes code (e.g., open-source software), contributions in online forums, etc. Terranova introduces the term 'outernet' to grasp a network of social, cultural, and economic relationships that both crisscrosses and exceeds the internet, and connects it to flows of labour, culture, and power. She questions the distinction between production and consumption as well as between labour and culture. The digital economy, according to her, comes with a new logic of value. The lines between exploitation and enjoyment are blurred in this type of labour: people contributing to open-source software, for example, might do so out of a spirit of community, not expecting anything in return and feeling a sense of accomplishment about having contributed. At the same time, capitalist businesses extract value from users' voluntary work. Along similar lines, Scholz (2017) refers to the extraction of value from activities that do not feel like labour, but rather like play, as 'playbour'.

Several authors build on this idea of the exploitation of free labour and the blurring of boundaries between work and play to create the image of 'entrepreneurs of the self' in digital capitalism. The underlying idea of this argument is that users of digital media perform free labour online not just for fun, but as investments in their 'human capital' (Feher, 2009). This has two implications: First, 'neoliberal subjects of value' (van Doorn, 2014) are not just producing value through labour, but also have a value assigned to them. Alison Hearn (2010) argues that digital social capital or 'reputation', earned for example by posting in online forums or increasing the number of followers on an online platform, has become a new currency, or source of value. She frames "[s]elf-branding [as] a form of affective, immaterial labour that is purposefully undertaken by individuals to garner attention, reputation and potentially, profit" (Hearn, 2010, p. 427). This implies that market value is assigned to users of digital media. Online reputation measures commensurate this value, that is, they integrate diverse practices into a common measurable framework (van Doorn, 2014).

Second, understanding unpaid online practices as investments in one's market value introduces an element of contingency, as the outcomes of one's investments cannot be predicted. Building on both Terranova (2000) and Hearn (2010), van Doorn (2014) points out an emotional dimension of digital practices in a neoliberal context: he argues that online reputation management is characterised by 'affective ambiguities', as users struggle to manage their market value in a context where it is unclear what constitutes this value and how it can be increased. According to him, entrepreneurial workers cannot control their human capital, "they can only invest in it, hoping that its value will increase when positive external evaluations enable self-appreciation in a competitive job market whose parameters have become increasingly uncertain" (van Doorn 2014, p. 358). This uncertainty is also the foundation for "hope labour" (Kuehn & Corrigan, 2013), that is, unpaid work performed as an investment in future earnings.

Drawing on ethnographic research in different business process outsourcing (BPO) agencies in Bengaluru over several years, Mankekar and Gupta (2016, 2017, 2019) expand the notion of emotional labour to work settings without physical copresence. They argue that call centre work is affective labour: Departing from Hochschild's idea that this means producing fake emotions starting from an 'authentic self', they argue that affective labour produces subjectivity (Mankekar & Gupta, 2016, pp. 24–25). What is more, they add the bodily challenges of going against one's circadian rhythm (Mankekar & Gupta, 2016, p. 30), the affective labour of linguistic, cultural, and experiential translation (Mankekar & Gupta, 2017, p. 71) and dealing with racist abuse (2017, p. 76), as well as the double burden that especially women face – they write: "most women agents experienced a double workday: they had to continue to perform affective labor at home because they were primarily responsible for taking care of their families" (Mankekar & Gupta, 2019, p. 424).

The freelancers at the centre of this study are not only characterized by how digitalised their work is but also by its creative nature. The context in which they work is highly flexible and often characterised by an erosion of the boundaries between what counts as work and free or private time. This development is discussed in cultural anthropology and neighbouring disciplines as part of a broader development of the 'de-bordering of work' (Gerber & Krzywdzinski, 2019; Huber, 2013; Voß, 1998). The de-bordering of work and life has been subdivided into different processes in the literature: subjectification of work refers to the development of ever more previously personal, emotional skills seeping into the work sphere. Marketisation refers to a de-bordering between the market or entrepreneurial principles and paid employment. Flexibilisation refers to the de-bordering of work and private life (Gerber & Krzywdzinski, 2019, p. 29).

These approaches to work provide useful hints as to how the concept of work can be expanded against the backdrop of digitalisation. They carve out a broader range of diverse practices than what is traditionally counted as work, including, for example, more playful practices that may not even feel like work. Moreover, they show how subjectivities emerge from digital practices in contingent processes. While these approaches add a useful view of how work practices are embedded within a broader context of capitalism, their unified perspective of workers in capitalism may lack the nuance of how workers are differently affected by changes in work practices. Workers relate to digital platforms and the overall system of platform work in diverse ways, and the dynamics of global platform work suggest that they have more agency to influence the overall system than what neo-Marxist approaches concede. Moreover, imagining an original clear separation of work and private lives, often connected to ideas of public and private spheres, renders invisible all the reproductive forms of work, often taken on by women, which make a 40-hour workweek possible in the first place. This non-recognition of reproductive labour is also where the feminist critique of concepts such as the 'entreployee' (German original: "Arbeitskraftunternehmer") (Voß, 1998), which refers to a transformation towards entrepreneurial practices in an increasing number of work constellations, comes in (Huber 2006, p. 127). While the perspectives outlined above have expanded the notion of work by adding unpaid practices, they still locate work within a sphere of economic productivity. Below, I draw on approaches that seek to go beyond economic productivity in how they define work in novel ways to develop a tentative framework for studying work practices in this thesis.

3.1.3 Deconstructing the category of work

Arendt (1969) does not conceive of work as a sphere that can be differentiated from life but as a fundamental human activity. She distinguishes three aspects of what she calls *vita activa*: labour, work, and action.[1] Labour, to her, is a continuous activity directed at subsistence: it is what humans do to sustain the processes of the human body. Labour does not produce a durable outcome – its effects are continuously consumed as they are produced (p. 86). Work, by contrast, entails producing something that lasts, and which is not subjected to the need for continuous subsistence (p. 7). Arendt describes labour as a cyclical activity, corresponding to the rhythms of growth and decay in biological life (p. 98). As such, labour never ends, or only ends with the end of human life. Work, on the other hand, ends when its object is produced. This distinction can be fruitfully applied to the study of platform work, as well: from this perspective, creating a logo, for example, can be considered work in Arendt's sense. Working on the logo

---

[1] Arendt describes action as activity that goes on between people without the intermediation of things. She uses this term to refer to the foundation for humans as political beings (Arendt 1969, p. 7). I will focus on her differentiation between labour and work here; her concept of action refers to political life, which would go beyond the scope of this thesis.

leads to a product, in this case, a source file that can be sent to and used by a client. This work is what is commonly taken into account and what is paid for by the client. However, I argue here that platform work also includes a considerable amount of labour as Arendt understands it: practices directed at keeping up the status quo. This could be understood in a much wider sense, too, but I will focus here on practices that directly support the 'work' aspect, such as keeping one's profile up to date or sending cover letters to clients. This labour is necessary to prepare the ground for work, but it does not have a durable product. In short, Arendt's (1969) differentiation between work and labour can be applied to differentiate interrelated components of platform work. Continuous labour is necessary as a foundation for work.

This interdependence of different forms of work is also present in feminist approaches to work. Over the past decades, scholars have pointed out that a narrow focus on paid employment renders especially work done predominantly by women, such as care work, invisible. Feminist scholars have introduced the category of reproductive labour to complement productive labour in the Marxian sense outlined above (Mackenzie & Rose, 1983). While productive labour is, for example, going to work in a factory to produce value in a capitalist system, the concept of reproductive labour originally included all the unpaid domestic work of cleaning, cooking, or caring for children. Building on this concept, some scholars have argued that the value produced in the domestic sphere should be recognised by including it in the GDP (Waring, [1988] 2016) or paying wages for housework (Federici, 1975). Further developing the notion of social reproduction, scholars have extended its reach to encompass "the fleshy, messy, and indeterminate stuff of everyday life [and] a set of structured practices that unfold in dialectical relation with production, with which it is mutually constitutive and in tension" (Katz, 2001, p. 711). While these approaches originally relied on a dualism between masculinised productive labour and feminised reproductive labour, there are also conceptualisations of work that carve out how these spheres overlap. In later approaches to social reproduction, scholars have critically examined the analytical separation of production and reproduction, integrating both into the concept of life's work (Mitchell et al., 2004).

Moreover, Haug (2008) expands the concept of work beyond the distinction between paid labour and reproductive labour to include political work and individual development. She creates a utopian vision for a society in which everybody, irrespective of their gender, can distribute their waking time equally between these four forms of work. Thus, she goes one step further and broadens the notion of work beyond the sphere of capitalist production or the reproduction of labour power. Digitalisation and, especially relevant in the context of this dissertation, the influence of online platforms, have further impacted how different forms of work and non-work interrelate and bleed into each other. Lizzie Richardson (2017) argues that with digitalisation, work is both extended and intensified. Thanks to digital technologies, work is extended both spatially and in terms of what spheres of life are touched by work, as it is less bound to a physical workplace and can be distributed over space and between producers and consumers, for example. As a result, work is also intensified as new tasks become necessary to make a space into a workplace or integrate more social skills into most kinds of work (Richardson, 2017, pp. 246–248). She argues that "[t]he emergence of the digital workplace means that what counts within the category of 'work' is open" (Richardson, 2017, p. 251).

While the approaches outlined above treat work as a concept that can be changed by adding new spheres and thus treat it as socially constructed and changeable, they remain within the logic of treating work as a bounded category that can be defined as the sum of distinct parts. As Cameron and Gibson-Graham (2003) argue, the "economy is thus expanded by conceptualising it as a dualistic whole comprised of a masculinised realm of paid work and a feminised realm of unpaid domestic, child-based, nurture-oriented, voluntary and community work" (p. 147). They contend that it is not enough to add new categories of production to the economy but still view it as a whole, the different parts of which can be added together. Instead, they suggest deconstructing the notion of the economy altogether and building it up anew from what can be observed. This move can also be applied to work more specifically: by opening the meaning of work, new aspects may become known. Similarly, Ivancheva and Keating (2020) argue that it is not the right move to attribute an exchange value to love, care, and solidarity. Instead, they "call for a profound rethinking and eventual reorganization of the productive domain around the concept of care" (p. 254). Within this framework, then, work and life, or productive and reproductive spheres, are not a binary but a continuum (ibid.).

3.1.4 Synthesis: Interdependent practices

To sum up, the approaches to work that I have outlined above have expanded the category in several ways that inform how I study work practices mediated by online platforms. I build on the feminist critique that has challenged work as an essential category to open up what work can mean. Drawing on perspectives on work beyond paid employment, I contend that work as a category is socially constructed and can thus also be deconstructed and opened up for new meanings. Taking on this critical feminist perspective, I focus especially on those aspects of work that are unpaid, unrecognised, and taken for granted. By doing this, I aim to go beyond the binary of work vs. nonwork, not excluding any activity from potentially being work. When I write about unpaid labour performed by platform workers, then, this does not automatically imply that all of what they do should ideally be integrated into the sphere of paid employment. Instead, I consider paid and unpaid practices, as well as emotional and affective labour, as different elements of platform work. Meaning and value are attributed to work practices as they are integrated into a larger context of relations.

Moreover, I argue that the different practices that make up the category of work are interdependent. This is reflected in the analytical perspectives outlined above in various ways: The invisible background work described by Star and Strauss (1999) provides a necessary foundation for the part of socio-technical work that is recognised. Work in Arendt's (1969) sense of producing or creating something would not be possible without the labour of subsistence. Moreover, productive and reproductive labour are closely intertwined. This interdependence calls for an approach to work that takes into account how different elements of work are distributed along the lines of relations, going beyond the single worker as an autonomous subject (cf. Ivancheva & Keating, 2020, p. 274). Although the practices that I am focusing on in this study would fit in the category of what Arendt (1969) has described as labour, I use the term 'work' here: this is because labour is predominantly associated with a Marxian frame of reference, foregrounding relations of capitalist production. However, I aim to understand work in a broader sense here, including, but also transcending economic productivity. Below, I will introduce the notion of assemblage, which I use to reflect the volatility of work connections as I construct the field of platform work.

3.2 Platform-mediated work from a global assemblage perspective

I argue that an assemblage perspective can contribute to a better understanding of the ambiguities of platform work. The concept of assemblage was originally developed by Deleuze and Guattari (1993) and has since been taken up and modified in various bodies of work, including Actor Network Theory (e.g. Latour, 2008) and New Materialism (e.g. DeLanda, 2016). It has been applied to diverse empirical fields, such as forest management (Li, 2007), social movements (McFarlane, 2009), and resistance in digital environments (Ettlinger, 2017). As Buchanan (2021) argues, assemblage theory is necessarily incomplete – it is an invitation to be developed further, held together by some core principles (p. 6). Below, I outline the assemblage framework as I use it in this thesis and relate it to the empirical case of platform work, drawing especially on Collier's and Ong's (2005) concept of global assemblages. First, I go into some broader characteristics of the term 'assemblage' and relate them to the volatility of gig work. Second, I outline how elements of an assemblage interact with each other. Third, I relate the assemblage framework to my perspective on space and the global in this thesis. Finally, I deduct an understanding of work as making and sustaining connections from the assemblage perspective.

3.2.1 Assembling volatile connections

An assemblage is formed by the practices of relating heterogeneous human and nonhuman actors (Ettlinger, 2018). In the context of this project, the actors include platform workers, clients, and platforms, as well as many more elements they relate to. As Marcus and Saka write, "[t]he time-space in which assemblage is imagined is inherently unstable and infused with movement and change" (Marcus & Saka, 2006, p. 102). That is, producing relations does not result in a stable structure, but actors' positions in relation to each other may change or it might disintegrate completely (Marcus & Saka, 2006). Assemblage, then, implies relations that do not necessarily form an organism: "[A]n assemblage is both the provisional holding together of a group of entities across differences and a continuous process of movement and transformation as relations and terms change" (B. Anderson et al., 2012, p. 177). Therefore, rather than trying to grasp its elusive structure, the assemblage can be approached as a continuous process. The volatility of connections makes it necessary for actors to continuously work on the assemblage: as Li argues, "assemblage flags agency, the hard work required to draw heterogeneous elements together, forge connections between them and sustain these connections in the face of tension" (Li, 2007, p. 264). I have shown above that both the work connections established via platforms in the form of gigs and the overall field of platform work are highly dynamic and volatile. The notion of assemblage can contribute to grasping this volatility beyond the promise of flexibility or the threat of precarity. Moreover, through the notion of making and sustaining volatile connections, the assemblage perspective provides an approach to the unpaid work practices that I want to focus on here. It thus complements the broad conception of work that I have established above.

3.2.2 Agency in an assemblage

From an assemblage perspective, all elements can affect the larger constellation (Ettlinger, 2018). In a configuration characterised by contingency, both power relations and the assemblage as a whole can change – or be changed (Ettlinger, 2018, p. 3). DeLanda (2016) describes the form of assemblages as a possibility space, which contains the multiple capacities of their elements. Power in an assemblage is not centralised on one actor but distributed between them (cf. Ettlinger 2018, Li 2007). Moreover, the notion of distributed agency does not mean that an assemblage resembles a level playing field: rather, power in this context can be conceptualised as "the capacity to assemble" (McFarlane, 2009, p. 567), that is, making connections in the assemblage. Making connections, then, is not only hard work but also harder for some than for others. The relations between elements of an assemblage are also power relations. On the one hand, this implies that platform workers are constrained in their actions within the assemblage of global platform work. On the other hand, it leaves space for agency and for them to shift relations in the assemblage. Connecting this to the existing studies on agency and control in platform work, the assemblage perspective, again, leaves space for ambiguities and negotiations. From this perspective, online platforms cannot determine workers' actions, just like workers cannot act independently of online platforms. Instead, they relate to and influence each other. Below,

I outline the implications of assemblage theory for the study of translocal connections.

3.2.3 The global in the space of assemblage

Assemblage as an analytic concept calls for a notion of space that is not bound to a material location but understood via relations. McFarlane (2009) argues that as a relational analytic, assemblage is open to multiple spatial imaginaries. The emergence of work relations mediated by online platforms is often connected to the globalisation of work and a notion of the world growing closer together in a process of time-space compression. However, just as social relations themselves, relational space is "by its very nature full of power and symbolism, a complex web of relations of domination and subordination, of solidarity and co-operation" (Massey, 1994, p. 265). Within a relational understanding of space, the idea of time-space compression has to be differentiated: As Massey argues, the time-space compression associated with globalisation does not affect everybody in the same way, as "different social groups, and different individuals, are placed in very distinct ways in relation to these flows and interconnections" (Massey, 1994, p. 149). This is true for the relationship between workers and clients in the context of this dissertation: the fact that there are world regions where mostly clients come from and others where mostly workers come from supports this. As Massey continues, "[t]his point concerns not merely the issue of who moves and who doesn't, although that is an important element of it; it is also about power in relation *to* the flows and the movement." (Massey, 1994, p. 149) This notion of "power geometry" (Massey, 1994) also connects back to the notion of power and agency in the assemblage explained above. From a spatial perspective, the capacity to assemble is reflected in the capacity to influence the flows and interconnections Massey describes. As digital connections permeate the global assemblage of platform work, the relational space constructed here transcends notions of physical and virtual.

To reflect the ambiguous ways in which platform work is dispersed globally, I use the term "global assemblage" (Ong & Collier, 2005) as a sensitising concept. The ontology of assemblage reflects the tension between the technological promise of a global labour market and the actual situated work practices and lived experiences of graphic designers using online freelance platforms in India. I argue that in the context of remote freelance platforms, work has developed into a global form, described by Collier and Ong (2005) as having "a distinctive capacity for decontextualization and recontextualization, abstractability and movement, across diverse social and cultural situations and spheres of life" (p. 11). Ong and Collier illustrate this with the example of organs becoming a global form through developments in medicine and technology that increasingly allow for them to be extracted from the context of one human body into another (ibid.). Similarly, the technological infrastructure of online platforms allows for work relations to be formed on a global level, integrating all actors into a shared context. Translocal work relations and an international division of labour are not new phenomena (cf. e.g. Massey, 1995), but through online work platforms, work relations span the globe in new ways, as I have outlined in Chapter 2.2.3.

Calling platform-mediated work 'global' here does not mean that online work platforms are present everywhere or that a single platform has a global reach, but that work becomes mobile "across diverse social and cultural situations" (Collier, 2016, p. 400). By conceiving of platform work as a global form, then, I do not suggest that it does not matter what social, cultural, or other contexts the work relations are formed in – they are "not unrelated to social and cultural problems" (Collier & Ong, 2005, p. 11). I also do not adhere to platforms' optimistic marketing statements promising that they create a global community or that everybody can make it on the platform, regardless of where they live. Instead, I consider global forms as elements in global assemblages, or a global assemblage as "the actual and specific articulation of a global form" (Collier, 2016, p. 400).

Collier and Ong argue that global forms interacting with other elements form contingent, uneasy, unstable interrelationships, constituting the global in the space of assemblage. They provide the example of neoliberalism as a global form, which becomes significant for forms of individual and collective life in assemblages with other elements in a specific context (Collier & Ong, 2005, pp. 13–14). It is these tensions and uneasy relationships that I aim to bring to light in this book. Thinking in terms of global assemblages also means turning away from the dichotomy between an abstract 'global' that is expressed in a specific 'local':

"In relationship to 'the global,' the assemblage is not a 'locality' to which broader forces are counterposed. Nor is it the structural effect of such forces. An assemblage is the product of multiple determinations that are not reducible to a single logic" (Collier & Ong, 2005, p. 12).

With regards to this study, this suggests that instead of viewing platform-mediated design work as an exemplary case for the principles of global platform work, I stay close to workers' specific practices to produce a situated account of how they relate to different elements in an assemblage of global platform work. Thus, I study how the assembling of heterogeneous elements performed by platform workers connects various places across the globe.

3.2.4 Synthesis: Work as making and sustaining connections

The assemblage perspective from which I construct the field of platform work builds on the broad notion of work that I have proposed above and connects it to the features of platform work that I have outlined in the literature review. This work encompasses a broad range of paid and unpaid practices of relating and, through relating, producing the assemblage. Work points at having to make an effort to keep things going, but it goes beyond common understandings within a framework of paid labour or capitalist production. This work is necessary because of the emergence and contingency of the assemblage: it is not stable, but actors' positions in relation to each other may change or it might disintegrate completely (Marcus & Saka, 2006). Therefore, what graphic designers do to keep this assemblage together can be considered part of their work, going beyond paid tasks they perform on online platforms.

Mirroring the volatility of the assemblage, I tentatively frame work as the continuous effort of making and sustaining connections. Against this backdrop, I assemble the global form of platform-mediated work with practices by graphic designers in India. By doing so, I contrast the broadly encompassing and mobile quality of the global form with the heterogeneous, contingent, unstable, partial, and situated character of the assemblage. Contingent, uneasy, and unstable interrelationships emerge. Reflecting the notion of a "life-work continuum" (Ivancheva & Keating, 2020), both relationships with clients and with platforms as nonhuman actors and relationships beyond the realm of platform work are included in this exploration. This comprises the following broad questions: How do gig workers relate to their clients and their peers? How do they interact with the online platforms that they use for their work? How do they view their role in these relationships? How do gig workers' relationships transcend the realm of platform work? How do they align platform work with different elements of their lives?

3.3 Working definition of practices of assembling

To approach the multiple interrelationships that freelancers make and sustain, I divide platform work into two analytical categories: practices of creating designs and practices of assembling. I consider 'creating designs' as the more direct, practical, and visible part of their work: for example, thinking of a new logo, making sketches and drafts, and producing a file. Practices of assembling encompass setting up and curating one's profile, browsing design briefs, writing proposals, discussing ideas with clients or collaborators, managing one's online reputation, and organising one's schedule – practices that are often taking place in the background. They also involve relationships that go beyond the realm of platform work. In this project, I focus primarily on practices of assembling. Practices of assembling and creating designs are not bounded from each other in the designers' everyday work: they are intricately connected and interdependent. The work of creating a logo depends on the designer setting up a profile and successfully attracting clients, for example. Practices of assembling add a dimension to the paid work of practices of creating designs, however, the notion does not cover everything that could be considered 'life's work' (Mitchell et al., 2004): While I incorporate relationships beyond the sphere of work in practices of assembling, I still focus on practices that are connected to and support freelancers' paid work.

The various aspects of practices of assembling are reflected in the analysis chapters. I weave in existing concepts of work with my observations of practices by freelance designers. The sets of practices I describe in the analysis section are also interwoven; they overlap rather than form neat categories. I will point out some of these overlaps while describing the practices and tie the different sets of practices together in the synthesis. Furthermore, I will embed the analysis of work practices within relations that go beyond the realm of platform work, including platform workers' support systems and the constellations of different forms of paid and unpaid work, of which platform work is only one part. The practices are not the same for all platform workers, but they have common threads, which I will describe as practices of assembling in Chapters 5, 6, and 7. Building on the analysis of these practices, I will then carve out central features of what work means in this context in Chapter 8. In the next chapter, I outline my research process and the methodological considerations undergirding the study.

4. Research Approach and Methodological Perspectives

As I have outlined above, the goal of this study is to explore and theorise remote gig workers' everyday work practices of making and sustaining global connections mediated by online platforms. To tackle this and to develop the lens of making and sustaining connections as work practices, I posed three interconnected research questions: First, *how do gig workers navigate the volatility of work relations?* Second, *how do online platforms mediate work practices?* Third, *how do remote freelancers align global work relations with local, situated practices?* In this chapter, I connect the conceptual framework that I have laid out above to the epistemological and methodological framework of the study. First, I reflect on the entangled processes of constructing the field of research and negotiating my position as a researcher. Second, I introduce the digital ethnography approach that I have taken in this study. Third, I trace the research process, which consisted of interconnected phases of theoretical sampling, online explorations, interviews, and digital photo diaries, as well as analysing material. Finally, I reflect on disruptions in the research process and ethical questions that my research entailed.

4.1 Co-construction of research, researcher, and field

I have argued above that the assemblage of global platform work is constructed by everyday work practices of making and sustaining connections. As the phenomenon I study is highly dynamic and volatile, it cannot be grasped by ideas of a static and bounded field. By constructing the field as an assemblage, I focus on the volatility of connections and acknowledge that they do not form a stable structure. As a researcher, I am not describing this assemblage from the outside, but I contribute to its emergence. Since the

Writing Culture debate in anthropology that started in the 1980s (cf. Clifford & Marcus, 1984), research has been widely accepted in the discipline as a social and context-dependent practice of knowledge production (Hess & Schwertl, 2013, p. 22). That is, the field is not simply there for me to become immersed in; instead, I am constructing it as the research proceeds. To reflect this entanglement of researcher and research, Hess and Schwertl (2013) propose to depart from notions of a spatially defined field; beyond the expansion toward multi-sited ethnography (Marcus, 1995), they argue that the field could be thought of as an assemblage in itself, in which the researcher is an actor. As I have described in Chapter 3.2, being an actor in the assemblage implies that I am enmeshed in interdependent relationships: I am both continually co-producing the field and the field continually co-produces my position as a researcher (cf. Robertson, 2002). Against this backdrop, I aim to reflect on the role that I as a researcher play in the knowledge that I produce.

As Haraway writes, "the only way to find a larger vision is to be somewhere in particular" (Haraway, 1988, p. 590). By constructing the field and selecting the relations that I consider most relevant to the situation, I am necessarily producing a partial account. It reflects my positionalities and the shared process of meaning-making by me and the object of research, labelled as a "material-semiotic actor" by Haraway (1988, p. 595). Both the research process and its result, this study, are entangled with my biography and my positionality as a *white* German researcher working at a research institute in Germany, as well as my gender, age, and educational background. To situate the knowledge that I present in this study within the power relations between me and other actors in the field (which I am co-producing), it is necessary to reflexively examine my positionality. Especially feminist scholars have called for this critical reflexivity – as McDowell (1992) argues, "we must recognize and take account of our own position, as well as that of our research participants, and write this into our research practice" (p. 409). However, this is not a straightforward task. My position is not stable, it shifts in relation to other actors, and distinct aspects of my positionality are relevant depending on the situation. In the different phases of field research, I was in the position of someone trying to sign up on various platforms without design skills, but with a German IP address; I was a *white* woman backed by a European academic institution asking for an interview, I was a stranger navigating the city of Bengaluru, and I was a client with the power to withhold payment or leave a low rating.

I negotiated these overlapping positions with online platforms and platform workers, and they were connected to different power dynamics, or "capacities to assemble" (McFarlane, 2009, p. 567). Throughout the research process, up to the claims that I make based on my observations, I have aimed to continuously reflect on my role in the various relationships that make up the field in memos and conversations with colleagues and research participants. Moreover, I have strived to take into account the limits of my knowledge and understanding of the field and to connect my account to where I am speaking from (Rose, 1997). The research participants in this study have contributed their perspectives and shared their knowledge as experts of their own everyday lives. I have aimed to incorporate their interpretations into this account, for example by using open interviews and digital photo diaries, as well as putting my preliminary results up for discussion with interested research participants. Still, I take seriously the privilege of being the one who can share her interpretations of this with an academic audience. In the remainder of this chapter, I will share reflections on my shifting positionalities along the phases of research, from delimiting the scope of my study to the steps of gathering and analysing material. This reflexivity also includes making struggles and frictions in the research process explicit (cf. Ouma, 2015, p. 89).

4.2 The lens of digital ethnography

As I have argued above, I study work practices from an assemblage perspective. The work practices that contribute to producing and sustaining the assemblage of platform work are dynamic and elusive. By constructing the field as an assemblage, I focus on the volatility of connections and acknowledge that they do not form a stable structure. As Marcus and Saka (2006, p. 106) argue, an assemblage perspective is most fruitful if it leaves space for heterogeneity and emergence, not trying to pin it down by depicting it as a 'final' state. To account for this, I have chosen an ethnographic approach for this study. The methodology of ethnography is suitable to study complex phenomena in their emergence for three reasons, as Knecht (2013) points out: First, it entails combining various perspectives, which is often reflected in a variety of data material. Second, ethnography is processual: the researcher adapts the approach and adjusts it to the observations they make throughout the research. Third, ethnography is based on being open to what comes up in encounters and willing to be surprised by what comes up in research participants' accounts. Ethnography aims to understand social phenomena in their complexity rather than explaining linear causalities (cf. Faust, 2019, p. 21). Its goal is not to uncover an objective 'truth' – instead, it is based on accepting that many truths can emerge from multiple perceptions. As Ortner (1996) describes, ethnography, then, means "looking at and listening to real people doing real things in a given historical moment, past or present, and trying to figure out how what they are doing or have done will or will not reconfigure the world they live in" (p. 2). Accordingly, I focused on freelancers' practices and perceptions, aiming to dive into their complexity and multiple entanglements rather than reduce them to seemingly stable categories.

As I have pointed out above, the everyday work practices that I focus on in this study are deeply entangled with digital technologies. The strengths of ethnography lend themselves to studying online interaction, as Star (1999) argues: "[I]t is capable of surfacing silenced voices, juggling disparate meanings, and understanding the gap between words and deeds" (p. 383). To account for online platforms as relevant actors in the assemblage, I embed this study in the field of digital ethnography (Pink et al., 2016). In doing so, I use a "non-digital centric approach to the digital" (Pink et al., 2016, p. 7), that is, I aim to understand practices of engaging with digital media rather than digital media themselves. Accordingly, I am more interested in the multiplicity of practices than the internal logic of 'the internet' (cf. Hine, 2015, pp. 28–29). In a similar vein, I do not intend to focus on a single online platform in my study but aim to trace "the multiple interrelationships and overlapping uses of digital technologies" (Ardévol & Gómez-Cruz, 2014, p. 7). As this perspective assumes digital technologies to be part of everyday practices, digital ethnography expands the toolbox of ethnography, but it does not leave behind established methods aimed at understanding everyday practices. Digital ethnography is thus also non-digital-centric in the sense of the methods used. Below, I outline the implications of a digital ethnography approach for how I constructed the field site and the combination of methods with which I proceeded.

4.3 Research process

My fieldwork consisted of three main phases between January 2019 and May 2021. As I have described above, ethnographic research is an adaptive process. This entails combining different methods to bring to light different aspects of a phenomenon, and adapting the approach to what the research process reveals (Hine, 2015, pp. 176–177). Accordingly, while I brought my own frames of reference and concepts to the table, I aimed to remain flexible and open to being surprised by the meanings that research participants ascribed to their situations and expanded the range of methods during my research process. Flexibility became even more crucial as the COVID-19 pandemic ruled out face-to-face interaction and international travel for a large part of my research process. In terms of methodology, I aimed to reflect this adaptability by iteratively switching between gathering and analysing material, using tools from Grounded Theory (Strauss & Corbin, 2003). Below, I will lay out the process in more detail, starting with how I delimited the scope of my research, and continuing along the three main approaches of unobtrusive explorations, interviews, and digital photo diaries. Moreover, I will explain how the phases of research informed each other.

4.3.1 Initial delimitations: Sites and protagonists

My first step towards grasping the global assemblage of platform work was choosing a particular entry point to access the practices that produce it. As I have described in Chapter 3.2, the global in the space of assemblage is characterised by friction between a global form and local, situated practices (Collier & Ong, 2005). To observe this friction, I chose a specific location and set of practices. I initially delimited the scope of my study to graphic designers who are based in India and connect to clients via online freelance platforms. I started with just these premises and aimed to continuously expand the variation within the sample by comparing cases (cf. Strauss & Corbin, 2003, pp. 72–85). The specific sample of research participants then emerged from the process, based on my theoretical sampling and what was possible for me to access. In this subchapter, I will outline the reasoning behind these choices and embed them within the research process.

I focused on freelance graphic designers' practices in my study, first, as the product of their work is easily transmittable online and does not strongly depend on language. Accordingly, tasks such as designing logos are commonly mediated by online platforms. Second, design is a complex task which requires specialised knowledge. By contrast to so-called microtasks, these types of tasks have received little attention in the literature on platform work so far, as I have argued in Chapter 2.1. What is more, I expected the need for unpaid work connected to standing out to clients, making emotional connections, and curating one's profile to be stronger in this type of work than with more standardised tasks. Thus, creative freelance work promised to be a good example of the practices of assembling in which I was interested.

Geographically, I delimited the scope of my research to freelancers based in India. The country was the largest provider of remote work in the world in 2020 (ILO, 2021, p. 53), followed by Pakistan and Bangladesh. Long before online platforms gained momentum, the country played an important role in the business process outsourcing (BPO) industry (cf. e.g. Aneesh, 2015; Mankekar & Gupta, 2016; Upadhya, 2016). Thus, I could expect many platform workers there. Moreover, due to my background as a South Asia scholar, I already had some contacts there and was familiar with the context, which made it easier for me to gain access to research participants. Bengaluru, where I stayed for a month in 2020 to conduct interviews, is characterised by contrasts and rapid transformations: the IT sector plays an important role in the city, and high-rise corporate buildings stand side by side with "a jumble of small shops, nondescript office blocks, modest bungalows crowded together on narrow roads, buildings half-demolished to make way for road-widening projects, proliferating construction sites, and garbage lying uncollected on street corners" (Upadhya, 2016, pp. 1–2). Thus, the city reflects the friction of the global in the space of assemblage, bringing together diverse experiences. While I could not follow through with my plans to visit further Indian cities, I included freelancers based in different regions of the country in video interviews and digital photo diaries to incorporate a greater variety of living situations and local contexts.

Although India is the physical location where the freelancers in this study work, other places play important roles in their practices, too – for instance, clients' locations affected their work rhythms. Moreover, while they are not physical sites that they move in, online platforms provided frameworks for freelancers' practices in important ways. Beyond combining online and offline strategies for gathering research material, digital ethnography also has implications for the understanding of field sites "as a heterogeneous network mapped out from the social relationships of the subjects and their connections to material and digital objects and to physical or virtual locations" (Ardévol & Gómez-Cruz, 2014, p. 7). Therefore, I will briefly outline the online platforms that I focused on in this study as another component of the research setting. At the beginning of my research project, I first gained an overview of online crowdwork platforms that mediate design jobs and target users in an international context. As Hine (2015) argues, combining the exploration of different platforms and juxtaposing their differences helps to assess how their technical setup, as well as the cultural conventions of their use, shape the practices of their use (p. 168). I, therefore, chose four platforms for closer investigation, 99designs, Fiverr, Talenthouse, and Upwork, aiming to contrast them along several dimensions. All four platforms target a global clientele and mediate design jobs. I differentiated them, first, by whether they are focused on design specifically or mediate a wide range of tasks. Within these categories, I chose platforms that differ from each other in their specific focus to cover a broad spectrum of user practices.

99designs and Talenthouse mainly mediate creative jobs through contests, with 99designs being more focused on professionals earning money through the platform, while on Talenthouse, contests are more playful and integrated into the use of the platform as a space to interact for creatives. As I have described in the introduction, 99designs is one of the most prominent online work platforms with a focus on design, with 42781 registered workers in September 2020 (ILO, 2021, p. 50). The platform connects designers and clients for logo or web design, illustrations, packaging design, and many more. The platform offers several ways of matching designers: the most common one is the design contest, in which designers compete by providing a full design. The winner of the design contest earns money depending on the level of the contest, while the others are not remunerated for their time. However, the platform also allows clients to directly approach a designer to work together, in which case the rate is negotiated between the client and freelancer. 99designs promotes its curation of designers, both by verifying design skills in the sign-up process and by classifying users in various levels, based on their design skills and experience. Moreover, the platform increases the visibility of some designers by displaying their work on the 'featured designers' page.

Talenthouse currently has around 14.7 million members.[1] The platform presents itself as a social media platform for creatives, which also provides freelance work opportunities, with a user interface similar to Instagram, for example. Users can post images, videos, or songs, as well as like others' artwork. They can link to their profiles on other social media sites; however, they cannot communicate directly through the platform, except for comments on

---

1 https://business.talenthouse.com, last checked on 05/05/2022.

others' posts. The platform is thus not purely focused on mediating work relations. It does, however, include so-called creative invites. These are design contests in cooperation with brands or organisations, where users are asked to submit artwork ranging from a poster to the design for the hull of a cruise ship, as well as stories or photographs. The user whose design is selected is rewarded with prize money of a few hundred up to a few thousand US dollars; in some cases, there are additional runner-up prizes. However, altogether, the focus of the platform is more on exposure than on earning an income. By contrast to 99designs, Talenthouse does not have any ranking or reputation systems and is more in the background of interaction.

Upwork and Fiverr mediate jobs across a wide range of different fields, with Upwork tending to more upscale and long-term jobs, and Fiverr being more geared toward smaller tasks. Upwork, which has emerged from the merger of its predecessors Elance and oDesk, is one of the oldest and largest work platforms, with an estimated number of eighteen million registered freelancers.[2] The platform mediates jobs in a wide range of fields, including, for instance, IT work, architecture, and legal consulting. Usually, clients post a job on the platform, specifying the task, potential milestones for bigger projects, and a budget. They can either directly invite freelancers to work together, or freelancers can apply for the job with a cover letter. Moreover, Upwork suggests freelancers who may fit the profile for the job. Projects can be paid per hour or at a fixed price. Differently from the other platforms in the sample, a longer collaboration between freelancers and clients via Upwork is relatively frequent. This includes larger projects, which may take several months and add up to higher rates, as well as a sequence of follow-up projects. Like 99designs, Upwork also limits who can sign up as a freelancer on the platform, and rates freelancers by job success rate as well as several 'top-rated' categories.

Fiverr currently has around 830,000 registered workers, who are called 'sellers' on the platform. The platform allows users to offer any service they wish and set a rate for it themselves; this comprises design jobs, but also a wide range of other tasks. On the platform, clients approach workers based on their profiles – accordingly, a convincing profile is especially important on Fiverr, with some freelancers adding videos in which they introduce themselves, for example. If clients are looking for a logo design, for instance, they can filter for design field, style, what language the freelancer speaks, their

---

2 https://cybercrew.uk/software/fiverr-vs-upwork/, last checked on 05/05/2022.

rating, where they live, as well as budget and delivery time. Based on these criteria, the client is then presented with a list of eligible freelancers. Like Upwork and 99designs, the platform uses ranking and reputation mechanisms: clients can leave ratings of up to five stars and written reviews for freelancers, and the platform classifies freelancers into four levels based on how many gigs they have completed and their activity over six months.

The setup of the online platforms themselves also reflects the global connections of platform work: 99designs, for example, was founded in Melbourne, Australia in 2008, where its headquarters still are. Currently, the company also has offices in Oakland, US, and Berlin, Germany. In 2020, the Dutch company Vistaprint acquired 99designs, adding another location to the global structure of the firm. While these platforms formed the core of my initial analysis, I also noted and explored online platforms that freelancers mentioned in the interviews.

4.3.2 Unobtrusive explorations

In the first phase of research, from January 2019 until October 2019, I explored the platform-mediated work environment from the vantage point of online platforms. I conducted walkthroughs (Light et al., 2017) of the four platforms I had selected for in-depth analysis, and looked at clients' and freelancers' profiles, as well as forum threads and blog posts within the framework of the platforms, without actively engaging with platform users. Hine (2015) calls this approach "unobtrusive exploration of online landscapes" (p. 157), and contends that it can be especially useful to better understand the unspoken elements of everyday life. My goal in this first phase was to establish an understanding of platforms' repertoire of structuring and framing practices, mainly to approach my second research question, *how do online platforms mediate work practices?*

Rooted in an ethnography of infrastructure approach (Star, 1999), the walkthrough method (Light et al., 2017) is based on the premise that apps – or platforms, in this case – can act as mediators, that is, they can change meaning or circumstances within a system (p. 6). It consists of two phases: In the first phase, the researcher explores the 'environment of expected use'. The platform's vision, operating model, and governance are studied via the narratives that they present on the platform itself and beyond, by their revenue system, and the terms of service. I started by collecting screenshots of the platform's homepages, as well as further info pages, and read interviews and news articles on the platforms. Moreover, I looked at their terms and conditions and advertisements to get an impression of how the platforms were presented there and what clientele they catered to. In addition, I captured common threads shared by the different platforms in memos to carve out characteristics of the environment. The platforms shared common narratives of global connections, for example. Especially the visual representations of world maps with connecting lines between various locations or expressions such as "global community of designers" (99designs) transported the idea of a seamless user experience irrespective of one's location. Moreover, success stories of workers having gained sudden wealth through platform work were amplified in blog entries or interviews. To explore the range of characteristics, I also took note of differences between platforms. While 99designs and Talenthouse as design-specific platforms centred on fun and playfulness in their self-presentation, for instance, Upwork focused especially on the verified competence of the service providers on the platform, and Fiverr on the ease of quickly finding someone for a wide range of tasks.

The second phase, called technical walkthrough, includes steps of signing up and using the platform, as well as discontinuing its use.[3] While exploring the technical affordances of the platform, I collected screenshots and took notes on the steps of clicking through the platform. Again, I reflected in memos on how the platforms structured what I could do and what categories I was sorted into. While Talenthouse and Fiverr only have one user category, Upwork and 99designs require users to identify themselves as clients or service providers when signing up. According to this choice, users can use the platform in different ways: 99designs offers a community forum for designers, for example, which users who are signed up as clients cannot access. I tried signing up as a service provider on 99designs and Upwork at first to get an impression of the work environment that freelancers encounter and to get access to the community forum and the design briefs posted on the platforms. I could sign up relatively easily on 99designs at first but stumbled over a change in their policy after a while: whereas simply signing up initially allowed me to access the designer forum and to view contest briefs, begin-

---

3 I focused on the process of signing up and the environment of everyday use in my exploration and left out the signing off process, as the access and everyday use were most relevant to my research questions.

ning in autumn 2019, designers could only use the platform once they had submitted a portfolio for review by the 99designs team. I tried submitting 'designs' that I had created in Microsoft Paint, which resulted in me learning that the platform does not accept just anybody as a designer. In Upwork, I also tried to sign up as a service provider but was rejected on the grounds of the high number of applicants for registration on Upwork. I learned later that this was a common experience among freelancers: it had taken many of my interviewees several tries to sign up on the platform they wanted to access. By contrast, I could sign up as a client on both platforms with great ease and without verification, which may hint at the differences in how different actors need to perform trustworthiness.

In the context of the everyday use of the platform, I focused on getting an overview of how users could curate their profiles, how they could communicate via the platform, how they were categorised in rankings and reputation systems, as well as in how far the online platforms provided options for linking to websites or social media accounts. Without interacting with them myself, I explored different briefs and contests, users' profiles, and reviews. At this point, I transitioned from studying only the framework for interaction toward combining these impressions with the accounts that were observable directly on the platform. Studying the platforms' forums, for example, brought to light biases and disjunctures among global users. Within the 'global community' that the platforms had proclaimed, users made sure to distinguish themselves from others, also by attaching varying degrees of professionalism to 'cultural' or regional backgrounds. To filter the overwhelming number of entries, I searched for South Asian or Indian subgroups in the forums, as well as threads in other forums that contained references to India or South Asia.

To sum up, the first phase of research helped me construct the first rough vertices of the field: I prepared the ground for interacting directly with the freelancers by familiarising myself with their work environment. Although I had not been in the position of a designer myself, I understood the basic mechanisms of the platforms, such as their reputation systems, and had an impression of how users interacted. Moreover, I generated preliminary hypotheses based on my observations, which guided the questions I asked in the interviews that I conducted in the next phase of research.

While this phase of my research was a helpful step, it also had its pitfalls. For one, as I was only studying the platform framework and interaction within this framework by lurking in the background, my preconceptions were hard to overthrow. For example, by looking for forum threads that explicitly mentioned the workers' national background, or by noting the option of showing or hiding it in one's profile, I got the impression that fault lines between the 'Global North' and the 'Global South' were much more present in platform users' minds than what I found to be the case in the interviews I conducted later. What is more, I found that while these methods were unobtrusive, I had to negotiate their intrusiveness. I only had the option of signing up as a worker or a client, both of which were not really the case. Within this categorisation by the platform, I had to negotiate how much of my identity I was going to reveal and how I was going to present myself: I was worried my account could be locked if I was open about using the platform for research, but I also wanted to be transparent about my intentions with other users of the platform. I chose in the end to use a photo showing my face and mentioning my being a PhD student researching design. However, when I started contacting freelancers later, there were sometimes misunderstandings about my role: for example, some freelancers assumed I was asking them to participate in a job interview for a design task. This illustrates how my practices and interaction with others were shaped by the range of possible uses afforded by the platforms, too.

4.3.3 Interviews

Based on the understanding of platforms' mechanisms of framing and structuring interaction that I had gained through the platform walkthroughs and further unobtrusive explorations, I set out to get more insights into freelancers' everyday practices and experiences, guided by the research questions *how do gig workers navigate the volatility of work relations?* and *how do remote freelancers align global work relations with local, situated practices?* To answer these questions, I conducted 25 semi-structured interviews, 17 of which took place face-to-face in Bengaluru, mostly in coffee shops. They usually lasted between 45 and 90 minutes. Most of the interviews took place during my month-long field stay in Bengaluru between February and March 2020; moreover, I conducted one pilot interview in advance and four further interviews via video calls until March 2021. All the interviews were recorded and transcribed for analysis. The interviews roughly fell into two categories:
    First, in 13 background interviews, I talked to designers and creative professionals from various fields, many of whom had experience working both

in India and in other countries, both freelance and employed. Moreover, I interviewed the CEO of an online recruiting platform for the creative industry in India. I attended events at design studios in Bengaluru, asked mutual friends for an introduction, and contacted designers online to get access to these research participants. I adapted my interview guides to the research participants' profiles, focusing on how they connected to designers, clients, and colleagues in different countries, and what role diverse types of online platforms played in their everyday work. Some of the designers had also tried gig work platforms for some time and then stopped – they reflected on what had attracted them to platform work and what led them to stop it. The conversations served as a backdrop to better understand the experiences of platform workers. While the research participants from the background interviews are only explicitly present in a few instances in the thesis, their assessments of design and their insights on working as a designer outside of freelance platforms have helped me tremendously in understanding what is special about working on a freelance platform.

Second, to understand freelancers' everyday work practices better, I conducted 12 semi-structured interviews with freelance designers who currently regularly use online freelance platforms to connect to clients. Getting access to remote freelancers was a challenge in the beginning and included a range of different strategies with varying levels of success. Before my field stay in Bengaluru, I joined various Facebook groups for gig workers on Fiverr, 99designs, and Upwork, and posted interview requests there. However, no interview came of this. As users can link to their social media profiles or websites on 99designs and Talenthouse, I also contacted potential interview partners via different social media platforms or by e-mail, which was slightly more successful. Moreover, I asked all my research participants if they could introduce me to further platform workers – however, this did not result in any further interviews. This is less of a surprise in hindsight, as many freelancers reported working in isolation from others. Similarly, my visits to co-working spaces in Bengaluru did not reap any interviews, which fits with what research participants told me about their splintered daily rhythms and odd working hours. The most fruitful approach by far was reaching out directly through the messaging function on Upwork and 99designs.

I loosely structured the interviews along three themes. Freelancers reflected on how they organise their everyday work, how they curate their profiles, and how they interact with clients and other platform workers. With some research participants, I combined the verbal accounts of their experiences with visual representations of how they curate their profiles. When we had an in-person interview and the research participants' time as well as the setting allowed for it, I opened their platform profile on my laptop and asked them to guide me through it toward the end of the interview, pointing out the features that they considered most relevant, and reflecting on the process of reworking different elements in their profile over time. I roughly followed the approach of a media go-along (Jørgensen, 2016), that is, combining interviews and observations of a personal communication service. Instead of following research participants as they move through a physical space, I asked them to give me a verbal and visual tour of how they navigate the online platform they predominantly use for work, prompting further elaboration by asking follow-up questions. I video-recorded the screen of my laptop during these parts of the interviews as a reference for the subsequent analysis.

How I contacted research participants had an impact on my position in relation to them: as freelancers' rate and speed of answering clients' messages are part of their reputation on the platform, they may have felt obliged to reply to my messages on the platform and we were integrated into the dynamics of a relationship between client and service provider, even if we did not make a contract. With some of them, we switched to Whatsapp or e-mail quite fast. Others did not want that because they were afraid it might not be in line with the platform's terms of service to use other media of communication to interact. I followed the freelancers' wishes and communicated with them via the media they suggested. Contacting the freelancers via the platform also means that those I have talked to were mostly workers with a high online reputation and visibility and who were actively using the platform. Those workers who showed up first in my search (I filtered for India and graphic design), are those that are favoured by the algorithm. That means that most of my research participants are long-time, successful platform users and that their experience of platform work is thus not the average one. Moreover, I only managed to recruit one woman for my freelancer interviews, which means that I could only contrast gendered experiences in a limited way.

Altogether, the different interviews I conducted led to a closer understanding of what freelancers' everyday work practices looked like. Moreover, the freelancers' accounts helped me critically probe my preconceptions; as I have mentioned above, the role of freelancers' location turned out to be much more differentiated than my initial distinction between clients from the 'Global North' and workers from the 'Global South', for example. My initial plan had been to stay in India for two months, conducting interviews in several cities and towns, and shadowing designers during their workdays. However, as the COVID-19 pandemic brought about contact and travel restrictions, I had to recalibrate and think of alternative ways to get deeper and more personal insights into everyday work practices.

4.3.4 Digital photo diaries

To go deeper into the affective dimension of freelancers' work and to add another layer to the material, I added digital photo diaries by freelancers as a third approach. The goal of this final method was to probe and refine my observations, and to allow more space for freelancers' reflections on their work. Between February and May 2021, I sent seven photo prompts and short questionnaires each to five freelancers. In addition, one freelancer provided written accounts without sending photos. With the photo diaries, I aimed to tie together the three research questions, integrating platform workers' routines and practices of making and sustaining connections with the affordances and constraints the platforms provided. Diaries have been used as a research method for a long time (e.g. Zimmerman & Wieder, 1977), and have since been adapted to capture experiences of digital media in everyday life (e.g. Hjorth & Richardson, 2020). They allow the researcher to indirectly participate in everyday practices, while also giving research participants the space to provide their own interpretations of and reflections. Clark (2021) further adapted the diary method by combining photo prompts with short questionnaires, arguing that pictures can capture affective and mundane elements of daily life and that they make it easy to also include non-human agents, such as the built environment.[4] As there is less focus on language or text than in classical diaries, photo diaries add another layer to the material. Moreover, participants are flexible in terms of when to do the entries and this type of diary requires much less of their time than writing longer descriptions of what they do. I roughly followed Clark's (2021) approach in my photo diaries, as I aimed to complement verbal accounts with visual ones and to still be mindful of my research participants' busy schedules.

---

4 Clark describes the method in detail in a YouTube video: https://www.youtube.com/watch?v=xRuxXp-ud54, last checked on 22/04/2022.

I prepared this phase by conducting follow-up interviews with some of my research participants, sharing my tentative hypotheses about specific challenges that remote freelancers face. I shared my hypotheses on negotiating value, aligning relations, and managing emotions with them, as well as the overarching category of uncertainty in the platform-mediated environment. Based on the participants' feedback, I refined my hypotheses and created seven photo prompts, which came with 2–3 questions each, to fill in the gaps in my material. The diaries covered research participants' workspaces, their daily rituals, their different responsibilities and relationships beyond platform work, their relationships with their clients, the emotions they connect with their work, and what they consider the value of their work. I then tested the first two prompts with three colleagues and friends to ensure that there were no technical hiccups and that filling in the diaries would not take more than 15–20 minutes per day.

When looking for participants, I first approached the freelancers working predominantly through online platforms whom I had originally interviewed, as well as some designers whom I had contacted for interviews but could not meet in person as my field stay was cut short. However, there was little turnout at first: only one of my initial interviewees agreed to take part, and two more initially agreed but did not respond to the photo prompts. To create a stronger incentive for participation, I decided to post the research diaries as a job on Upwork,[5] remunerating up to five participants with 50 US dollars each. I briefly described my research project in the brief and mentioned that I was looking for freelance designers who are based in India and use Upwork regularly. In the end, five people participated: two of my initial interviewees and three new participants who fit the profile.[6] I sent them daily photo prompts over seven days, accompanied by a link to a short questionnaire. In the questionnaires, I asked participants to describe the photo and what it meant to them and added one to two questions that prompted further reflection on the respective theme. When participants had sent their replies,

---

5 I chose Upwork for this because most of my interviewees use the platform and the system of clients posting briefs that freelancers can directly apply to was more suitable for my project than design contests or freelancers advertising their services.
6 One of the participants, Janbir, is based not in India but in Bangladesh. As I expected his work experiences in a neighbouring South Asian country to be similar, and to add further participants to the sample, I also included his account. Moreover, another participant, Advik, agreed to answer the questions in a written form without sharing photos.

I sent them the next prompt the following day. If they did not send a reply after two days, I sent them a short reminder.

Against the backdrop of what I had gathered in the previous phases of my research, the digital photo diaries added insights into the wider context of the interdependent relationships in which freelancers are integrated. As workers in a creative field, expressing themselves through visual means came easy to the research participants, and provided an extra step of reflection, which made them stop and think before answering my questions. Altogether, they provided a helpful addition to the research material. Moreover, my impression was that writing their answers down made it easier for some participants to share more personal stories. They provided accounts of their mental health, for example, which they may not have done in an interview situation in a busy coffee shop. However, there were also limitations to the process. Especially using the platform as a frame for the project was an ambivalent decision: On the one hand, it helped me make sure I did not simply take from research participants without giving anything back. On the other hand, it also changed my positionality in relation to them: I was now officially their client. Accordingly, they knew that they would only be paid if they finished the project, and that I would be able to leave them a rating in the end. Thus, participants may have left out overly critical thoughts in the photo diaries, especially about clients.

4.3.5 Analytical strategies

I used the software MAXQDA as a tool for managing and analysing the diverse types of material: I collected screenshots from online platforms, interview transcripts, and participants' digital photo diaries in the programme and marked them with codes, from which I proceeded to build overarching categories through open, axial, and selective coding (cf. Strauss & Corbin, 2003). As Faust (2019, p. 28) contends, creating neat categories through coding can be at odds with the goal of ethnographic research to capture ambiguities and the complexity of social phenomena. Coding thus entails walking a fine line of grasping a phenomenon without oversimplifying it. To bring to light the messy overlaps between categories, memos were an important part of the analysis process. I started with open coding of online documents, writing memos on observations, and making first hypotheses on connections. In this phase, I assigned codes inductively line by line, revising them through memos and grouping them into categories. For example, I created the codes 'loving designers' and 'loving designs' from the homepage of 99designs, where clients were promised to be connected to a designer that they would love. I reflected on the emotional component of the product of the freelancers' work and the need for establishing an emotional connection with clients in memos and grouped both codes in the category 'clients' emotions'. To refine these observations and compare them with further cases, I integrated the questions that this first phase of coding hat prompted into my interview guideline.

In the interviews, I aimed to find out more about how freelancers manage their clients' emotions and added further codes, such as 'building rapport' and 'being reliable'. In addition to adding depth to the online observations, the interviews also added variety: for example, the platform emerged as an important actor mediating trust, as is reflected in the code 'platform mediates in conflicts'. What is more, the range of freelancers' own emotions about their work emerged from the interviews, leading to the codes 'mundanity' and 'feeling appreciated', for instance. Again, I used memos to feather out the dimensions of the category and to weave in the ambiguities inherent in how freelancers relate to their own and clients' emotions. To refine my hypotheses, I asked about freelancers' emotions in one of the photo prompts, adding the codes 'joy of creating' and 'thrill' to the category 'managing one's own emotions' based on the entries. Subsequently, I used axial coding to subsume these codes under the higher-order category of 'managing emotions', which I turned into one of the analysis chapters.

While I built up an image of practices of assembling in this way, I continuously returned to the material that I had gathered earlier, probed the codes that I had created, and added dimensions via selective coding. From this process, the overarching categories of shooting in the dark, managing emotions, negotiating value, and aligning relations emerged. Finally, I integrated these categories into characteristic practices of assembling: 'shooting in the dark' as the constant need to guess and anticipate outcomes turned out to cut across the previously established categories, and they furthermore had in common elements of adapting to constant change, producing relatable selves, and creating momentary alignment, on which I will elaborate in Chapter 8.2. In the following subchapter, I will reflect on the role that disruptions and dead ends have played in my research process, and how I navigated ethical questions of "doing no harm" (Sultana, 2007) and reciprocating what research participants shared with me.

4.4 Concluding reflections on methodology

4.4.1 Disruptions and dead ends

Throughout this chapter, I have mentioned various instances in which my original plans failed, and I had to recalibrate my research. Following Ouma (2015, p. 89), I aim to make struggles and friction in the research process transparent as I reconstruct it to further elucidate the situatedness of the knowledge that I am producing. The COVID-19 pandemic was certainly the most prominent disruptor in my research process: instead of spending two months in India, interviewing designers and getting insights into their everyday work practices, I went home after four weeks without a realistic perspective of coming back before the end of my study. The flexibility and adaptability that is part of ethnographic research projects thus became relevant in other ways than I had anticipated. However, travel restrictions were not the only factors mitigating access to the information that I was looking for. Gaining access to research participants was often tricky: many of the strategies that I deployed, such as joining designer groups on social media or visiting coworking spaces, amounted to nothing – at least in terms of finding interview partners.

Looking back on the process, these experiences all contributed to the final image in some way: not being able to conduct participant observation led me to explore more experimental approaches to gaining insights into everyday practices. My unsuccessful attempts at recruiting interviewees through social media helped me understand the challenge of sifting through the opaque and complex platform landscapes, and the instances where I did not manage to get across to freelancers that I was looking for participants in a research project and not a job improved my understanding of how difficult digitally mediated communication in a second or third language can be. Thus, it may be helpful to think of the research process as similar to my field of research: not a straight road, but rather a continuous effort to make and sustain connections.

4.4.2 Ethical considerations

As I was making and sustaining connections with research participants, I also continuously navigated ethical questions. As a researcher, I felt the responsibility of "doing no harm" (Sultana, 2007). Research participants trusted me with personal information, also regarding how they bent or broke the rules of the platforms they used. This put them in a potentially vulnerable position, as being excluded from the platform would mean a loss of their main source of income for many. I dealt with this by assigning them pseudonyms to make sure that what they shared could not be traced back to them, while still reflecting them as individuals in the story that I am telling. However, contacting research participants through the online platforms they used for their work also entailed navigating what was potentially detectable by the platform. This was especially relevant once I had left Bengaluru, as we had to use some digital means of communication in any case. On the one hand, communicating directly via the platform interface may have prevented some designers from sharing all they wanted, and it left me worried about being cut off from my contacts. On the other hand, continuing the conversation outside of the platform was against the terms and conditions – in Upwork, for example, when I typed the word 'Skype' in a message, a notification would pop up that the platform provided the means for communicating directly via video chat, and that users were advised to keep communication on the platform.

Another challenge was navigating my role as a researcher while using online platforms. I have mentioned above that I was automatically categorised as a client or a freelancer when I signed up on a platform, which came with a set of affordances for me, but also with certain expectations from others. I dealt with this by explicitly stating that I was a researcher when I contacted somebody, but as the example of the digital photo diaries has shown, it was not always possible to clearly distinguish between roles. Even trickier was the question of navigating my role when I was not directly interacting with people but lurking in the background. Community forums, for example, are accessible to all registered users, but users may still consider them as a more private space. Some freelancers strategically post there to increase their visibility, but others also use it to share their personal struggles. To navigate this ambiguity, I read forum contributions and produced fieldnotes on them but did not collect screenshots and do not quote them directly.

Finally, reflecting on the research process also entails thinking about reciprocity. While I hope that the results of this study may benefit platform workers indirectly by shedding light on some of their challenges, I also aimed to keep in mind how I could give back to the research participants who had so generously shared their time and stories with me during the research process. As I have mentioned above, I remunerated participants for submitting their digital photo diaries. In addition, I asked research participants at the end of each interview whether they would be interested in me sharing the results of my study. Moreover, many of them were interested in getting to know fellow platform workers and hearing about their experiences. To report back my preliminary results to them and provide an opportunity for them to meet other platform workers, I set up several online group discussions in spring 2021. However, as many freelancers are very busy with multiple forms of paid and unpaid work, committing to a time and date to come together was difficult. In the end, both group discussions were just follow-up interviews, as only one freelancer, respectively, attended. This suggests that other formats, such as processing my results in a concise format, may be a more promising way forward.

In the following chapters, I formulate the results of my study along three sets of practices that I observed: negotiating value, managing emotions, and aligning relations.

5. Negotiating Value

The large-scale mediation of work relations by online platforms has raised new questions about the value of work. The extension towards a "planetary labour market" (Graham & Anwar, 2019), facilitated and dynamized by online platforms, has lifted opportunities for labour arbitrage to a new level: while business process outsourcing (BPO) to so-called low-income countries has been around for quite some time, it is now possible even for small-scale enterprises or individuals to use the services provided by freelancers around the world with relatively low transaction costs (ILO, 2021, p. 108). Platforms catering to a global workforce often hold the promise of making the world grow closer and granting access to those previously excluded from the field due to their location at the economic margins. For example, item 2 of the "5 things to know about 99designs" in the self-description of the gig work platform reads: "Design doesn't do borders – Having offices located around the world is a pretty sweet deal, but we think it's even more amazing that any designer – from Sydney to Serbia – can succeed on our platform".[1] This may be true in terms of logistics; the chances of succeeding on 99designs and similar platforms are not equally distributed, however. Clients would often rather award a contract to a designer from Los Angeles than one from Lagos and are prepared to pay the latter less for the same task (Beerepoot & Lambregts, 2015). With collaboration being less and less anchored to specific locations, what are the reference points for the value of a service?

Moreover, the mechanisms of negotiating the value of work are transformed with platforms, as wages are no longer subject to collective bargaining but supply and demand. With a general oversupply of labour on gig work platforms (ILO, 2021, p. 50), making a living on platforms means that plat-

---

1 https://en.99designs.de/about, last checked on 12/06/18.

form workers have to put in considerable time and effort to negotiate the value of their work. Girard and Stark (2005) reflect on a similar degree of openness in their ethnographic study of a new media start-up firm, proposing to open the notion of value to account for different frameworks and to grasp its ambiguities:

"In this move, the polysemic character of the term – worth – signals a concern with core problems of value while recognizing that the task of valuation can work with multiple evaluative frameworks. We see this in everyday life. 'What are you worth?' is a question that can be unambiguous when constrained by context (as, for example, when applying for a mortgage). But the question 'Yes, but what is it worth?' already suggests that value might be different from price. And the question, 'Girl, do you really think he's worth it?' is one that brings several evaluative criteria into play. Social life is a place of perplexity and sometimes wonder precisely because of these problems of incommensurability" (Girard & Stark, 2005, p. 293).

This points to an important question: how is the value of a service measured? Moreover, the quote illustrates that value is an elusive notion, going beyond what can be measured as a price. In addition, the processual character of valuation as an open process, subject to various frameworks, is stressed.

They outline how in the highly uncertain context of the new media start-up firm they studied, not just the allocation of value to different products is up for negotiation, but what might be considered a product at all (Girard & Stark, 2005, p. 294). With the term "heterarchy", they describe a mode of organising that is characterised by relations of interdependence between heterogeneous actors (Girard & Stark, 2005, p. 303). The openness and uncertainty inherent in heterarchies of value also reflect the work practices in a global assemblage of platform work, as structures of organising work have partially dissolved and work practices must be continuously adapted. Moreover, authority is distributed in a heterarchy, departing from hierarchical structures of accountability (Girard and Stark 2005, p. 304). This can also be observed in platform work: how work is organised and what is paid for a job is not clearly structured, but subject to continuous negotiations.

Based on this notion, I open the perspective on the value of online freelancers' work in this chapter. I argue here that it is neither straightforward nor completely freely constructed, and that value is not adequately reflected by considering wages alone. Against this backdrop, I outline different dimensions of value in the global assemblage of platform work, and how it is negotiated between freelancers, clients, and platforms. First, I explore the value associated with a single job on the platform. I show what freelancers themselves consider as relevant for the value of their work and point out instances of friction where their valuation collides with clients' ideas. Moreover, I relate these negotiations to the affordances and constraints the platforms provide, framing and mediating the process of valuation. Second, I show how freelancers interact with different elements of the assemblage over time, investing in their market value as 'entrepreneurs of the self' (Hearn, 2010; van Doorn, 2014). The boundaries between the value of a service and the value of the service provider become blurry in these practices. Third, I show how valuation goes beyond what is paid for a service. I explore how being 'valued' and appreciated – or, the opposite, being 'devalued' – affects freelancers on a personal, emotional level. Value, then, does not only refer to the outcome of work but also to the platform-mediated work process. Finally, I tie these elements together to reflect on specific characteristics of platform work when it comes to negotiating value.

5.1 What is the value of a logo? Negotiating fair rates

In this first part of the chapter, I focus on the value of a single job performed on a platform, reflected in the rate that is paid for the product. At its most basic level, the value of a logo, for example, could be measured as the outcome of the freelancer's work of creating it, for which they are remunerated by the client, while the platform receives a commission. However, the value of a design also relies on practices of assembling on several levels. With macro tasks, such as designing a logo, valuation is more complex than with microtasks, as there are many shades of completing a job successfully. Beyond following instructions, designers face the task of creating something their client is happy with, even if the clients may not be able to express or imagine the result themselves. This also creates more space for misunderstandings or diverging interpretations. How a job is valued, then, depends on the interacting perceptions of freelancers and clients, mediated by the online platform. I focus on the freelancers' experiences and perceptions here, exploring how they navigate different evaluative frameworks when it comes to the value of their work and their value as workers. Taking their relation to their work as a starting point, I will branch out to consider how they negotiate value within contingent relations with clients and platforms.

5.1.1 Negotiating value with clients

When I asked freelancers about the value of their work, they came up with several different criteria. Concerning the rate they expect for their service, they consider the hours they put in as well as their skills, creativity, and experience. Moreover, they stress the service aspect of their work, focusing on making the client happy instead of producing what they like themselves. Freelancers' and clients' ideas of what constitutes a job well done do not always match, which often results in implicit or explicit tension. Reflecting on the value of his work, Arnav writes:

> "Generally, we only feel happy when client likes our work. Sometimes though we know we have created something awesome, a client may not like it at all. In that case; that work doesn't mean anything. We have to start all over again and create something different though we know is not as good as the previous one because client is the Boss!" (Arnav's photo diary, day 7).

Arnav refers to himself as a service provider with little power to define the value of his work. Once they have accepted a contract or successfully taken part in a design contest, designers' opinions on the value of what they have created are just one factor and must be negotiated with their clients and the platforms they use. Even if Arnav thinks what he has produced is great, it is ultimately up to the client to decide whether it was a job well done. Krishnam expresses something similar in his photo diary. His account shows that based on their limited knowledge of design principles, clients sometimes do not appreciate the skill that goes into creating a design:

> "Its mostly the clients who decide what they're going to pay me. What i think is, there is a huge lack of perception of a good design. There are certain principles in designing and what it seems that most think it is just photos and text. This creates a distortion of real value of work" (Krishnam's photo diary, day 7).

The designers' work process usually remains in the dark for clients, and based on their limited knowledge, they might see no reason to pay a large sum for 'just photos and text'. These two quotes illustrate that the value of the freelancers' work is negotiated within unequal power relations. What they think about the value of their work is not always reflected in what they are paid for it or how much credit they get.

Accordingly, the value of freelancers' work varies in different situations and with different clients. It is not inherent to the practice itself, but rather established within the relation, as Krishnam reflects:

"It's a little complicated to address the value of my work. I've done jobs in companies and firms as a graphic designer and videomaker, I've done freelancing and in some cases I have had to do work for free. So there's nothing fixed in my case" (Krishnam's photo diary, day 7).

Considering clients' power to decide whether a job has been successfully completed, it is no surprise that freelancers deem their service and the relationship they build with a client as part of the value they create. This also influences their work process: Ankit, for example, finds it important as a designer

"to explain why you came up with a design or to basically include the client in your process a lot. So that it builds trust and communication. And, I think, making the client feel like this is a safe design space and to basically trust me as a designer" (Interview with Ankit, 01-03-20).

To the freelancers I have talked to, whether they have done a good job depends on the product they have created, but also on the service they provide. Delivering on time, following clients' instructions, and valuing their opinions, all play into the value of their service. How the designers manage their relationships with clients will be considered more in-depth in Chapter 6. At this point, it is especially important that freelancers also manage their clients' perceptions of what their work is worth by communicating their thought process and being responsive to clients' wishes. In short, the value created by practices of creating a logo, for example, is entangled with practices of assembling, in which its value is negotiated. In the next subchapter, I explore the role of online platforms as actors in these negotiations, and how freelancers interact with and within the framework that platforms provide to them.

5.1.2 Online platforms framing and mediating the process

Online platforms frame and mediate the process of negotiating value. First, they set up different ways of allocating and organising jobs, which affect how freelancers' work is reflected in their pay. In Upwork, for example, clients initially set a budget when they post a job. Clients can either pay a fixed price for the whole job or a completed milestone or set an hourly rate. In the cover letter with which they apply for the job, freelancers can accept the client's offer or state a counteroffer. The contract is closed when both parties agree on a rate. In 99designs, by contrast, the platform plays a bigger role in the pricing: designers can only take part in certain design contests, based on the design level the platform assigns them. How much money the winning designer is awarded is stated in advance – freelancers' agency consists of the decision to take it or leave it. Moreover, freelancers can advertise their rates on the platform, offering, for example, a logo design for a fixed price. These different mechanisms frame the valuation between freelancers and clients and make platforms important players in the negotiation. By pre-defining the rate for a service, for example, platforms can counteract the stratification of rates along the lines of so-called high- or low-wage countries. At the same time, platforms that are highly involved in pricing also leave workers with less room for manoeuvre.

Freelancers, in turn, interact with the framework that the platform provides to find arrangements that make sense for them. Whether applying for a project or entering a contest is worth their time is a complex decision for freelancers, and it is based on a lot of unpaid work, including, for example, sorting through briefs: there is an overwhelming number of design briefs they could potentially reply to, and it requires time and effort to go through them, make choices, and to create structure within this complexity. Coming up with a structure and creating a system for themselves can be considered 'shadow work' (Illich, 1981), that is, work that is neither recognised nor paid but needs to be done for wages to be paid. Some platforms reduce this complexity, for example by making suggestions for what they consider to be a good match for both clients and workers. Still, as I have outlined in the introduction, platform workers spend a lot of time doing unpaid work to prepare the ground for gigs (ILO, 2021, p. 166). Accounting for this unpaid work would bring the average hourly rates down significantly.

To generate a continuous and sustainable income, designers must weigh the risks and rewards of what they do on the platform. In platforms with different levels, this means that freelancers calculate if they should enter a contest for a higher paying design, thereby risking not being chosen and having worked in vain, or enter a contest for a lower paying design, where their chances to succeed are higher. In addition to weighing risks and rewards, freelancers also invest time and effort to come up with their own structure and schedule. Ankit describes this as follows:

"So, then I look at some briefs, I've organised them on a weekly basis, like what kind of projects I'm going to be working on Mondays or Tuesdays or Wednesdays. [...] Just to be a bit more organised because there are, I mean, a thousand briefs. It's really hard to navigate between all of them. So, then I take about an hour to look at some briefs, just to see what I'm going to work on during the day. Then I select three to four briefs out of these. And then I start designing, or sketching, or conceptualising basically. And sometimes I'm stuck on a brief the entire day, sometimes I can go through two to three briefs, I mean, complete two to three briefs in about five, six hours" (Interview with Ankit, 01-03-20).

When they accept a job, freelancers assess what is worth their time based on different factors. Working for an hourly rate makes it relatively easy to calculate whether it pays off to accept a job. It gets more complicated when there is a fixed price for the whole project, as there are usually several factors that cannot be overseen in advance. Creating a logo, for example, does not always involve the same amount of work. Therefore, Ankit does not feel that the fixed-price function on 99designs offers enough flexibility to reflect the diversity of work processes in different contexts:

"I don't think a fixed price for something like a logo design is actually fair […]. Because, I mean, if somebody hires me, then I have to look at the project and what the project is about or what the company is like, so basically, I would like the pricing to be value-based more than just a fixed service price" (Interview with Ankit, 01-03-20).

Moreover, accepting a job for a fixed price can be quite risky. After gaining experience and a good reputation on Upwork, Jiya switched to only accepting jobs with an hourly rate to avoid working on a project for a long time without it being reflected in her earnings:

"Because, sometimes what happened was, we agreed with some fixed price job for a client, but […] they don't like the design. I have to re-do the entire thing. Sometimes it's my fault, I'm re-doing, sometimes it's the client's fault also, some, they misplaced something, miscommunicated something, we did something, now they need something else. So, I have to re-do the entire thing. […] I know it will take two hours; I can finish it in two hours. I'll bid according to that. But if there's some miscommunication, I have to do the entire thing – two plus two, I invest four hours in a particular job. But I'll get paid for only two hours job. Because I know it'll take two hours, maybe I'll bid for 50 Dollars or something, if it's a small job. But if I re-do the entire thing, it's a complete loss for me" (Interview with Jiya, 08-03-20).

Especially if Jiya does not know the client, she cannot tell how the project will unfold from the design brief alone. At the same time, the working arrangement does not leave her much space to renegotiate the terms if she is asked to do more than she anticipated or more than she feels is fair for what she is paid. At the same time, she does not feel like counting how long one takes for a job is an adequate way to determine value because it includes more elusive aspects – what she comes up with is a result of her creativity and of the experience she brings to the table. With design contests, it is even harder to assess where a freelancer's hourly rate falls, as the work is done in advance without knowing yet whether the designer will be paid for it at all. Especially when they are new to the platform, freelancers often spend many hours creating designs for contests without ever winning and thus also without ever getting paid. Moksh reflects: "When I was first into a freelancer platform, I was literally doing lots and lots of contests and stuff, but nothing was working out" (Interview with Moksh, 10-03-20).

The second way in which online platforms influence the process of negotiating value is by mediating conflicts between clients and freelancers. Platforms invoke trust in prospective client users by promising them that they must only pay for the service if they are happy with it. Accordingly, freelancers must sometimes deal with clients who refuse to pay them, saying that the job was not properly completed. In Upwork, freelancers can bring their grievances to the platform if a client refuses to pay or leaves them a review that they consider unjustified:

> "And there are clients which I told you, they ask for refund. They give you a rating of one star, even after all the hard work, and they don't want to pay you as well. So, I fight for that actually, to be frank, with Upwork, giving them all the proofs. [...] So, I show them all the proof what I have given, what was their conversation. Basis that I asked them to remove the comment, because it is not ethical to be giving someone after doing all the hard work, even after you put in that much. If I have not done anything or I have not delivered, then, even if I want to, I will not be able to remove that rating, even if they have given me a one-star" (Interview with Moksh, 10-03-20).

This quote by Moksh illustrates not only the relations between freelancers, clients, and platforms but also the difficulty of assessing whether a design job has been successfully completed. Moksh reflects on a conflict with a client: although he had done his best to deliver, incorporating requests for changes the client had made, and putting in many hours of work, the client ended up giving him just one out of five stars and refusing to pay him. In this situation, the platform acts as a mediator: if Moksh does not agree directly with the client, he can fight for his payment by providing details of his work and the conversation with his client to Upwork. If he can convince the platform that he has completed the job as it was agreed upon, the low rating will be removed, and the client must pay. Thus, the platform is also directly involved in negotiating the value of a job.

So far, I have argued that the value of freelancers' work is elusive: what they consider to be the value of their work sometimes clashes with clients' perceptions. The designers balance their perceptions of value as a reflection of their creativity and hard work with their work as service providers, trying to understand clients and be nice to work with. Both clients and freelancers navigate value within a framework provided by the platform and relate both to the infrastructure of the platform and each other in their negotiations of value. This subchapter has illustrated the interdependence of practices of assembling and practices of creating designs: the value of a design is not simply the product of practices of creating designs, but it is contingently negotiated in practices of assembling. Having started with a focus on the value of single jobs, I will now shift to the freelancers' subjective value, that is, negotiations over their capacity to assemble.

5.2 Investing in subjective value: Trade-offs and long shots

While the calculations of assessing the time that a freelancer spends on a task in relation to the money that they receive for it are already complex and contingent, they are only one part of the story about value. Otherwise, there would be no explanation why Krishnam has "had to do work for free" (Krishnam's photo diary, day 7), or why Janbir did not care about the payment for his participation in the photo diary project if he could expect a five-star rating for it: Janbir was the first designer to react to my brief looking for participants who would document their everyday work practices in digital photo diaries. I had mistakenly set the budget as 250 US dollars, thinking it was the overall budget for five freelancers. When I countered his bid to do the job for 250 US dollars with the offer to give him 50 US dollars for it, he immediately agreed, writing: "No problem, I will participate in your project. All I need is a 5 star review" (correspondence in Upwork messages, 30-04-21). Working for free or for one-fifth of what one expected would not make sense from the perspective of earning a fair rate. However, in the long run, it appears to be useful or necessary for freelancers to take more than the financial gain of a single job into account. Platform workers consider more than just the immediate payment they may receive when they decide whether or not to apply for a gig or accept a work offer.

Freelancers' practices on the platform, be it how they fill in their profile, how they interact with clients or the design they create, always have a component that goes beyond their current interaction. They also consider jobs as investments in potential value, hoping that they will be rewarded with higher pay and success rates later. Like negotiating the value of a single job, negotiating one's 'market value' is also a continuous process between freelancers, clients, and platforms. In this subchapter, I outline how freelancers negotiate their subjective value, that is, the value that is attributed to them as workers. In doing so, I will consider different dimensions of value to accumulate or invest in, and the platforms' role in mediating this value. Finally, I will connect this process of negotiation to van Doorn's (2014) deliberations on 'human capital' in digital capitalism.

5.2.1 Ascribed and projected value

As I have argued above, freelancers' work does not only consist of producing a design, but they also provide a service to clients. Accordingly, clients do not only consider how a job is done but also by whom. Clients can usually choose from a large pool of freelancers on gig work platforms, and they assess whether they would like to work with a specific freelancer, as well as what they are willing to pay, based on the information that they can find on the platform. The subjective value that is ascribed to a freelancer sometimes depends on features and biases out of their control, such as their location. The freelancers who have participated in this research project are sure, for example, that being based in South Asia affects their job prospects and the rates they can expect for a service: Sarabjit reflects that "people outside of India think that we Indians are cheap labour" (Interview with Sarabjit, 09–03-20) and mentions that some clients refuse to work with Indian freelancers at all. Reflecting on the rates she can expect from a client, Jiya faces the "hard truth" that overseas clients are prepared to pay her less than someone from their own country because she is based in India: "That is one of the reasons why they are in that platform. Otherwise, obviously they can find a local designer and do it at their local price" (Follow-up interview with Jiya, 23–02-21). Contrary to the image of a neutral digital labour market, then, the value of the freelancers' work is also attributed to them based on very analogue things, such as their nationality.

At the same time, freelancers also compare platform work to what they earn in local projects. Ankit, for example, finds that providing a service for a lower rate than what a client from a high-income country would pay someone there still leaves him with more than he would get for the same job locally:

"Online, I just work on 99designs primarily and I take local projects. But the thing about local projects is that they don't pay as well as online platforms. I mean it's just because I'm in India. Because a lot of these other, I mean the clients that come on these websites find it a lot cheaper than their local talent. [...] So, but for me it works out because what they pay locally is less than what I would get on an online platform" (Interview with Ankit, 01–03-20).

Moreover, freelancers also categorise others in this way. While I have focused on their positions as freelancers providing a service here, some designers also buy services from others via the same platform they use, for example, to subcontract elements of a design job they are providing. Ishaan, for instance, operates through Upwork with a small design agency he has set up with two colleagues. Having established himself on the platform, he has now moved on to a more managerial role: he regularly receives big and complex orders from a US client and subcontracts the actual design work to around eight further designers. He explains: "Most of the graphic designers are from Pakistan, Bangladesh, Nepal, Philippines – countries which have lower cost of living than India" (Interview with Ishaan, 11–03-20). What can be considered a fair rate, then, is measured against local contexts on several levels. The translocality of the work relation does not mean that local contexts cease to matter but rather that they overlap and sometimes clash. In their day-to-day practices, the freelancers I have talked to appreciate that they are paid more than in most local contexts, but also critically reflect on being categorised as someone from a 'low wage country'.

Consequently, the information that freelancers can project via the data in their profile, for example, is crucial. Whether a client selects them for a job and what they are willing to pay them depends partly on very subjective factors; beyond their location, this also extends to their profile picture or what they write about themselves in their profile description. What is more, platforms mediate both freelancers' visibility and how they are presented to clients, as Ankit's example illustrates: Ankit regularly posts in the 99designs community forum to catch staff members' attention; he hopes to be featured on the 'inspirations' page and thus become more visible to clients, and ultimately get more direct invitations to work together instead of having to go through the contest stage. In Chapter 6, I will explore the need to project a 'professional' image to prospective clients in more detail. Below, I elucidate how freelancers negotiate their value as workers by learning about the mechanisms of the platform-mediated work environment and by managing their reputation.

5.2.2 Learning the unspoken rules

Freelancers need work experience to be successful. While designers certainly increase their skills over time and may learn to work more efficiently, enabling them to ask for higher rates and complete jobs in less time, I will focus specifically on the value of experience on the platform here. Many of the freelancers I have talked to are relatively successful on the platform they use, having earned a considerable amount of money, and established more long-term connections with clients who trust them with multiple follow-up projects. They have developed strategies over time that help them find the right words in cover letters, assess what jobs are worth their time and whether a client might be difficult to work with and manage their time efficiently. When designers start using online platforms to connect to clients, they go through a phase of trial and error, where they often spend a lot of time writing unsuccessful cover letters or taking part in contests without standing a chance. This account by Vikas resembles a typical beginning story that designers go through when they are new to platform work:

> "Before, actually I have a very strong experience in graphic design. That is the main thing I wanted to start that. After I quit the job, I wanted to learn and I thought, only I have design skills only, I don't have anything else. I don't know how to manage projects, I don't know how to send proposals. And I don't know anything else actually. So, a few things I wanted to know: How to contact with the client? How do I reach them? I even don't know about proposal, what it is. So, I was supposed to learn that, because I sent a lot of proposals on Upwork, I did not get any jobs" (Interview with Vikas, 15–03-20).

Although Vikas was already experienced in graphic design when he signed up, he had to learn how to use Upwork and manage his work as a freelancer. Many freelancers who sign up on a gig work platform never get a single job, and some of my interview partners stopped trying after a couple of unsuccessful attempts. Those who stay must have a steep learning curve, as platforms usually limit how many connections new users can make. Sarabjit started his career working for an agency that operated through oDesk and decided to work directly as a freelancer through Elance after some time.[2] Having just signed up on the platform, he was allowed to send job proposals to 30 prospective clients. This is how it went:

"So, first project was on Elance, and after that, there was, 30 or 40 connects in Elance. So, only in a single day, I spent all 30 connects. I submitted all 30 proposals on, I think, logo design projects only. [...] I spent all 30 connects, but I didn't get any projects, so I understood that this is not the way we can work as a freelancer, submitting the proposal with blind eyes" (Interview with Sarabjit, 09-03-20).

After using all his free opportunities to connect to clients on unsuccessful attempts, Sarabjit had to wait for some time until he was allowed to write a new cover letter. Thus, he was not completely free to try out different strategies but had to find a successful one quickly if he wanted to make it on the platform. Most freelancers told me that it makes sense to be very specific in their proposals and to rather spend more time on a proposal than to send out as many proposals as possible as quickly as possible. Instead of having one standard proposal that they send out to every brief, experienced freelancers pick up on what is mentioned in the brief and argue why they are the exact right person for the job. The communicative skills the freelancers gain on the way further support them in finding jobs.

One way of getting value out of one's time on the platform is choosing deliberately what offers to reply to. Freelancers must learn to assess their chances for a particular job, weighing the risks and rewards of aiming high. Moreover, experience on the platform means being able to assess what job might not be worth their time in the end. Jiya, for example, has come up with a strategy to tell whether working with a client will be pleasant when she reads a design brief:

"I have a very specific way to decide that. If somebody says that 'it will take only 1 hour for this job', I do not work with the client. My logic is that I am the professional here, let me decide how long it will take, if you are deciding the time for me, you better do the job. It may sound arrogant but most of the time it works. They specify the time to decide the price but price does not always depend on time, quality and creativity also count because this is creative work" (Jiya's photo diary, day 4).

By navigating design briefs, she does not only consider the payment she can expect to receive but also tries to assess if the client takes her seriously as a

---

2 Elance and oDesk merged in 2013 and were rebranded as Upwork in 2015.

professional. This processual aspect of value will play a role later in this chapter.

After just having started on the platform, freelancers often take jobs that do not pay well in the hope of gaining experience. In addition to trying out different strategies for themselves, freelancers also get in touch with others who have more experience on the platform, either through the community forum on the platform or groups on social media. One of my interview partners, Kanav, even hired a more experienced user through PeoplePerHour to provide him with insights on how to use the platform efficiently. Over time, freelancers develop "gig literacies" (Sutherland et al., 2020), that is, they learn how to leverage the platform environment to their favour. They can build up this experience to some extent; however, the mechanisms the platforms use change regularly. Even the most well-adapted designers may have to start over from time to time, find new strategies, and gain new experience. Even if a designer figures out a system of interacting with the platform that works perfectly for them, chances are that the algorithm that affects their visibility will change again. Moreover, platforms regularly introduce new features or mechanisms for allocating jobs, as well as changes in their pricing structure. Accordingly, freelancers must continuously adapt their strategies to a changing environment.

5.2.3 Demonstrating skill

But even designers who have ample experience and know how to write a great cover letter or how to choose a gig wisely face challenges when they are new to a specific platform: it is not enough to be good at one's job, one also needs to persuade others of one's qualifications. This is another, closely connected aspect of long-term value: beyond their skills and experience, freelancers also build a portfolio to present themselves well to prospective clients. Growing one's portfolio, then, is also part of the calculation that leads especially new freelancers to accept jobs for which they are paid little or even no money. When they create a design, freelancers are paid for their service with money, but they may also add the design to their portfolio and thus potentially attract further clients' attention or put them in a position where they can ask for a higher rate. As Kiaan recalls from starting on PeoplePerHour:

"And then, once I got some information on how that works in terms of basic process, then I thought: Let's jump start. Even if your gigs are not that good but let me do few gigs for free and then eventually let me build the portfolio and then eventually expand. So, when I started doing things for free, I got more gigs compared to the paid ones. So, there is a lot of designers who are experienced, they were charging approximately 10 dollars, 15, 20 an hour. So, I decided: let's do it for free. So, I got approximately five or six. And then, once I built the portfolio, then I started charging people" (Interview with Kiaan, 29-02-20).

While freelancers outside of digital platforms must find ways to showcase their portfolio, too, there are some differences. For freelancers doing platform work, the platform sets the framework for how the freelancers can present themselves and therefore structures self-presentation along their chosen criteria. Most platforms allow freelancers to show their portfolios on their profile pages. Thus, designers can transfer their experiences from working as a designer to the platform to some extent, for example, by including previous jobs in their portfolio or linking to an external portfolio website, and by entering their job experience and educational background into their online profile. Some freelancers also create designs just to have something to show in their portfolio. In Upwork, for instance, freelancers can create several sub-profiles that focus on the different services they provide. Moksh, for example, has a general profile, one for graphic design, and one for virtual assistant jobs. The platform provides designers with pre-established categories and sometimes also limits the number of designs to be added to the portfolio.

Freelancers who sign up on a gig work platform often spend considerable time working for little or no money, hoping that their investment in experiences and their portfolio will pay off eventually. There is a stage of trial and error involved, but they learn how to handle clients well, how to read the subtle signs that will tell them whether a job will be worth their time, and what designs in their portfolio will increase their chances of being hired. However, there is another powerful aspect of their 'market value' that is much more volatile, namely, their reputation on the platform.

5.2.4 Platform-mediated reputation

Freelancers' reputation on the platform plays a big role in what jobs and what rates are accessible to them. In addition to improving their design skills and their specific skills of acting within the platform-mediated environment, then, freelancers also need to earn a certain reputation on the platform. This reputation is mediated by the platform, which commensurates job history, client relations, and many more factors into a logic of performance metrics that allow for assigning a 'market value' to freelancers.

First, before freelancers can start working on a platform, their applications are filtered by some of the platforms, judging their initial market value. In 99designs, for example, applicants must provide work samples and information about their previous experience working as a designer; in Upwork, the decision is made based on background information and specifying what services freelancers are planning to provide, as well as their specific qualification for that service.

Second, platforms sort freelancers into a hierarchy. Depending on the platform, this hierarchy may impact what jobs a freelancer can apply for or more subtly influence their chances of being hired. In 99designs, for example, users start as entry-level designers, and can then work their way up to mid-level and finally top-level designers. Higher-paying design contests are only accessible to top-level designers. The decisions about promoting a designer to the next level often remain opaque to the designers, however. Similarly, going through a verification process with Upwork earns designers a blue check next to their profile picture and evokes trust with clients, which, in turn, adds to the freelancers' market value.

Third, more volatile measures, especially client reviews and ratings, also impact freelancers' reputations. In Upwork, clients can leave reviews and ratings of up to five stars. In addition, their job success rate is shown next to their profile picture. This is a form of market value that freelancers cannot build up but need to constantly work on. It is hard to get started without any reviews, but even a freelancer with a lot of great reviews may lose jobs for a long time after just one bad review (Wood & Lehdonvirta, 2021b, pp. 18–20). Moreover, freelancers usually cannot transfer reputation scores when they move to another platform. What is more, if they do not constantly accept new jobs, their success rate will go down – according to rules that, once again, remain in the dark, as this quote by Moksh illustrates:

"So, you only are top-rated when you are having a good feedback, continuously, and you are having work regularly. And this used to be 100 per cent, but I don't know, it fluctuates sometimes. Maybe because one week I don't have a work, some weeks I have" (Interview with Moksh, 10–03–20).

Thus, long-term market value, again, is continuously negotiated between freelancers, clients, and platforms. At times, platform workers do extra work for free or even offer a refund to avoid a low rating by a client (Wood & Lehdonvirta, 2021b, p. 27). Even if this means they lose money, a low rating might mean losing even more in the future. Platforms do not only frame this by setting up rating systems and by sorting designers into a hierarchy; they also influence ratings 'backstage' by penalising inactivity, as Moksh's quote has shown.

Van Doorn (2014) describes managing one's online reputation as an investment in human capital. He argues that the value that is created by users of digital platforms is not created because rewarding activities are performed and then exploited, as Terranova (2000) would argue, but because people invest in their human capital to increase their market value. Accordingly, the neoliberal worker acts as an "entrepreneur of the self", who invests in their human capital:

"In this way, human capital — at once a 'measured measure' and a 'measuring measure' — represents a powerful subjective form that is a defining feature of neoliberal reason, extending the economic speculation on one's market value to spheres that were previously exempt from such calculations" (van Doorn, 2014, p. 358).

This notion of speculation illustrates the volatility of the value that is assigned to the freelancers' work. Their practices do include unpaid work of filling in their profile, for example, to attract clients' attention. Yet, what forces them to constantly keep negotiating and speculating is their integration in a dynamic assemblage of actors. They are in a paradoxical situation, as their market value is embodied, but at the same time dependent on others' valuation and thus not completely in their power. They do not really 'own' their human capital but can only invest in it and hope that its value will increase (van Doorn, 2014, p. 358).

What is more, individual choices, such as trade-offs between financial rewards and the opportunity to build experiences, harm platform workers' situations on a larger scale. Decisions that make sense to an individual freelancer within the framework that the platforms provide, such as working for free as an investment in one's human capital, may make it harder for freelancers collectively to make a living on digital platforms. Thus, even though many freelancers who use online platforms are not directly in touch with their platform 'colleagues', they have an impact on each other's work practices and situations.

5.3 Process matters: Being valued as a creative professional

I have elaborated so far on how value is framed differently with different freelancers, and how it is continuously negotiated between different actors in the assemblage. In this section, I will show how value goes beyond the price of a service. I outline how value is entangled with the work process rather than only its result. In doing so, I extend the notion of value to an emotional dimension: value, to the designers, also has a component of being valued, of being appreciated. This notion of value relates to financial value: being appreciated is sometimes reflected in payment, and freelancers feel valued when they are paid well. However, payment is, by far, not the only important aspect. Designers also want to be taken seriously as creative professionals and be involved in the process.

When freelancers feel that they have done a good job, it can be quite an emotional experience: they identify strongly with their work and bring a lot of themselves into it. They feel responsible for the result and their ambition to create something great has value for them beyond what the client thinks about it. This is how Krishnam reflects on creating a poster for a client:

"[...] while i was making it, i experienced a burst of emotions. The emotions were a mix of happiness and proudness like getting an achievement. I was swearing myself like 'how i did that', 'its better than what i was trying to make', 'this gonna blast'. I was really happy when i was making that poster and at the same time very excited. At last I was very proud. This infers that i really enjoy what i do" (Krishnam's photo diary, day 6).

The quote points to a dimension of value that is untouched by financial rewards. The designers feel that there is value in what they create, and their work is rewarding to them. The price for a service, thus, cannot fully express its value.

When the designers in this study describe their work processes, they often differentiate between working *for* a client and working *with* a client. In the process of working *with* a client, the designer is taken seriously in the process, which includes clients trusting their assessment and giving them some discretion. When working *for* a client, the designer has little freedom to make their own decisions but is asked to simply follow instructions. Designers differentiate this along various lines – some argue that the international clients they get in touch with through online platforms have more appreciation for good design than their local clients; some say that big firms usually understand better that design is more than "just photos and text" (Krishnam's photo diary, day 7), and some say that the systems put in place by the platform decrease their influence on the process.

How the work process is structured impacts both how much designers are paid for a job, that is, the valuation from outside, and their own feeling of satisfaction, that is, the value of their work to themselves. Freelancers see themselves as creatives, but also as skilled professionals. They stress that design is more than just creating something nice to look at – it follows certain principles that they need to learn, and that they adapt their designs to specific companies and their goals.

This is not a simple difference between local and platform-mediated work – a lot of the designers I have talked to have told me about experiences where local clients did not trust their judgment. Saanvi, a very established graphic designer, told me about her struggles when she returned to India after having studied and worked abroad for several years:

"Because you have to spend a lot of time trying to convince your client why you have done something; they will challenge you for everything, you know? And they think they know a lot, even though they don't know design or anything. But they will constantly suggest things that you know won't work. [...] So, a lot of my effort went into advocacy about design, because people did not know what it is. They all thought [it is just] making a pattern or something. Clients used to tell me 'Okay, I will show to my wife and tell you what she says', you know?" (Interview with Saanvi, 04–03-20)

As the quote indicates, local clients do not necessarily take designers seriously as a professional or value their opinion highly. Moreover, in all arrangements, clients usually have the final say about the design, which means that designers must sometimes follow instructions that run counter to their ideas. However, the way the process is structured especially on contest-based online platforms reinforces clients' influence, as this quote by Ankit indicates:

"So, recently I've been struggling with what design really means to me and what a design service means to me and how valuable it is to me. So, basically, I feel like a lot of these online platforms, even 99designs, basically design contests, are, actually I don't really believe how that, a design contest should be. Because ultimately the client has all the power. Basically, the client makes the decisions, the design decisions, without any prior information of design. So, the client can make a lot of, you know, poor choices, based on just aesthetics, that might not be right for his company, that might not be, right for the future of his company. And a lot of this is missed in online competitive platforms, where they have these competitions" (Interview with Ankit, 01–03-20).

As I have described above, spending extra time on re-doing a design impacts the financial value a job entails for a designer, as the money that they earn stays the same for a longer time spent working. This quote points to another dimension of value, that is, being able to shape the work process. While Saanvi spent a lot of time trying to convince her local clients of her design ideas, freelancers working via online platforms often do not have this option. This aspect of value goes beyond payment. Ankit describes how the mechanism of design contests leaves him little room for manoeuvre as a designer. Although the client usually does not know as much about design principles, he must follow suit if he wants to win a contest.

The process of creating a design brief for a logo on 99designs, which I have already touched upon in the introduction, illustrates this: to start a contest, clients fill in a standardised form. They can describe the design they are looking for, propose a colour palette and place the design they are thinking of along several spectrums: classic-modern, grown-up-youthful, feminine-masculine, playful-sophisticated, economic-luxurious, geometric-organic, abstract-specific. Based on this information, designers can submit their logos and hope to be selected. They can contact the client to ask for specifications, there is little room for a shared process or working *with* the client. Accordingly, they rather create "a design based on an educated guess of what they would like" (Interview with Ankit, 01-03-20). As Ankit puts it: "99designs offers a pretty linear way to communicate with clients. Basically, you post the design, and they'll give you some feedback and then you revert and then they select your design" (Interview with Ankit, 01-03-20).

Moreover, design processes tend to be more fast-paced in platform work, as Ankit argues. Keeping in mind that he will be rejected instantly if the client does not like his design, he tries to "dish out designs pretty fast" and "give them the gist of the design" (Interview with Ankit, 01-03-20). In local projects, by contrast, he will usually prepare three different concepts and explain to his client where he is going with the design. The platforms thus make it harder for clients to be an active part of the thought process, valuing their contribution to the process less. In combination with the power imbalance between freelancers and clients outlined above, the designers I have talked to often feel that their skills are not reflected in their role and that they are, thus, not properly valued in the work process.

5.4 Synthesis: Heterarchical negotiations of value in platform work

I have elucidated several aspects of value in this chapter: First, I outlined how freelancers, clients, and platforms contribute to valuating jobs. Second, I showed how freelancers negotiate the value attributed to themselves and their work over a longer time, again, continuously relating to clients and platforms. Third, I detailed how value is part of the work process beyond payment, how processual value emerges from the relation between freelancers and clients, and how platforms structure this process. The various aspects of value cannot be separated: being paid a fair price is part of valuing someone's work, and the emotional reward of having produced something one is happy with may be overshadowed by a client's negative feedback. Moreover, I have argued in this chapter that value is not something that a freelancer can accumulate or own – it is continuously re-negotiated and situationally produced within relations. Accordingly, the question of the value of work in global platform work can only be answered concerning specific situations. Demirel et al. (2021) use a Bordieuan framework to study how hierarchies of value are reproduced in the online labour market. They argue that differences in economic, social, and cultural capital lead to the reproduction of inequality between the Global North and South. In a context where clients are predominantly from the Global North, some social and cultural practices are valued while others are devalued. The insistence on English proficiency and "articulation of Global North business etiquette and specific client-focused corporate practices" (Demirel et al., 2021, p. 13) is one example of this and can explain to some extent how differences in the valuation of work are reproduced. Some of the practices I have observed can be understood as building up capital: for example, work experience on the platform as cultural capital, or getting follow-up clients as social capital. Moreover, value is embodied by freelancers in the form of skills and creativity and in the experience that they have gained on the platform. This capital is expressed in online ratings or, more broadly, online reputation.

However, I would argue that a framework based on capital has some drawbacks when it is applied to platform work. First, considering online platforms simply as a field where certain forms of capital are useful downplays their role in mediating value. Platforms are not simply a work context but actively and dynamically shape work practices. They mediate how freelancers can transform their time and skills into money, and they shape the work process. Second, as I have shown in this chapter, there is no single definition of what constitutes value in platform work. As Girard and Stark (2005) have described for heterarchical organising, several different evaluative frameworks meet: platform workers themselves include time spent on a job, the quality of the final product, as well as the level of service they provide in their assessment of the value of a job. In addition, clients have their own ideas about the value of a job, which is further mediated by platforms. These heterogeneous actors interdependently produce the valuation of services on a platform, negotiating not just rates, but also what exactly constitutes a job well done. Third, value is continuously negotiated over time, making it necessary for freelancers to adapt to changing structures. They must constantly work on aligning their idea of value with new clients and re-negotiate with clients and platforms. What is more, as the subchapter on investing in one's market value has shown, future value is negotiated in a context of uncertainty. Accordingly, value is not built up by accumulating different forms of capital but produced with a range of different practices.

The dissolution of structures does not necessarily translate into more freedom for workers. Allocating jobs individually to workers who are considered independent contractors makes it extremely hard to strive for better working conditions through collective bargaining. Instead, rates are often subject to supply and demand – which often leads to extremely low rates in the context of an oversupply of labour on platforms (ILO, 2021, p. 50). Moreover, there are also notions of hierarchy within platform work. First, as I have described above, access to higher-paying jobs is often conditioned on being sorted into a higher-level category by the platform, such as a top-level designer on 99designs or a top-rated user on Upwork. Value is dynamic, but not equally distributed. Second, platforms direct and structure work practices, for example with their terms and conditions. Therefore, while freelancers, clients, and platforms are interdependent, platforms have more power to make changes to the overall system. Third, platform work interacts with unequal structures beyond the platform and these structures have an impact on how platform workers can interact with the platform.

How freelancers experience platform work depends to a large extent on how financially dependent they are on the income generated there (Schor et al., 2020). Not all workers can afford to pick only attractive jobs; it is thus mostly those who have other options who can enjoy the flexibility associated with platform work. As I have described above, freelancers can often be pickier after they have built up experience; however, they are also generally in a more difficult position to negotiate their market value if they or even their whole family rely on a regular income from the platform. Moreover, while online platforms extend access to work geographically, they are still integrated into unequal global valuations of work. As I will argue in more detail in Chapter 7, the global assemblage of platform work produces tension between the global form and actual situated practices. Transforming work into a global form, online platforms hold the technological possibility to disintegrate and reintegrate work practices from one place to another, and to transcend income structure, purchasing power, or integration into postcolonial dependencies of national contexts as evaluative criteria. The actual situated practices of working together via online platforms, however, are still affected by these factors.

While I have focused on freelancers' practices of negotiating value here, it is important to also think about the embeddedness of these negotiations over value within the context of the platform economy. Considering the revenue models at the heart of how platforms structure interaction (van Dijck, 2013) adds another layer to the negotiation of value as the freelancers contribute to the platforms' revenue not just through the commission they pay, but also by supplying different kinds of data. When freelancers work on their digital reputation, for example, by replying to help requests in the forum, they perform a service for free that the platform would otherwise have to hire paid workers for. Moreover, the data generated by selection and valuation processes are analysed to contribute to the algorithmic evaluation of designs (Rest, 2016).

6. Managing Emotions

In Chapter 5, I argued that the value attributed to freelancers is negotiated within relations between them, their clients, and the online platforms they use. Moreover, their success depends on how well they can convince clients to pick them out of a large number of potential service providers. Creating a design for a client is quite subjective and requires them to understand their vision, often with very little information to rely on. The freelancers' work requires creativity and discretion – accordingly, they also face the challenge of convincing their clients to choose them by standing out and demonstrating their trustworthiness. In this chapter, I further explore how freelancers make and sustain connections by focusing on the emotional and affective aspects of their work. I carve out how managing both their own and clients' emotions is a part of freelancers' practices of assembling.

The exploration is guided by two central sensitising concepts: First, Hochschild's ([1983] 2012) concept of emotion work and emotional labour. Based on her research on flight attendants, Hochschild argues that in addition to physical and mental strain, managing and regulating one's emotions, too, is an aspect of work. The second concept, affective labour, is closely related to emotion work, yet sets a different focus: first established by Hardt (1999), the term affective labour denotes the effort of managing others' emotions and producing affect through one's behaviour. Taking a relational perspective, the term departs from the notion of a bounded, authentic subject. While Hochschild frames emotional labour in terms of acting, affective labour includes a notion of subjectification, that is, working subjects are produced through affective labour practices (Mankekar & Gupta, 2016, pp. 26-27). However, I will not treat the two concepts as clearly separated here but as joint elements of managing emotions: affective labour includes the emotional labour of managing one's own emotions: when freelancers put on a friendly face with a difficult client, they partly do so because they are hoping for a positive reaction, for example.

While the concept of emotional labour was developed from a vantage point of face-to-face interaction, the freelancers in this study mainly communicate with their clients via online platforms. Getting the right emotions across remotely requires specific practices of emotion work and affective labour, as Mankekar and Gupta (2016) have argued based on their study on business process outsourcing (BPO) call centre workers in Bengaluru. Based on the entangled concepts of emotion work and affective labour, and taking into account the platform-mediated context, I will explore how freelancers manage their own and their clients' emotions, and how platforms mediate emotional connection, in this chapter.

First, I explore the role of emotions in freelancers' everyday work, looking at how they relate to their work on an emotional level. Second, I focus on how they relate to their clients emotionally while interacting through online platforms. Third, I turn to online platforms' role in mediating emotion more closely. Finally, I bring these aspects together to reflect on the notion of trust in a platform-mediated work environment.

6.1 Between thrill and frustration: Managing one's own emotions

In this first part of the chapter, I outline how freelancers' work practices are interwoven with emotions. Their everyday work – both practices of creating designs and practices of assembling – can raise positive emotions, such as joy, pride, or excitement but also difficult emotions, such as frustration, sadness, or anger. Below, I explore how freelancers deal with these emotions, as well as how emotions influence their work process.

6.1.1 Emotion as a motivating factor

The freelancers describe how emotions of joy or excitement motivate them. A lot of them express a deep passion for their work, and they are driven by the joy and excitement they feel when creating something new. Krishnam, for example, describes how he felt about a design he completed in his photo diary like this:

"The reason i decided to put that picture for this day's topic because while i was making it, i experienced a burst of emotions. The emotions were a mix of happiness and proudness like getting an achievement. I was swearing myself like 'how i did that', 'its better than what i was trying to make', 'this gonna blast'. I was really happy when i was making that poster and at the same time very excited. At last I was very proud. This infers that i really enjoy what i do" (Krishnam's photo diary, day 6).

He even surprised himself with what he had created and felt immense pride about it. Other designers have shared similar accounts of being in a flow state and happy with what they produce – their work, thus, is a source of joy and fulfilment for them. The designers describe this role of passion and the joy of creating as a motivating factor on two levels: on an everyday level where their passion for artistic work motivates them to keep going with their work, and on a more general level as a rationale for choosing to work as a designer in the first place. Divyansh, for example, explains how his love for films motivated him to enter a creative field:

"I fell in love. Like, I fell in love with that subject, I fell in love with these directors and I just, went deeper and deeper. I saw world cinema and I saw styles of directors, and then I knew that I wanted to get into films" (Interview with Divyansh, 27–02–20).

How strongly emotions motivate freelancers for their work varies. Some frame their work strongly in connection with emotions. Especially those that rely less on the income they generate with platform work stress the happiness that creating designs brings them – like Nitin: "Talenthouse is a platform, still I do stuff on my own, it's for my happiness" (Interview with Nitin, 04–02–20). For those who are more focused on stability and a steady income, emotions also play a role. Jiya, for example, finds joy in the steadiness of being able to work every day:

"The emotions I feel for my work are happiness, thrill, and excitement because I have clients, I am still able to work every day makes me happy. Work, in general, makes me happy" (Jiya's photo diary, day 6).

While the uncertainty of the platform-mediated work environment is often described as stressful, and Jiya, for example, feels satisfaction at finding some regularity in her work, some freelancers appreciate precisely the dynamic nature of their work. Arnav, for example, states: "This is something so addicting about freelancing, it has life, a job can be boring but freelancing is always exciting!" (Arnav's photo diary, day 6). Joy, gratitude, and excitement, then, are emotions that motivate freelancers to sit down at their desks and create a new design.

In addition to the creativity of designing something new and the joy they find in the rhythms of their work, relating to clients, too, is interwoven with emotions. Janbir, for example, states that it is "fun working with people from different countries" (Janbir's photo diary, day 3). I will elucidate how freelancers work on their relationships with clients in a later part of this chapter but will focus on the emotions these relationships bring them here. Feeling appreciated by their clients is a great motivation for freelancers. What is more, being trusted by clients fills them with a sense of pride and can make them happy. I have described in the first part of this chapter how strongly many freelancers identify with their work on an emotional level. Accordingly, when their work is appreciated, they also feel appreciated as a person. Their feelings are affected by how others perceive them, and positive feedback feels like a valuation of themselves, not just their work. Nitin, for example, recollects an instance where he won a contest on Talenthouse with a poster design:

"Yeah, so that made my day. [...] So, looking at all this, at least I achieved something in life. I mean, not much and all, but, small small things is like big things to you right? When people notice something which you did, right? That is where you win. That's all – it's not about the money. But it's about winning there" (Interview with Nitin, 04-02-20).

People noticing and appreciating his designs felt exciting and rewarding to Nitin, beyond the happiness he felt while creating the design and even more than earning money with it.

What the freelancers perceive as signs of appreciation by their clients varies. In Upwork, for example, clients can pay freelancers a bonus if they are especially happy with their work – something that Kanav counts as a sign of appreciation. Moreover, clients' reviews and ratings are a central potential source of appreciation. Freelancers feel pride and joy about positive reviews – to the extent that they can almost become addictive. Arnav, for example, writes: "[...] excellent feedback from clients, I read more than 100 times; a feedback that says good things about me. It gives me a strange kind of confidence" (Arnav's photo diary, day 6). At the same time, getting a negative review can be very frustrating. Sarabjit, for example, recalls how disappointed he was when is rating on Elance dropped: "It was a five-star rating system, and when it went to 4.9, I was very sad, throughout the day" (Interview with Sarabjit, 09-03-20).

While emotions like joy or passion for what they do motivate the freelancers, to what extent they can let themselves be steered by their emotions also depends on how dependent they are on the income they generate with platform work. Their work is not always fun – as Krishnam explains: "Sometimes its just nothing, i got a stack of work and have to complete it somehow till the end of the day." (Krishnam's photo diary, day 6). Moreover, being evaluated by and working with diverse clients can also raise negative emotions, which the freelancers then have to deal with. In the following subchapter, I will take a closer look at how freelancers manage their less-desired emotions when they deal with clients and with their everyday work.

6.1.2 Powering through and putting on a brave face: Deep and surface acting

While the emotions I have described in the first part of this chapter generally drive work or make it easier for the freelancers, dealing with difficult emotions concerning their work or their clients requires emotion work and emotional labour from them (cf. Hochschild, [1983] 2012). Hochschild differentiates between deep acting or emotion work, that is, inducing or suppressing one's feelings, and surface acting, that is, managing outer expressions of feeling (Hochschild, [1983] 2012, pp. 38–45). Both deep and surface acting are necessary for freelancers in their everyday work practices.

First, freelancers must process negative emotions and still manage to stay motivated, regulating their own negative emotions, resembling what Hochschild has called deep acting. Designers' work experiences include being rejected on multiple occasions. A common occurrence, which I have described in more detail in Chapter 5, is being rejected when they start working on a platform. At that point, designers often do not know yet how they need to communicate with clients. They may not put enough time and effort into a design for a competition or a cover letter for a job, thus ending up being rejected for all jobs and having wasted time. This gets better with experience, but with the oversupply of labour, rejection is still a common experience even for long-term platform designers. It takes strength and determination to keep trying even if the results remain bad for a long time. While not hearing back for a cover letter does hurt, the emotional impact is even stronger when a freelancer has already created a design, which is then rejected. Akarsh, for example, remembers an experience when an acquaintance from college had asked him to create a logo for his mother's shop:

"I told 'Okay, I will create it'. But at that time, I don't know how to do business, means how to ask for the money. So, I did not tell him anything. And in the morning, I thought I have to give him the logo, I will say what I want and how much I want for the logo. So, in the morning, after I created a logo, I was just sending him, the file was just uploaded half, he called me and said 'Bro, I don't need the logo right now, my mom said somebody also had done'. So, on that day I cried, I was just looking into the mirror and 'So, what happened?', yes? 'You just wasted your time" (Interview with Akarsh, 31-08-20).

Although Akarsh did not arrange the logo design for his acquaintance through a platform, it still resembles an experience that the platform workers go through regularly, especially if they take part in design contests. Considering that freelancers often feel a personal connection to what they create, having invested something of themselves and it being rejected can be tough.

Second, designers' work also includes surface acting in the sense of projecting positivity even when it does not reflect how they feel. I will go into greater detail about how the freelancers manage their relationships with clients below – at this point, the focus is on how they try to stay friendly when dealing with difficult clients. I have described in Chapter 5 how designers' work does not only include producing designs, but also producing a positive experience for their clients and being nice to work with – even when they are "getting annoyed when client is requesting too many changes" (Krishnam's photo diary, day 6). Janbir contrasts his work experiences with diverse types of clients like this: "An appreciation from a client gives me the motivation to work hard. On the other hand, I hate doing kind of work from a bad client but stay positive" (Janbir's photo diary, day 6). Staying positive in this situation takes work, as it does for Kanav when he tries "to keep patience even when I get the hard clients to work with" (Kanav's photo diary, day 6). This surface acting is also present in work environments not mediated by platforms. However, as I will explain in the following subchapter, some of the emotional strain that the freelancers in this study experience is closely tied to the uncertainty of the platform-mediated work environment.

6.1.3 Dealing with the anxiety of a highly flexible work environment

First, as I will carve out in more detail in Chapter 7, remote freelancers are often living out of sync with their immediate surroundings. Moreover, they do not have colleagues to vent to, to keep them company, or to share experiential knowledge about the job with them. While BPO call centre workers, too, often follow different rhythms than those around them, they share an office with others who are in the same situation, and they often have a range of joint activities organised by their company (cf. Mankekar & Gupta, 2016, p. 31). By contrast, the platform workers whom I have talked to hardly know any other online freelancers. If they do know someone from the same platform, it is usually based on a previous connection outside of the platform. The platforms do provide ways to connect to other freelancers online, such as community forums, or even occasional local events. However, the reality of the designers' everyday work experience is far removed from the picture of a global community of designers that platforms like 99designs paint. Ankit, for example, regularly posts in the online community forum of 99designs, but this is less about connecting with other designers and more about attracting attention and, hopefully, getting featured on the website someday. The platform interface is geared towards enabling connections between freelancers and clients, but it is relatively hard for freelancers to connect to other freelancers through the platform. When they use the community forum, their conversations are under the eyes of the platform operators, which makes it harder to openly chat about their grievances with the platform, for example. Some of the freelancers in my study connect with others via groups on social media, such as Facebook or WhatsApp, where they can talk more freely about their work. While there are accounts of freelancers who organise to fight for better working conditions (cf. e.g. Wood & Lehdonvirta, 2021b), the experiences that the freelancers whom I have talked to share sound more like Krishnam's:

"There are very few real social aspects in a freelancers life. I have some local freelancers that i can connect and there are worldwide people i can connect through my work. I do have some people in my profession in my city whom i can meet with and discuss some talks together but pandemic has made it more difficult. Virtual connections are no fun" (Krishnam's photo diary, day 6).

Second, in addition to the loneliness and isolation that remote freelance life entails, the uncertainty inherent in platform work can bring a lot of anxiety. As Gregg (2011) notes, precarity has an affective dimension, as workers always have to be prepared for change and try to anticipate their next steps:

"In the language I have been using in this book, precarity is another manifestation of work's intimacy: its irrepressible invasiveness over one's thoughts, regardless of time or locations, is symptomatic of the unpredictable nature of jobs increasingly facilitated by communications technology. Anticipation and preparation for work's potential presence are the 'immaterial' of [sic] 'affective' dimensions to work in knowledge professions" (Gregg, 2011, p. 155).

Moreover, what Gregg (2011) has called "presence bleed" (p. 2), also takes an emotional toll on the platform workers. As Gregg notes, dealing with the volatility of the workplace and with a never-ending to-do list is emotionally taxing. Compared to Gregg's study of office workers in Australia, gig work is characterised by even more uncertainty and volatility: as risk is increasingly shifted to workers and contracts only last as long as it takes to complete a single design, the freelancers grapple with the anxiety of continuously having to make sure that work keeps flowing in. Below, I will go one step further and explore how freelancers manage the emotional dimensions of their relationships with clients.

6.2 Emotional relations

In this subchapter, rather than focusing on freelancers' emotions, I ask how they leverage and manage emotions when they relate to clients. Emotions are not just the freelancers' or the clients', but they are part of the relationship between them. I show how the freelancers interact with the platform infrastructure to evoke clients' trust along the lines of the process of finding and performing work. Before they start working with a client, freelancers must attract their attention and convince them that they are the right person for the job. They need to evoke an initial basic level of trust with the clients as a prerequisite for them to hire them. The number of competing freelancers and the opaque mechanisms of the platforms that have an impact on their visibility is an important part of their practices of assembling. Here, I will focus specifically on how freelancers work on standing out to prospective clients as professionals – and what being professional means to them. To be hired, it is not enough for designers to be visible to clients, they must also convince a prospective client to trust them with the job. Proving this in a context where clients and workers cannot see each other and where their communication is streamlined by the platform is a challenge, and I argue here that proving one's trustworthiness online is part of the affective labour that the freelancers perform. Being professional, then, does not contradict emotions; by contrast, freelancers are supposed to professionally manage emotions.

6.2.1 A leap of faith

For both clients and freelancers, closing a contract is a leap of faith. As I will carve out in more detail below, the risk for clients varies according to how jobs are allocated on a platform, as clients make their decision based on a design that has already been created when they choose to launch a design contest, for example. Especially when they want to hire someone for an extensive job, clients sometimes ask designers to do a test job for them, that is, they hire them for a small task and make their decision about hiring them based on the results of the job. A lot of times, however, the hiring decision is made based on limited information on both sides. As Jiya describes: "It's a complete virtual thing. The client cannot see you. I cannot see the client. So, trust is very important. Your credibility is very important." (Interview with Jiya, 08–03-20)

Freelancers, too, take a risk when they start working with a new client and use different strategies to assess whether a client will be a good fit. To do this, they take hints from the initial conversation with a client or even from the design brief. Arnav, for example, not only checks the ratings that a client got, but he also takes a closer look at what the freelancers who have previously worked with a client leave in the comments. He reckons that freelancers would usually not leave a low rating or a negative comment, so he takes it as a bad sign if the reviews are not accompanied by any comments, as this is how he deals with unpleasant experiences with clients himself:

"I will be reading all the feedbacks. [...] So, then we can come to know whether to work for this client or not. [...] Even if it is like, fine, then we go to the comment what they have made. Sometimes, like the people don't give bad comments. Like for me, I have never given a bad comment to any client. But if I don't have anything to write, I'll just leave it. Five stars, and I don't write anything there" (Interview with Arnav, 09–03-20).

Assessing the clients extends to assessing what the experience of working together will be like but also includes questions of how the client is likely to rate them in the end. Others go by the design brief, trying to judge from the clarity of instructions whether the client has a clear idea about the scope of work or from the tone of instructions whether the client will take the designer's judgment seriously.

Generally, designers are confronted with the task to evoke a feeling of security in the clients in a context where it may be tough to trust someone at first, as they cannot easily verify whether what they say about themselves is true. I understand their practices of demonstrating how professional they are and working on a positive and memorable first impression as a form of self-branding. As Hearn argues: "Self-branding may be considered a form of affective, immaterial labour that is purposefully undertaken by individuals in order to garner attention, reputation and potentially, profit" (Hearn 2010, p. 427). That is, by presenting themselves in a certain way, freelancers seek to invest in a future relationship with clients, hoping that they will be rewarded by a profitable working relationship. Within the opaque and complex environment of the platform, freelancers face the challenge of making their clients feel that they can trust them without seeing them and that they are catering to them personally.

As they are trying to anticipate the reactions of both their prospective clients and the platform mechanisms, freelancers face double uncertainty. In this context, they produce theories about what makes them stick out to clients. I rely on their interpretations here because I am focusing on work from their perspective, and it is more important for me to know what incomplete knowledge motivates them for specific practices than to know what clients want from them. Ankit, for example, who mainly uses 99designs, would like to move towards working directly with clients instead of participating in design contests, and he tries different things to gain their attention and trust:

"1-to-1 projects is what I'm hoping to do on this platform. I mean, 1-to-1 projects is basically where the client finds you on the platform. It could be from a design that I've done before, it could be from a showcased design, could be that he stumbled upon my profile, or from word of mouth. And he contacts me, and he hires me directly for a project. [...] So, in the last three years I've been only approached, about 15 times, 15 to 20 times. And out of those 15 to 20 times, I've actually managed to bag a project, I guess 11 times [...]. So that's what I've been trying to do on 99designs is basically, reach a level where my designs are featured, and to grow to a position where my designs are regularly featured so that clients keep approaching me and I don't have to compete in contests" (Interview with Ankit, 01–03-20).

He goes on to talk about how he tries to be featured: winning contests helps, but he also posts in the community forum, for example, to try and get the platform operators' attention and increase his chances of being featured. This quote illustrates the uncertainty of the affective labour performed by the freelancers: Ankit does not know if it was his portfolio that attracted clients, whether someone has recommended him, or whether being featured on the 99designs website has pointed them towards him. Within this context of uncertainty, I have identified two central strategies that freelancers apply to perform as a professional before a contract is closed: proving one's authenticity and putting oneself in the client's shoes.

6.2.2 Initiating contact: Performing professionalism

First, being 'authentic' is important for freelancers to gain clients' trust and to make them feel like it would be worthwhile to hire them. Being in a virtual work environment where they cannot see each other means that freelancers must work extra hard on proving to clients that they can trust them. When I asked them what is important to be successful as a designer on an online platform, a lot of the freelancers answered along the lines of being honest, being credible, and being reliable. On the one hand, there are many possibilities to cheat online. For example, people might fill their portfolio with designs they have not created themselves or they may even use other designers' work and submit it for design contests. This is also a major topic in the forum on Fiverr, for example, where freelancers call out others whom they suspect to have stolen their work to submit it for a job.

On the other hand, it is also hard for freelancers to prove that they are authentic – whether what they put up on their profile reflects them and their skills can usually only be assessed in hindsight. However, being transparent in the information they share in their profile picture is something they perceive as helpful in coming across as a professional. In their accounts of their work practices, freelancers often made a close connection between being professional and being authentic. Coming across as professional, to them, entails granting clients insights into who they are and providing them with a notion of authenticity. One example of this is the profile picture they choose. As Sarabjit reflects:

"It should look professional, and it should not look funky. Although we can do some artistic things, like upside down and all. But I don't think Upwork will verify that [...] because they want a professional designer instead of a funky designer (laughs). [...] Keeping the photograph gives the client a personalised touch, instead of putting the logo. [...] Because they can find a logo on Google. [...] So, they are not interested in our logo. They are interested in with whom they are working" (Interview with Sarabjit, 09-03-20).

Sarabjit's account illustrates that choosing a professional profile picture entails adhering to shared standards, such as being serious rather than funky, on the one hand. On the other hand, it means sharing one's face with a prospective client, that is, providing information about who is going to work for them. Thus, professional self-branding means that freelancers need to find just the right balance between sharing and holding back, presenting those aspects of themselves that they anticipate being relatable and reassuring to the client. Being professional, then, does not mean being emotionally neutral but connecting their profile to a person beyond the platform. However, there are also aspects of gaining clients' trust beyond the designers' control. For example, Gerber and Krzywdzinski (2019) have found that clients often prefer freelancers of the same nationality when they hire someone through a platform. Moreover, as I have described in Chapter 5.2, some of my interview partners have reported that they have come across clients with reservations against designers from India or South Asia. In these instances, self-branding can also include hiding parts of one's identity hoping to come across as more professional.

Proving one's authenticity is a novel challenge that digitally mediated tasks pose. A freelancer who communicates directly with their client would not have to prove that they are a real person. The importance of being personal and relatable also hints at the emotional dimension of platform-mediated work relationships: although the process of working together is structured by the platform, it is still relevant for clients to work with a 'real' person. Moreover, as the quote illustrates, the platform – Upwork, in this case – plays an important role in how being professional is understood and reflected in practices of self-branding.

Second, in addition to proving one's authenticity, being professional is associated with empathizing with clients and anticipating what information they need. This starts with the profile description: Jiya, for example, explains that she makes a point of choosing carefully what she writes in her profile description to make sure her profile is professional. When I asked her what she meant by being professional, she replied:

"Professional, previously what I had, the description, it was like me what I am as a designer, I do this this this, and that's what. [...] I don't want to tell any history in that. It has to be brief enough, we can use some software, whether you have some experience, you have some degree, in designing, you can show that, that's it. That's all they need to know (laughs). They don't need to know anything else. It has to be brief enough, to know that. That is how, it should be brief. Professional is, it has to be brief. Nobody has time to read everything. Everybody's busy" (Interview with Jiya, 08–03-20).

Being professional, to her, means putting herself in the clients' shoes and assessing what information they will find useful, rather than making it about what she finds interesting or important.

Similarly, as I have described in Chapter 5.2, the freelancers who persist on the platform spend considerable time writing personalised cover letters. Instead of writing generic applications, they refer explicitly to what the client mentioned in the design brief and explain how their qualifications meet the requirements of the job. A lot of them go through a learning process when they start on the platform, where they first write a lot of generic cover letters, which mostly get rejected, and then learn from their mistakes and start taking more time for a single cover letter. Reflecting on this process, Sarabjit explains:

"I understood that this is not the way we can work as a freelancer, submitting the proposal with blind eyes. Then I made some strategies how to submit proposal. What should be written in there, that's all. I have noticed, I have been working as a client also, you know, on freelancer.com. So, I noticed that many freelancers are submitting proposal without looking at the job description. So, I started writing customised proposals. We should be focused on what is the client's problem. If we are giving the solution of that problem in that job proposal. Then it will be definitely awarded" (Interview with Sarabjit, 09–03-20).

While the freelancers are part of a 'crowd', they make sure that their clients feel unique. This requires empathy, attentiveness, and diligence on the freelancers' side. In a context that is characterised by complexity and opacity, the freelancers perform affective labour to make the clients feel like they are just the right person for the job. It is not a singular characteristic of platform work that emotional labour is performed by designers – those freelancers who also work on local jobs have told me that getting along with a client is important for them in both contexts. However, the affordances and constraints that the platform provides to them mean that they perform this affective labour in a challenging setting, where they must put a lot of effort into purely written communication. Once they have successfully closed a contract, affective labour remains an important aspect of working with their clients, as I will show in the following subchapter.

6.2.3 Being nice to work with

In this subchapter, I outline the freelancers' practices of making and sustaining emotional connections with their clients. As I have touched upon before, emotional and affective labour is part of many service jobs and not a singular characteristic of platform work. What is new, however, is the setting in which this emotional labour is taking place, which creates specific challenges. Both the setting of communicating through the online platform and the translocal connections pose specific challenges for freelancers. As Hochschild [1983] 2012) describes, emotion work also has a social dimension: different social situations have different 'feeling rules', that is, they call for different ways of displaying emotion, such as sadness at a funeral, for example. These feeling rules are also relevant in business contexts, and they vary across cultures. Mankekar and Gupta (2016) describe, for example, how BPO call centre workers in India were "trained to adopt particular kinds of affective repertoires – of courtesy, familiarity, friendliness, helpfulness, and, above all, caring" (p. 26). Depending on whether they communicated with clients from the US or the UK, they learned to speak more informally or with more courtesy; more than just what they said, they underwent training of the body and the voice "to produce the right affect in agents' unscripted encounters with customers" (Mankekar & Gupta, 2016, p. 27).

Not all freelancers perceive their relationships with clients as very emotional. Jiya, for example, differentiates between personal and professional relationships – her clients are not her friends, and she would not discuss personal matters with them, for example:

"Actually, the entire relationship is based on work. Without work, we don't even interact with the client. So, it is mostly on a professional and work relationship, no such emotions involved in that mostly" (Follow-up interview with Jiya, 23–02-21).

At the other end of the spectrum, there is Advik: he continually works as a virtual assistant for a client in the US and considers him one of his closest friends, even though their relationship is centred around work. He writes:

"I am friends with one of my clients though and enjoy chatting with him. I have been working for him for more than 2 years. We only text through Slack. I have never called or video chatted with him as my spoken English is bad. But, he's my closest friend after my mother." (Advik's digital diary, day 3)

The two of them have talked about their mental health struggles with each other and connected over their shared interest in metal music, thus going beyond topics that are directly work-related.

While these two examples show that freelancers relate to their clients emotionally to different degrees, I argue that even those who perceive the relationship as purely professional do perform affective labour.

When freelancers' performance is evaluated, it is not just the design they have created but also the process of working together that counts towards their performance, as I have argued in Chapter 5. They are service providers and making their clients happy extends to the experience they create for them. As Divyansh explains from his experience as a freelance filmmaker:

"I'm very casual that way, so it doesn't feel like work for them. I make their work easy. So, people who are like that, I don't think they would need anybody else to do my job, you know. Because I make sure it's more fun than work" (Interview with Divyansh, 27-02-20).

In this sense, freelancers perform affective labour to create a positive experience of working together. They go to great lengths to keep their clients happy and to sustain positive relationships with them. Kiaan, for example, explains that he would rather work for less money than risk an uneasy relationship with a client:

"So, if I am charging people 250 dollars for a project and the client says 'Okay, my budget is only 200', I would rather do that for 200 to maintain that trust and relationship instead of taking it off. Unless I have 100 projects coming in every day" (Interview with Kiaan, 29-02-20).

Below, I will carve out how freelancers interact with their clients and with the platform to make and sustain emotional connections with their clients. Some of the things that just happen implicitly when working together locally need to be made explicit in a platform-mediated environment. Freelancers use various strategies to show clients that they are trustworthy while working with a client.

First, being reliable is an important aspect of reassuring clients. This is intricately connected to what I have described earlier as authenticity and credibility: within a context where it is hard for clients to verify information about freelancers, freelancers must work extra hard on gaining clients' trust. They demonstrate their reliability by strictly sticking to the deadlines that they have agreed on with a client, for example. This can just mean agreeing on a deadline once and then not trying to push it if something comes up for them. But, as I have described in Chapter 5.1, it is sometimes hard to assess beforehand how long a job will take because they do not know how many iterations the client will ask them for, and they also do not know if the client will change the deadline at some point. Within their uncertain working environment, then, being reliable sometimes entails flexibility rather than stability. Moreover, being reliable also includes an aspect of demonstrating activity. As Gregg (2011) has described for office clerks working from home, the flexibility of remote work is often undermined by the need to signal to employers (or clients, in this case) that one is working: Gregg describes that one of the workers in her study tries to respond to e-mails extra fast because she wants to demonstrate that she is working although she cannot be observed directly, for example. She needs to perform this by always being reachable, as she is afraid those who work at the office would suspect her "baking a chocolate cake or at the coffee shop" (Gregg, 2011, p. 42). The freelancers I have interviewed pointed out how important it is to be fast to reply to their clients' messages, for example (see also Chapter 7.2). This is not only important to make collaborating a smooth experience on a technical level, but it also serves to reassure the clients.

Second, the freelancers strive to perform transparency throughout the work process to evoke trust. The work that the freelancers in my study perform entails quite a lot of discretion and being on the same page about the client's vision is simultaneously more important and more elusive than with many other types of platform work. As Krishnam explains:

"The main thing which comes in order to provide satisfactory work is to understand the needs of the client solely from the instructions provided. The one who's better in this, nails the work" (Krishnam's photo diary, day 4).

At the same time, how they can get the message across is limited by the infrastructure of the platform. Janbir, for example, reflects: "Sometimes it feels very difficult to describe a project, we have to send messages and images to get feedback. On other hand, online communications are fast and interesting" (Janbir's photo diary, day 3). Relying on digitally mediated communication sometimes poses an additional challenge for communicating ideas, both for freelancers and clients. For freelancers, this often means additional unpaid work of sharing their thought process extensively with their clients. At the same time, Janbir and others also stress the positive aspects of using digital tools for communication if they provide the right infrastructure for their work. Krishnam reflects in his photo diary entry, where he shared a screenshot of a chat record with his client:

"The picture is sent is one of my favourite client whom i like to work with on a regular basis. We use discord* for communication. [...] I faced some other clients with whom the process becomes difficult due to lack of understanding or communication. The discord itself have a great influence here, the app designed for minimal distraction and provides seamless experience with few notifications. Some clients prefer to work through mail or social media apps, which in my experience will not provide the environment needed" (Krishnam's photo diary, day 4).

While some emotional components of the relationship between freelancers and clients are reduced in the platform-mediated environment, then, there are also new forms of making and sustaining emotional connections. The freelancers are not simply released of the work of making emotional connections, but they transport these connections to a new format. Ankit's practices of sharing his thought process with clients illustrate this. Reflecting on what he thinks makes clients book him for repeat jobs, he explains:

"I think, if they're comfortable with me, working with me, they have good communication with me, they really like my work, they really like my thought process, which I try to explain a lot. Which I've realised other designers don't do as much, to explain why they came up with a design or to basically include the client in your process a lot. So that it builds trust and communication. And, I think, making the client feel like this is a safe design space and to basically trust me as a designer" (Interview with Ankit, 01-03-20).

Building this safe design space, as Ankit calls it, requires him to perform unpaid work, making his thought process explicit by sharing it mainly in a written form. However, trust and a perceived emotional connection between the freelancer and the client are not entirely in the freelancers' hands. While all the freelancers whom I have interviewed have English skills that allow them to communicate clearly, speaking English as a second language and not knowing some of the cultural codes is sometimes read as a lack of professionality (cf. Oechslen, 2020, p. 90). In the following subchapter, I explore relationships with long-term clients, which are often initiated by affective labour, and which provide more space to deepen emotional connections between freelancers and clients.

6.2.4 Taking it to the next level: Long-term clients

The work freelancers put in to establish trust with a client may pay off if this client decides to continue working with them on further projects. Especially in Upwork, a lot of the freelancers I have talked to work with the same clients for quite a long time. The practices of establishing trust that I have described above are like an investment in future relationships, as Jiya explains:

> "Credibility is very important. For, if it is not a one-time job. If you want to sustain, you want your client to come back to you for the next project. So, you have that credibility, you can give them that trust, as a designer, they will come back to you" (Interview with Jiya, 08-03-20).

Divyansh, too, explains that his efforts to be nice to work with have often paid off in the form of clients coming back to him:

> "I had worked with them. [...] And then like people started approaching me for music videos. And then I kept like a nice rapport with them, like I've been putting out work, being a nice guy to work with. And any number of iterations et cetera, I have been nice, and people came back, and now I have like a client list, you know?" (Interview with Divyansh, 27-02-20).

Divyansh points out two elements here: building a rapport with clients on an emotional level and going the extra mile, that is, putting in extra work as an investment in the long-term client relationship.

When freelancers' practices of establishing trust work out and clients rehire them for further projects, they have several advantages compared to working together just once. On a personal level, freelancers feel appreciated and valued in their work when a client decides to work with them again. This also has a positive effect on their online reputation: Upwork, for example, shows the number of repeat clients on a freelancer's profile. Against the backdrop of the uncertainty and risk associated with hiring a new designer, which I have described above, knowing that other clients have decided to work with them repeatedly is a strong selling point on a freelancer's profile. But working continuously with a client also reduces uncertainty for the freelancers and gives them some stability in an otherwise highly flexible working environment.

In their relationships with clients, then, working together for repeat projects is something many freelancers strive to do. However, they cannot tell in advance whether a client will ask them to work together again. This is something they often cannot quite put their finger on, an experience of 'just clicking', getting along and communicating well. Moreover, some factors are completely outside freelancers' control, such as whether the client even needs another design. This means that they can do things the same way, but different clients may react differently.

Their making emotional connections with their clients does not result in stability for them, but it is necessary to continuously perform employability. This is part of a development that goes beyond platform work – Gregg describes something similar for office workers, for example:

"In fact, [...] job security is no longer attained as a consequence of social networking. Rather, networking is an additional form of labor that is required to demonstrate ongoing employability" (Gregg 2011, p. 13).

Within this context, freelancers need to continuously work on their future hireability, without being able to rely on the results of their performance. For remote freelancers who perform complex tasks, there is potential for some degree of a personal connection and continuity with the same client, which sets them apart from delivery riders, for example. However, the system of the gig economy is still geared towards treating workers as disposable. The gig economy and long-term relationships between clients and freelancers can exist together, but the respective logic underlying them is different. The gig economy is about hiring someone for just the job you need to be done, not for longer. So, there is less commitment on the side of the client. This also means that the freelancers must keep working on making their clients happy, as they still want to be hired for the next gig. In the next subchapter, I will turn to the ambivalent ways in which platforms mediate trust and emotional connections.

6.3 "Finding you a designer you'll love": How platforms mediate emotions

On the one hand, platforms leverage emotions, even love, and leave the more mundane aspects of working together backstage. They create the image of an exciting, playful, fun experience. On the other hand, they provide quite a rational, detached notion of trust, based more on reducing risk than on an emotional connection.

6.3.1 Creating the image of a 'magical experience'

As I have touched upon above, design jobs are more intricately connected to emotions and, in a way, more personal than many other jobs that are mediated by platforms. This shows in the way that 99designs presents itself. On the website, the process of working on a design together is promoted as "a magical experience". Moreover, platform operators promise users to find "a designer you'll love", or "100 % design love" for them.[1]

In a media interview, the CEO of 99designs, Patrick Llewellyn, also frames designers' activities on the platform as mainly passion projects, where the money they potentially earn is rather a by-product than the goal:

"You talk about professional freelancers who calculate very strictly. But let's be honest: How many freelancers do you know who really act like that? Typically, I'm a designer because I'm creative. Out of passion. The last thing I'm good at is calculating exactly what my real labour costs are. I want to do creative stuff and on 99designs I can do just that. We take the tedious bureaucracy away from designers" (Rest, 2016; own translation).

I want to stress two aspects of this narrative: First, the platform creates an image for both clients and designers implying that what they do with the platform is more a fun experience than a business transaction. The work practices that I have described so far, however, are not always fun – the freelancers enjoy their work, but they also do have to calculate their labour costs and it does matter to them if they take part in a lot of design contests without ever winning and thus also without ever being paid. Second, the platform is presented as an important actor in the emotional experience and connection between freelancers and clients: clients can just rely on the platform to create a magical experience and to find just the right designer for them, and freelancers can just follow their passion, relying on the platform to take care of the more tedious, bureaucratic parts. Here, too, the work practices that I have described so far suggest that there is more backstage work involved than what is implied in this image. At the same time, it is important to take the platform's role in mediating emotions into account. Below, I will outline the platforms' role in creating a notion of trust that centres on reducing risk.

6.3.2 Mediating trust as reducing risk

With the help of different mechanisms, platforms mediate trust between clients and freelancers. I have shown above that the remote setting of work-

---

[1] https://99designs.de/how-it-works, last checked on 28/01/2019.

ing together creates challenges for establishing a relation of trust without knowing each other in the beginning. This varies with different platforms, depending on how the hiring process is organised. In 99designs, for example, clients already have quite a high degree of safety because designers produce a design before they are hired. The clients can then just choose a design and go with it. In Upwork, clients must rely on other features to evoke trust. They hire a designer first and pay them per hour or for the whole service or single milestones.

The platform mitigates some of the risks involved in having transactions with someone you cannot see or the information about whom you cannot verify. A lot of the mechanisms that platforms put in place are aimed at creating trust – with both clients and workers. The platform acts as an escrow for the payments, so the risk of not being paid is lower for designers. At the same time, clients know that they must only pay for a design they are happy with. Thus, clients and freelancers do not have to trust each other completely – it is enough for them to trust the platform. It is also in the interest of the platform to be the bearer of trust – if freelancers and clients did not perceive it as a risk to circumvent the platform, the business model of mediating the relationship would not be viable anymore. Kiaan, for example, reports from his time as a freelancer on 99designs that it was a regular occurrence that freelancers contacted clients while a contest was going on, offering them to provide a design outside the platform for a lower rate. The main reason that not more people did that was trust, in his opinion:

"I would say those clients who did not establish trust. I think that was the main criteria that I would say in my opinion. Because unless you develop trust on people, and then you cannot really take it outside. [...] 99designs were also offering them a refund if the contest did not happen. So, maybe these are the few criteria my client could still be on. Because for them, the money is still safe" (Interview with Kiaan, 29–02-20).

Trust is not the only reason to follow through on the platform – the terms of use of the platforms in my study prohibit circumventing the platform, in the case of 99designs even for more than a year after the first contact. Still, it seems reasonable that more users would still avoid paying the platforms' fees if it felt safe for them.

Platforms mediate trust between freelancers and clients in all the phases of working together that I have described above. Especially in the first part of establishing trust, before a contract is closed, the platform plays a central part in pre-selecting, vetting, and curating designers. By mediating authenticity, platforms mitigate the perceived risk of hiring someone whom the client does not know. Different platforms do this with different rules, but the rules have in common that they increase accountability by tying workers' profiles to their identities in the 'real' world. Upwork does this, for example, by asking freelancers to use photos that clearly show their faces and not verifying photos otherwise, as Sarabjit's statement about his profile picture at the beginning of this chapter reflects. On 99designs, new members must verify their identity with an official ID and provide proof of their design skills before accepting jobs on the website. Moreover, the rating and review systems put in place by the platforms are supposed to help clients decide whom they can trust with their projects. Platforms sort designers into different categories, thus reducing complexity for clients and providing them with indicators about whom to choose. By highlighting freelancers as top-level (99designs) or top-rated (Upwork) designers, the platforms show clients that these designers will most probably be a viable choice. Along similar lines, 99designs features designers that stand out to them on the website and Upwork suggests potentially suitable freelancers to clients who publish a design brief.

Once a contract has been closed, platforms mediate the connection between freelancers and clients by setting the stage for communication. Ankit, for example, explains that communication with clients feels rather neutral to him when he works on 99designs:

> "99designs offers a pretty linear way to communicate with clients. Basically, you post the design, and they'll give you some feedback and then you revert and then they select your design. So, it's quite linear in that sense" (Interview with Ankit, 01-03-20).

The platform environment does not leave much space for connecting to different clients, compared to local projects, where the designers report that they often meet up several times to discuss a design. Contrasting his remote jobs with other design jobs that he accepts locally, Ankit explains:

> "A contest brief [on 99designs] is basically just reading what they've shared with us about their company, and it's just making a design based on an educated guess of what they would like. While over here it's actually guiding the client, of why I am making these decisions for your company, design-wise. And why I think, your targeted demographic would like this. It's a lot more in-depth, locally. And it's a lot more intricate. But, online, it's pretty fast, I have to dish out designs pretty fast, [...] it can get rejected instantly, so, I have to just give them the gist of the design. I have to just show them, [...] whereas locally, I have to prepare an entire presentation of my three concepts, and I can talk to them, and I can make them understand why I've made these decisions" (Interview with Ankit, 01-03-20).

That is, when Ankit works for a local client, there is a continuous process of negotiation between the client and the designer. On the platform, by contrast, the process can hardly be altered. This can be a relief to some extent, as the platform takes over some of the work of establishing trust. However, it also means that the freelancers are less in control of the situation.

Moreover, the platform is also involved as a mediator if there is a conflict between freelancers and clients, as I have described in Chapter 5.1. If a client refuses to pay for a service, for example, the freelancer can take the issue to the platform and try to convince the platform representatives that they have completed the job. Again, this makes the platform the ultimate bearer of trust. It is important to note, however, that freelancers often choose not to rock the boat and to keep silent if clients do them wrong, as they often feel in a weaker position and do not want to risk a low rating. Generally, the trust that is produced through the platform is not so much about making emotional connections but rather about minimising risk. Freelancers' opportunities for action, and for making emotional connections, are constrained by the platform infrastructure.

6.3.3 Structuring the work environment

On a more general level, abstracted from single jobs, some platforms enable more stable – and potentially emotionally closer – long-term relationships with clients than others. Freelancers on Upwork, especially those who have been on the platform for a longer time, often have a substantive part of long-term clients, sometimes working with them for years. The platform is also geared towards more long-term projects. When a project is completed, clients are invited to rehire the freelancer for the next project. This is quite different on 99designs, for example. There, the focus is much more on taking care of a single job than establishing long-term relations. Platform work is thus not homogenous and there are different experiences of working together on different platforms.

What is more, freelancers on the online platforms at the centre of this study do not connect to clients on an equal level. This is shown in the review systems, for example, which I have explained in more detail in Chapter 5.2. Freelancers must make clients happy and manage their emotions, sometimes sacrificing time and money for this goal because they are so dependent on how clients feel about them. Moreover, against the backdrop of the oversupply of labour on most gig work platforms, freelancers must work extra hard to attract and keep clients with them. This is exacerbated by the review and rating systems that platforms put in place. Trying to satisfy their clients means that freelancers are working for an elusive goal: their reputation and success depend very much on how they come across and how they can communicate, but that is not fully in their control. The uncertainty of this brings extra unpaid emotional labour with it, trying to win long-term clients but also "as a means of reducing the threat of bad ratings" (Wood & Lehdonvirta, 2021b, p. 34). In short, platforms mediate emotional connections between freelancers and clients on several levels and in ambivalent ways. While they transport an image of playfulness and evoke strong feelings, the reputation systems and communicative affordances of the platforms, as well as the allocation of jobs as single gigs, rather contribute to a working environment in which connecting on an emotional level is difficult.

6.4 Synthesis: Limited knowledge and volatile trust

To sum up, I have elucidated the emotional aspects of the freelancers' work practices from two vantage points. First, I have described the roles that the freelancers' own emotions play in their everyday work practices. Both their practices of creating designs and their practices of assembling raise emotions like joy or excitement, which play a key role in their motivation. On the flipside, dealing with clients and, more generally, working within a highly flexible platform environment can be emotionally taxing. Managing their own emotions and keeping up appearances even when they are sad, angry, or frustrated takes emotion work in the forms of deep and surface acting (cf. Arlie Russel Hochschild, 1979). Second, being a successful freelancer on an online platform also includes continuous affective labour (Hardt, 1999; Hardt & Negri, 2000; Weeks, 2007), that is, managing others' emotions. Freelancers use the tools which the infrastructure of the platform provides to reassure prospective and current clients of their trustworthiness, creating a relatable image of themselves. The platform-mediated work environment, where clients and freelancers have only limited points of contact, makes it both more relevant and more difficult to perform the authenticity and transparency that are necessary to get clients to trust them. To balance this and to increase their chances of winning and keeping clients, freelancers perform unpaid labour, for example by extensively explaining their thought processes to clients. However, they still have no guarantee that their clients will be happy or that making clients happy will result in them returning. Finally, I related freelancers' practices to the online platforms they use for their work. I argued that, while they create the image of a magical and emotional experience, gig work platforms do not contribute to trust between freelancers and clients. Instead, they remain the bearer of trust for both parties, for example, by securing payments and mediating in the case of conflicts. Moreover, the rating and review systems on platforms and the oversupply of labour contribute to an unequal distribution of unpaid emotional labour.

This is intricately connected with the fact that freelancers' success depends on clients' satisfaction and the rating by clients. They work on pleasing their customers without knowing which actions exactly will result in a good or bad rating, and they do not have a lot of information on the clients' contexts. As results depend on interaction and on producing affect, they are incalculable. Similarly, Mankekar and Gupta have argued for call centre workers:

"Workers now had to labor to please their customers without knowing which actions would result in a 'good' rating versus a 'bad' one, and without any control over the consumers' contexts. Since affective labor depends on interaction, the 'output' is always uncertain, even less than the worker's control over a product being made on an assembly line. It is for this reason that we contend that call centre work cannot be categorized as just another example of Taylorized, assembly-line production, no different than producing cars, washing machines, or electronics: in this important sense, then, the affective labor of our informants was distinct from the labor of factory workers" (Mankekar & Gupta, 2016, p. 28).

For graphic designers working through an online platform, this uncertainty is exacerbated as they additionally deal with opaque platform mechanisms. Accordingly, their efforts at self-branding consist of trying to invest in the market value of their personal brand without really being able to tell what a successful strategy looks like. This leaves designers with a sense of what van Doorn (2014) has called "affective ambiguity": the structures of the platform give workers a sense of security about their value, but at the same time they cannot foresee if they are following the right strategy. This is expressed in trying to master the rules of a game which are both obfuscated and changing all the time. The freelancers are thus confronted with an ambiguous situation that suggests agency while also bringing a lot of uncertainty.

One of the central goals of freelancers' affective labour as I have described it in this chapter has been establishing trust. There are several aspects of trust in a global assemblage of platform work that I want to point out here.

First, the notion of trust illustrates the relationality of the freelancers' work practices. Trust is not individual but produced in relations. Accordingly, freelancers contribute to evoking trust with their practices, but they are not the only ones on whom this trust depends. Even if they put the same amount of effort into every single client, the results will always be different. Sometimes they "just click" (Interview with Jiya, 08-03-20), and other times, they will just not get along.

This relationality resembles how Mankekar and Gupta (2016) conceive of affect in their study of BPO call centre workers in India:

> "[I]n our characterization of the labor of call center agents as affective labor, we theorize affect as a field of intensities that circulates between bodies and objects and between and across bodies; as existing alongside, barely beneath, and in excess of cognition; and as transgressing binaries of mind versus body, and private feeling versus collective sentiment. Affects cannot be located solely in an individual subject, nor can they be relegated to the psyche or to subjective feelings" (Mankekar & Gupta, 2016, p. 24).

By defining affect in this highly relational way, they go beyond Hochschild's notion of emotional labour as (deep or surface) acting, arguing that working subjects are produced in and through affective labour. This ties in with the practices of self-branding and the anticipative interaction with reputation mechanisms that I have described in this chapter. Hearn (2010) argues that producing affect is an important aspect of labour today, reflected in the constant work on one's online reputation. Moreover, she argues that it is not just the self at work, but the self is produced through work: "In the post-Fordist era, then, we see a shift from a working self, to the self *as* work in the form of a self-brand with reputation as its currency" (Hearn, 2010, p. 426).

But how are freelancers' selves produced in their practices of affective labour? This is the second aspect of trust in a global assemblage of platform work: in their statistical analysis of how people's earnings in online labour markets are connected to their online reputation, expressed through ratings by previous clients, Gandini et al. (2016) have found that reputation measures have a significant impact on workers' chances of being chosen for a job. They conclude that trust in online labour markets is mediated in similar ways to e-commerce platforms, based on reviews, where a third-party entity regulates interactions between clients and buyers. Consequently, they argue, trust in online labour markets, where strangers have to find ways to trust each other, is less like social capital embedded in a network and rather like Luhmann's conception of trust as reducing the risk of interacting with non-intimate social actors (Gandini et al., 2016, pp. 39–40).

Third, the way that online platforms mediate the relations between freelancers and clients contributes to this notion of trust as a reduction of risk through the mechanisms that I have described in this chapter. Connecting Hearn (2010) and Gandini et al. (2016), I argue that it is not just labour that is transformed into a commodity here, but that the freelancers produce a "persona for public consumption" (cf. Wernick 1991, cited in Hearn 2010) on their profile and in their practices of interacting with both clients and the platform, which they invest in, hoping for a value increase. Thus, the worker, who is produced in affective relations, becomes the commodity that is traded on online labour markets.

7. Aligning Relations

In the previous chapters, I have focused on unpaid and invisible aspects of gig work, such as setting up a profile, relating to clients, or managing one's online reputation. As components of a global assemblage of platform work, I view a broad range of freelancers' practices of making and sustaining connections as part of their work. I have established above that platform work is characterised by a high degree of uncertainty: the freelancers' income and their volume of work vary greatly, and one bad review could result in being out of work for months (Wood & Lehdonvirta, 2021b) – making them examples of "the flexible and uncertain working and living conditions in the contemporary world" (Ivancheva & Keating, 2020, p. 252). I have explored how boundaries between the value of their work and their own 'market value' blur in Chapter 5 and how complex emotional relations are involved in their work in Chapter 6.

In this chapter, I go one step further and relate these practices of assembling platform work to the multifarious relationships that make up freelancers' "life-work continuum" (Ivancheva & Keating, 2020, p. 254) and how they are interwoven with each other. As Ivancheva and Keating (2020) argue, "[p]aradoxically, both the Marxian proletarian and the autonomous, rational actor championed by neoliberalism feature indifference to the affective domain, ignoring the relational life of humans as interdependent, loving, caring and solidaristic beings" (p. 274). Moreover, they contend that life and work are much more interwoven than most perspectives on precarity and exploitation give credit for. Building on this notion, I argue that platform work is deeply interwoven with further elements of freelancers' lives: the various interdependent relationships that make up their everyday lives affect how they approach and experience platform work. Against this backdrop, I explore the implications of the volatility of platform work for freelancers' lives beyond the platforms they use for work. I outline how flexibility can have different connotations, depending on what role platform work plays in a freelancer's life. Thus, I extend the notion of practices of assembling to ask how platform workers align different elements of their lives with the platform-mediated work environment.

In the first part of the chapter, I focus on variations in freelancers' experiences to show how their respective circumstances of combining different forms of paid work as well as their varying ways of sustaining interdependent relationships characterised by love, care, and solidarity (cf. Ivancheva & Keating, 2020, p. 256) touch their experiences and practices of working through online platforms. In the second part of the chapter, I focus on what freelancers have in common, based on their shared experience of working through online platforms. Along the lines of the translocal, freelance, and platform-mediated character of their work, I explore the tensions that arise in the process of aligning different relations in gig workers' lives in time and space. I argue that they live and work in "seamful spaces" (Vertesi, 2014) and must continuously work on aligning different relations.

7.1 Assembling the life-work continuum

To understand freelancers' work practices on the platforms they use for work, it is important to also look at their lives beyond the platform. In this first part of the chapter, I outline how freelancers are integrated into relationships of mutual care and responsibility and how their work using online platforms is embedded within these relations in diverse ways. Deconstructing the conception of work and life as separate spheres, I argue that different forms of paid and unpaid work are interwoven and influence each other. As I have carved out at the beginning of this study, platform work is very volatile and the earnings from platform work fluctuate a lot. Accordingly, many freelancers cannot just rely on platform work financially but combine it with other forms of paid work. How they approach and experience platform work differs with what the rest of their lives look like. In the following paragraphs, I will provide examples from research participants' accounts to illustrate how platform work is embedded in various constellations of paid work.

7.1.1 Aligning different responsibilities

In some cases, my research participants work via online platforms just to a small degree while they are employed somewhere else. They do not depend on an income from platform work, which makes a great difference in their experience of platform work. Nitin, for example, works full-time as a graphic designer at an agency in Bengaluru. Sometimes, when things are slow at the office, he participates in online design contests on Talenthouse or 99designs. He approaches the design contests playfully and sees them as a pastime, something to keep him busy and make him happy. For him, creating designs online is more like a hobby with the added benefit of feeling appreciated when he wins a contest, more than earning money with it. He says that "it's for my happiness, or maybe in my free time I just want to do something" (Interview with Nitin, 04–02-20). For him, the complexity of the platform means being confronted with many different options to choose from – options that he is free to make use of or to leave aside.

Some of my other research participants have moved on to employed positions after working through platforms for some time. They do not look for new jobs via platforms regularly, but still use them to work for long-term clients. While their use of the platform is more serious and less playful than Nitin's, they still get around a lot of the more tedious parts of platform work: as they are working with clients they already know and have a connection with, they do not have to perform the invisible, unpaid work of applying for jobs or establishing a connection with their clients. For the same reasons, they also bear less of the risk of clients giving them a low rating or refusing payment. Sarabjit, for example, moved on to a job as an employee with an online retailer in Bengaluru after having worked as a full-time freelancer for around four years. However, he still works for some of his long-term clients – he says: "these clients have been with me for the last three or four years. So, I can't say no to them" (Interview with Sarabjit, 09–03-20). Even after working together for several years, they still use Upwork to connect, and he regularly monitors the messages he gets there but does not submit any new proposals. In these constellations, freelancers have less time to dedicate to platform work, but they are also less dependent on an income from the platform. This puts them in a position where they can choose what jobs are attractive to them.

A lot of platform workers also combine their work on the platform with local freelance work or switch between different platforms. Ankit, for example, is a top-level designer in 99designs, but also regularly accepts local freelance jobs in his hometown, Pune. He started his design career with small local freelance jobs, which he got through recommendations from friends. After a while, he signed up for an online platform to find more jobs and has settled on 99designs now, after trying out different platforms for a while. On average, he spends 70 percent of his time working for clients on 99designs and 30 percent on local projects. Compared to the designers described above, who have fixed working hours in their day job, he can be quite flexible and spontaneous in how much time he dedicates to his online freelance work. At the same time, there is less security for him, and he must put in more work to make sure enough jobs are coming in. The local and remote jobs have very different temporalities, as he describes:

"Locally, I have a lot more control over the project and I spend a lot more time [...]. A contest brief [on 99designs] is basically just reading what they've shared with us about their company, and it's just making a design based on an educated guess of what they would like. While over here it's actually guiding the client, of why I am making these decisions for your company, design-wise. [...] It's a lot more in-depth, locally. And it's a lot more intricate. But online, I have to dish out designs pretty fast, and I cannot spend a lot of time designing online, because, as I said, it can get rejected instantly, so, I have to just give them the gist of the design. I have to just show them, I have to design enough so that they just understand the direction and not the entire design, whereas locally, I have to prepare an entire presentation of my three concepts and, I can talk to them, and I can make them understand why I've made these decisions" (Interview with Ankit, 01–03-20).

Ankit combines different jobs and adapts his routine to his clients' timelines, making sure he gets enough jobs to get by, but not more than he can manage. Up until this point, his experience is not so different from freelancers who do not use gig work platforms for their work. However, for him, additional work is needed to bring together different temporalities and different ways of working together to do justice to his different responsibilities. Moreover, the possibility of being rejected instantly for jobs on the platform implies that phases of high or low activity are even harder to anticipate. He may be rejected for all his proposals on online platforms and glad he took on a lot of local jobs, or he may be accepted for all and not know how to oversee them. Thus, combining local and remote freelance work brings about challenges of aligning different jobs, both providing and requiring flexibility on the workers' part.

Some of the remote freelancers whom I have talked to also combine platform work with other forms of income beyond paid employment or local freelance design jobs. Arnav, for example, has created several websites through WordPress. He uses these sites to promote his work, but their main purpose is to generate a passive income, as he says. He keeps up websites, such as a blog or a personal website for ad banners, mainly to get money through Google AdSense, that is, being paid for advertisements that are shown on the website or for sponsored links to other websites. He promotes the websites through his social media account on Facebook and uses the websites as his portfolio to show clients his skills as a WordPress developer in action. That way, he tries to get some extra security and be prepared for the volatility of remote freelancing:

> "Because you cannot depend on freelancing forever, you have to do something for your own. [...] It is kind of a very messed-up thing. Yes. So, like now, you see the corona virus. Because of this, the market may go down. And tomorrow, it will be very difficult to find a project there" (Interview with Arnav, 09–03-20).

Still, several of the freelancers that I have talked to do just that and rely completely on freelancing for their income. Jiya has been working as a designer via Upwork for a couple of years now and earns a considerable amount of money there. She moved towards fully working through an online platform gradually: after finishing her studies, Jiya worked at an agency in Kolkata that operated through an online platform and specialised in work for clients outside India. Thus, she was already working through a gig work platform back then, but not immediately and not as a freelancer. After getting married, she moved to Bengaluru and joined a local software company there. Her job there did not include a lot of design work, so she started looking for alternatives that would allow her to work more creatively. From her previous job in Kolkata, she already knew a little bit about platform work, so she decided to try and create a profile on the online platform Elance for herself. She started small, bidding for freelance jobs and creating designs beside her day job. She was able to use designs she had created in her previous jobs as work samples, which gave her a head start in filling her portfolio. For six months, she did both her local job and freelance work through an online platform side by side. When her earnings from freelance work exceeded what she made in her day job, she decided to start working full-time as a freelancer. This transition phase was quite important to help her gain experience in dealing with clients and getting enough good reviews to make sure she would be able to get jobs.

Focusing on platform work completely, especially on a single platform, has some advantages. In Chapter 5.2, I have outlined how the reputation systems of online platforms penalise longer phases of inactivity, for example. Working through Upwork almost every day and having acquired a high proportion of long-term clients to work with, Jiya has been able to rise to the top-rated designers of the platform and currently has a rate of 100 percent successfully completed jobs. However, this also means that she must prioritise platform work and keep up being available for her clients. She used to get anxious handling many clients at the same time but has created structures for herself to manage her time accordingly. However, creating a schedule only works to some extent: her working hours depend on her clients' working hours in their respective time zones in Europe, the US, or Australia, and she must regularly adjust her schedule when clients come up with spontaneous requests for changes, for example.

Ishaan, too, works exclusively via Upwork. After working on the platform on his own for some time, he joined forces with two of his friends and created an agency profile on Upwork. They operate the agency from their respective homes and mostly online, except for their Friday team meetings in Ishaan's colleague's living room. The three friends are the only ones working directly for their agency, but they hardly accept design work now: instead, they manage and curate bigger projects for their clients. One client for whom he works outsources bigger projects to Ishaan's agency, which supervises around eight graphic designers in turn. In one example that Ishaan spoke about, the team was tasked with sketching out illustrations for truck engines. When Ishaan sees special challenges, he creates a template for the graphic designers working for him. Mostly, he splits the projects into smaller tasks and gives weekly assignments to his subcontractors. When they are done, they discuss the results via WhatsApp or Skype, Ishaan checks the quality of the designs and then delivers them to the client. The graphic designers performing the partial tasks for the projects are also connected with Ishaan's client via Upwork, but most communication runs via Ishaan. This way, while he also uses Upwork full-time, Ishaan has created a more fixed structure for himself. He does not work in isolation but has colleagues close to him. Moreover, like Jiya, working mostly for long-term clients emancipates him to some degree from the review and reputation systems of the platform and from the unpaid work of sending out proposals.

Both Jiya's and Ishaan's examples are indicative of how freelancers who rely completely on online platforms manage their work lives. Those who persist are often the ones who manage to introduce some regularity, for example, by working predominantly with long-term clients. Relying on platform work also means having to dedicate a lot of time to managing one's online reputation and sometimes managing clients from various time zones at the same time.

To sum up, the different constellations of paid jobs in which the designers integrate working on gig work platforms translate to differences in their experiences of platform work. Platform work is one element in their work lives and the different elements have an impact on each other. Schor et al. (2020) also find that there is not just one singular platform worker experience. They argue that platform work can be satisfying if workers do it for supplemental income rather than as a main source of income. Therefore, they call for an analytical approach to platforms that takes these variations into account. I would like to go one step further here and argue that it is not only different forms of paid work but also unpaid work and the multifarious relationships workers have with others that makes a difference in their experiences using gig work platforms. While it is true, for example, that Jiya focuses on Upwork for paid work, her daily schedule also includes caring for her young son. She dedicates the first half of her day to her family and household chores and the second half to platform work – unless a client's time zone makes it necessary for her to shuffle her tasks around. Understanding her daily schedule would be incomplete without considering these care responsibilities. For Ishaan, the fact that he works with his friends, who live close by and whom he meets regularly, brings more stability into his work life. His work and private lives blur and both feed into each other.

7.1.2 Interdependent care relationships

Haug (2008) has proposed a fourfold concept of what people dedicate their waking time to: she differentiates between paid work, care work, self-development, and political work or taking care of the community. I argue here that platform work as a form of paid work interacts with the other three elements, which are present to different degrees in the platform workers' lives. The designers I have talked to care for their personal development as well as for their families and others around them. Moreover, they support others financially with their income from platform work. Again, I will use examples from my research participants' stories to illustrate how they combine different forms of caring for themselves and others with their work on gig work platforms.

Kiaan has a background in computer engineering and used to work freelance as a user experience (UX) designer via 99designs when he was still in college. Later, he founded his own start-up firm and stopped using gig work platforms when his firm was up and running. This is what a normal work week looked like for him when he was in college and working on 99designs:

"It was every single day when I was on a project. Because as I said, I wanted to complete the work as soon as possible to jump on to the next one. So, the work week was more towards in the night-time because that would be the daytime for the US. So, it has to be the night over here. My college ended at 4 pm, so I would be home by 6. And then probably from 8 till 12 is when I worked. So, I was working probably five or six hours, probably as low as four hours and as high as six hours. So, that was my weekly thing. But eventually, when I had exams, I was not working at that time" (Interview with Kiaan, 29–02-20).

For Kiaan, platform work was his only source of income during his college days, but not the only responsibility he had. He had to fit his platform work in the time he had besides his college syllabus, balancing phases of high activity at college, such as exam times, with cutting back on platform work and getting in as many projects as he could when he had the time. Moreover, he had to keep both his college schedule and the working days of his US clients in mind and thus worked mostly at night. Working on his education and his paid work on 99designs, then, left him with little time for anything else, including sleep.

Sarabjit, who has already made an appearance earlier in this chapter as someone who has moved on from platform work to working as a full-time employee, only catering to his long-term clients, did so because he was left with hardly any time to be with his family. He reflects: "If we are working as a freelancer, we are submitting proposals in the night, working on the projects in the day. So, at what time we are going to spend our time with the family?" (Interview with Sarabjit, 09–03-20). When he was working full-time as a freelancer on Upwork, there was nothing flexible about his job. Of course, he did not have fixed working hours and could have taken time off in theory, but in practice, making ends meet through platform work alone meant always being on the clock. However, designers integrate their care responsibilities in different ways, also depending on how paid and unpaid work are arranged in their families. For Jiya, working from home and not having fixed working hours as a freelancer enables her to spend quality time with her son, as she says. As her husband works outside the home and they have agreed not to leave their child at day-care, the task of caring for their son during the day has fallen to her. Different constellations of responsibilities and different interdependent relationships, then, connected also with different priorities, all affect how platform work is integrated into daily life and what challenges platform workers face. In their photo diaries, both Jiya and Arnav sent pictures of their children to symbolise what they considered their most important responsibility (cf. Figure 1).

Except for Jiya, all designers currently working via online platforms in my interview sample are men but comparing her and Sarabjit's experiences of combining platform work with caring for a family, respectively, hints at gender differences in platform worker's work-life constellations. While caring for his family and working through Upwork meant prioritising paid work to the point of working day and night for Sarabjit, Jiya is continuously working on a balance between paid work and unpaid care work. This adds another layer to the perspective on flexibility – or precarity – in platform work:

"[I]n spite of the vulnerabilities created and exacerbated by precarious working conditions, within the current system, highly flexible labour can be more compatible with care responsibilities for workers seeking to negotiate life within globally unequal geographic locations and oppressive social realities" (Ivancheva & Keating, 2020, p. 267).

That is, although the challenges of uncertainty remain for Jiya, in the constellation she is in, she needs the flexibility of working from home and adjusting her working hours to her son's needs. Wallis (2021, p. 6) makes similar observations in Germany and Romania, stating that it is often women who turn to gig work for the opportunity to work from home and with flexible hours. Although Jiya is not the only one of my research participants who has children, she was the only one who brought her child to our interview. While she was answering my questions, she simultaneously kept an eye on her son, who was roaming the coffee shop and occasionally asking her for chocolate or playing with my laptop and recording device. Working from home with her son around is probably quite similar to that experience: in her everyday practices, the boundaries between paid work and care work are blurry.

In addition to caring for one's children, both financially and through care work, designers also care for and connect to others in many ways. Advik, for example, lives with his parents and supports them financially. Ankit makes time to meet his friends in the evening, adjusting his daily work schedule by working until the late afternoon and, if he has a project to finish, night sessions after coming back from seeing his friends. In addition, freelancers

Figure 1: Arnav's daughter
Source: Arnav's photo diary, day 5

also want to spend time just for themselves, working out or pursuing their hobbies. While the specific responsibilities and setups vary widely between designers, every one of them has various things to do and relationships to care for that compete with their work on the platform over the time they have in a day.

On the flipside, freelancers often also have others in their lives who care for them and support them. This support can take many forms, such as buffering financially hard phases. Thus, even if online freelance work is the only paid work they do, how dependent they are on their income from the platform also depends on their support system. Moreover, they have others around them to provide emotional support or to take care of food or household chores, to varying degrees. How they are integrated into interdependent relations of mutual care and responsibility plays a key role in their paid work on the platform, too. When they work long and flexible hours, a lot of platform workers rely on their parents or their partners to cook meals, clean the house, or take care of their children – in short, they have time and energy for productive labour because others ease their load of reproductive labour (cf. Federici, 1975). Suveer, for example, says, after outlining his daily schedule:

"My wife is making sacrifices for me, for this working style. [...] But she knows, I am doing this for my family. [...] She understands each and everything in there. That's why I am sitting freely on the computer" (Interview with Suveer, 27-02-21).

While Suveer's wife's unpaid work of managing everything in the background so that he can do his paid work plays a significant role in his work on the platform, of course, there are also friendship and family relations that do not fit a clear distinction between productive and reproductive labour. Moksh's story provides an example of how family ties and informal support can be interwoven with working together. He is based in Bengaluru and works as a graphic designer and virtual assistant on Upwork and FreeUp. He learned his design skills from his sister, who used to work as a designer herself. Moreover, she was already experienced in platform work when he was just starting, so she taught him what it takes to work on an online platform, making the phase of entering platform work easier for him. In addition, Moksh's sister has introduced him to fellow freelance designers and thus broadened his professional network. She does not regularly do paid work now, but she supports him with his designs when he has taken on more jobs than he can manage. When I asked him if he ever subcontracted any work, he replied: "I actually do most of the work myself. Or my sister, [...] who taught me, I take help from her, because we are in the same home. We manage the work" (Interview with Moksh, 10-03-20). Wallis (2021) has made similar observations in her qualitative study of gig work in Germany and Romania: a lot of gig workers in her sample "share their accounts with household members, friends or family, or even work on gigs together" (p. 10).

Sarabjit's early ventures into platform work were also connected to people close to him: before he got married, he shared an apartment with some other young men. They had a profile on Elance, and he occasionally helped them out with designs, especially when they had more to do than they could manage to deliver in time. He did so for free, as an act of friendship rather than considering it as his work. But it was also not completely outside the sphere of work. He recalls, for example, how he accidentally landed a client, who ended up working with him for two more years: His roommates had accepted a project that consisted of several parts. After Sarabjit had completed the initial design, he went home to visit his family for a couple of days and when he got back, he found that the client had contacted him via e-mail to say that he was not happy with what his friends had delivered and that he would prefer working with him instead from now on. When freelancers work on projects that are paid by the hour on Upwork, the platform takes screenshots of their desktops to make sure they are working on the project. Through one of these screenshots, the client discovered Sarabjit's e-mail ID and understood that it was Sarabjit who had created the design he preferred. So, to his roommate's disappointment, Sarabjit took over the client.

These examples have illustrated that work and life are not separate spheres for freelancers. Their lives beyond the platform play a vital role in their work on the platform – other forms of paid work pre-structure their days to varying extents and give them different degrees of financial freedom. This also affects how much time they spend on unpaid work like sorting through and applying for briefs, and how invested they are in managing their reputation on the platform. Moreover, their relations to others, the care work they do, pursuing education, or time they spend on what is personally important to them, all play a role in how much time freelancers have for platform work and when they can take the time for it. It takes work to align these different elements of their lives. In addition to how much time the freelancers have, their lives beyond platform work are interwoven with their work on the platform in further ways, leaving the boundaries between 'work' and 'life' blurry. Designers' families and friends contribute to their work on the platform, for example, by taking over care responsibilities, by providing emotional support or a financial safety net to buffer phases when they cannot find a job for some time, or by helping with performing a job in phases where they have more jobs than they could do on their own.

After setting the stage by illustrating the variation that exists between different platform workers in terms of their work-life setup, I will now move on to looking at specific challenges connected to platform work. Up to this point, the experiences I have described are not unique to platform workers: nurses, teachers, or engineers are embedded in interdependent relations of mutual care and responsibility, too, and are also tasked with fitting different elements of their lives into their days and weeks. I do, however, argue, that there are challenges in aligning elements of work-life that are specific to platform work, which I will outline below.

7.2 Everyday practices of aligning relations in platform work

In this subchapter, I go into more detail about what I consider specific challenges of aligning platform work with other elements of life. I argue that practices of creating designs and practices of assembling have different spatialities and temporalities. I consider 'creating designs' as the more direct, practical, and more recognised part of designers' platform-mediated work: for example, thinking of a new logo, making sketches and drafts, and producing a file. This part of the designers' work is usually solitary and depends on being able to focus and shut out distractions. While creating designs is about setting boundaries, then, practices of assembling are about making connections. Practices of assembling encompass setting up and curating one's profile, browsing design briefs, writing proposals, discussing ideas with clients or collaborators, managing one's online reputation, and organising one's schedule – practices that are often taking place in the background. In designers' everyday work, practices of creating designs and practices of assembling are closely connected and interdependent. The work of creating a logo depends on setting up a profile and successfully attracting clients, for example. However, the practices also show some distinct characteristics, which I will carve out here. I begin by exploring the spatiality of platform work, showing the ambiguities of creating boundaries and making connections. Furthermore, I outline the temporal disjunctures of remote platform work by carving out similarities with and differences from work in the business process outsourcing (BPO) industry. Finally, I show how platform mechanisms create challenges for aligning different elements of life by simultaneously demanding flexibility and continuous effort.

7.2.1 Working from home, working from anywhere

While they connect to clients and other workers who are mostly far away, at the same time, freelancers' work is often tied very closely to their homes. Nearly all the freelancers I have talked to for this study work from home. Only one of my research participants, Thomas, worked out of a coworking space in Bengaluru at the time of our interview in March 2020. Working from home has ambiguous implications for how platform work relates to the freelancers' lives beyond the platform.

On the one hand, working from home can make it easier to combine platform work with other responsibilities, such as care work. I have mentioned Jiya in the first part of this chapter, for example, who chose working from home to be able to combine paid work with caring for her son. Having different elements of her life in proximity, she can flexibly react to changes and switch between different responsibilities faster. Thus, temporal and spatial dimensions are once again closely interwoven here. On the other hand, working from home can also bring about challenges in terms of setting boundaries, as Gregg (2011) argues, for example. She contends that technology contributes to the de-limitation of work and that professional and personal identities are increasingly blurred when work is done from home. I will point out below what my specific observations on platform work and its frayed rhythms can add to this.

For their design work, freelancers require a big screen and specialised software. Accordingly, while they are not bound to an office, this part of their work can only be done in a fixed workspace. The freelancers whom I asked about their workspace on the first day of their photo diaries pointed out the importance of a large screen to work on minute details of a design (Jiya, Krishnam), powerful hardware and software (Krishnam), and an ergonomic desk setup (Janbir). Moreover, they stressed the importance of keeping distractions at bay while they are working (Jiya, Krishnam, Arnav). Keeping distractions out also means creating boundaries in different ways: Krishnam, for example, has set up his computer in a separate room, while Kanav creates an acoustic boundary by wearing headphones. He writes:

"The picture I sent is my airpods, it always helps me to mind my own business, whether I need to take any client's call, or listen to any music, I don't disturb anyone else" (Kanav's photo diary, day 3).

This points to another aspect of working from home: freelancers often share their homes, and, by extension, their workspaces, with others. Accordingly, they are not only potentially distracted, but also potentially a distraction to others.

In addition to the practical requirements, some designers also pointed to ways in which they personalise the space and create a pleasant work atmosphere for themselves: Advik, for example, has placed some Hindu idols on his desks, listens to music while he works, and likes to have his pets around when he is working. Krishnam has decorated his work area with a wall sticker, a small panda figure, and a photograph of a video game he enjoys playing (cf. Figure 2). When they are creating designs, then, freelancers are required to work in a focused and solitary way. Their work rhythms are still dependent on others to some extent, as they agree on deadlines with their clients and as their responsibilities beyond the platform affect what time they can allocate to platform work. However, the work itself is rather based on retreating from connections with others and making time for uninterrupted work.

Practices of assembling, by contrast, have a very different character: they are based on making connections with others, and they are much more elastic (Nadeem, 2009) in both time and space. While the design part of freelance designers' work is predominantly stationary, the surrounding elements of their work are more mobile. Janbir, for example, usually takes clients' video calls from other places than his desk: instead, he moves to another room in his apartment with his laptop. While his desk setup works well for creating designs, he prefers presenting a different background to his clients. Moreover, many freelancers have the gig work platforms they use installed as apps on their smartphones in addition to their computers. The apps are predominantly used for the latter part of their work, for example, connecting with clients via the messaging service of the platform. In addition to the platform itself, some freelancers also connect to clients via further tools, such as WhatsApp or Skype. This means that they carry their work with them almost everywhere and not just at set spaces and during set times. While gig workers are generally free to organise their time as it suits them, working efficiently on one or more gig work platforms entails being fast to reply, as I will elaborate on below.

In short, platform work has a twofold impact on how freelancers can align different relations spatially: On the one hand, their work takes place at home, which brings opportunities as well as challenges for alignment. On the other hand, being able – and expected – to work from anywhere via their smartphones further contributes to expanding work time, as freelancers carry their work with them on the go and in different situations. Thus, work seeps into different situations and they are always 'on call'.

7.2.2 Work across time and space: Global work relations

Connecting to clients mainly in the US, UK, and Australia means that the designers must adapt their circadian rhythm to be awake when their clients

Figure 2: Krishnam's workspace
Source: Krishnam's photo diary, day 1

need them, to talk over a draft, for example. Working and living in a rhythm that is out of sync with most people around you can take an emotional, physical, and social toll, as Aneesh (2006) describes. In his ethnographic study of work relations between India and the US, he argues that for software programmers in India who work during the night to be available during US working hours, "local contexts and the social times of people's lives" (Aneesh, 2006, p. 92) are reconfigured. Mankekar and Gupta (2019) make similar observations in their study of call centre workers in Bengaluru, who are employed in the BPO industry and connect to clients mainly in the US. They argue that as work rhythms are adapted to the needs of clients in the Global North, "disjunctive temporalities" emerge:

"The modes of embodiment enjoined by BPO agents' affective labor were profoundly imbricated with the temporal disjunctures between biorhythms and cycles of affective labor, the disruption of circadian rhythms by the durée of business cycles, and the complex relations of articulation and disarticulation between the temporalities of BPO work and those of family and community" (Mankekar & Gupta, 2019, p. 422).

The authors describe how workers' bodies are challenged by their dislodged circadian rhythms, messing up their menstrual cycles, for example. Moreover, being in a different time zone than those immediately around them meant that they regularly missed out on family or community events and being awake when those around them were asleep left some of them feeling estranged. At the same time, some of the call centre workers appreciated being able to combine work and care responsibilities.

The platform-mediated work at the centre of this study shows some important parallels to BPO work in that its translocality creates temporal disjunctures. Although working together across large distances has become easier in terms of technology, aligning platform work with other elements of remote gig workers' lives still entails tying it to local, embodied rhythms. However, there are also crucial differences and new aspects brought about as this work is done freelance and mediated by platforms. Differently from call centre work, only part of the freelancers' work must be performed synchronously with their clients' business hours. When freelancers create designs, they usually do not have to work synchronously with their clients. Moreover, practices of creating designs and practices of assembling are affected by these temporal disjunctures in separate ways.

As freelancers, they do not need to stick to schedules created by employers. Depending on the type of project they work on, freelancers may be paid for every hour they work, for milestones, or a final product. This affects how they manage their time. Altogether, their work time is organised around deadlines rather than schedules, as Arnav describes: "A freelancer doesn't have any work schedule. We have targets" (Arnav's photo diary, day 2). This provides them with some flexibility, as they can usually choose at what times to work:

"Most of the maintenance of my day comes from me. I've to complete projects within certain timelines, ending up sleeping and waking late. Outside influence is much less because the only instruction affecting my workday is deliverable deadline, which in most cases is sufficient enough" (Krishnam's photo diary, day 2).

As Krishnam describes, no one tells him when to start his workday or how much time to spend on a job. He can organise his workday himself if he meets his deadlines. Usually, the intensity of his work increases as he approaches a deadline. Freelancers can choose autonomously when to perform a task and over what time. Accordingly, they can move this part of their work around to align it with other elements of their lives. However, they are not completely free in how they organise their work – Krishnam adds: "Oh, but sometimes when client want some changes or multiple changes, it definitely interrupts my structure" (Krishnam's photo diary, day 2). This is the flipside of his flexible days: while he does not have anybody to give him a fixed structure from the outside, he is not always able to defend his structure against outside influences, either. Working as a freelancer does not mean that he is free to plan his days as he pleases, but that it consists of moving parts – some of them within, some beyond his control.

Reacting flexibly to clients' wishes presents additional challenges in the translocal work contexts of the platform workers, as this account by Kiaan illustrates:

> "I mean, in terms of challenges I would say there were a lot of times when the timeline got really used by the clients, because, I mean, the entire process got shifted. [...] Plus, you have to maintain the time zone. [...] Because you cannot contact them when it is nighttime over there [...]. Mostly, it was the deadline, so you get some requirements from the client and the requirements eventually got changed in the middle. [...] And then, it was much more difficult in terms of having that right communication with the client, because they were not available all the time. They had a fixed time, 'I can give you two hours of the day'" (Interview with Kiaan, 29–02–20).

As I have described in Chapter 5.1, it is often hard for freelancers to assess how long a job will take, as it includes a process of negotiation about the results with clients. Moreover, they cannot always rely on the deadlines that were agreed upon in the beginning. Sometimes, clients change the deadlines, or they require freelancers to quickly react to a request. In Kiaan's account, the time difference between him and his clients exacerbates this challenge, reducing the time frames for them to discuss ideas. What is more, the quote shows that in relation to his clients, Kiaan did not have much power over the process – in theory, he could use his time flexibly, but at the same time, he was expected by clients to adjust if they changed the deadline and to be available to them during their business hours. While his schedule was flexible, then, this flexibility did not mean complete freedom, but aligning his schedule with that of his clients.

For asynchronous work, the time difference between gig workers and clients can be an asset, for example, if a job is done during Indian business hours and can be submitted by the time US business hours start. This phenomenon has been coined "time arbitrage" (Nadeem, 2009, p. 21). Jiya, for example, explains:

> "See, mostly my clients are offshore clients, so out of India. It depends, actually most clients are from the US. Mostly we have US clients. So, most of the time, the works, if you're 1-to-1, you directly contact your client, it begins, you know, after 12 o'clock or 3 o'clock, it will start. Because there's a time difference, different time zones. And actually, sometimes it helps. Because the entire day I can do my job. I can submit, you know, here in the evening,

they can review, next morning I have next feedback and I can start working. So, it is very helpful in that" (Interview with Jiya, 08–03-20).

Jiya creates her designs during the day and takes turns with US clients in giving and incorporating feedback. Platform work is part of her daily rhythm, but it is not all-encompassing. She combines platform work with caring for her son and structures her workday according to what she finds important. For the most part, she can decide on her own when she works for the platform, and she has come up with a general structure for herself: in the mornings, she takes care of her son and household chores, and in the afternoons, she works on her designs. However, the quote also illustrates that time arbitrage is only feasible for part of the freelancers' work. While Jiya can make use of the time difference when she is creating a design, she also adapts to her clients' time zone when she schedules calls with them. This assembling work is affected by different time zones much more, as it often requires the freelancers to work synchronously.

There are also variations between the different freelancers in how synchronised their work rhythms are with those of their clients. While Jiya mostly works independently on bigger projects, Advik, for example, is in close contact with his client during his working hours. His work rhythm is quite similar to that of a BPO worker in that he works mainly for one client and adapts to his work rhythm. He works as a virtual assistant for several clients in the US, taking care of admin work for them and only occasionally creating designs. As he is mainly tasked with things that must be done immediately, he cannot choose freely when to work but must be available during his US clients' business hours. Creating designs (or mostly spreadsheets, in his case) and assembling work are both tied to his clients' time zone. He has shifted his circadian rhythm completely, usually waking up around 2 pm IST and going to bed at around 5 am. He has built his life completely around his work schedule, leaving little space for anything but work and recovering for work. He describes that he does not have many social connections beyond his family and a friendly relationship with one of his clients. His mother keeps him company when he is working but usually falls asleep before the end of his work hours. He lives with his parents, works from home, and does not leave the house much except for taking a walk. While Advik feels quite comfortable with living and working according to a different rhythm from those around him, it also means that he has little contact with others. However, working freelance and from home still affords him some freedom to allot his time flexibly: he has spread his work across his waking hours, usually alternating between around 30 minutes of work and rest, respectively.

For some of the freelancers whom I have talked to, there is another moving part in the assemblage: inspiration. They explain that as creative professionals, they cannot schedule creativity – as Kiaan puts it, referring to the timeframes his clients used to set: "as a freelancer [in design] you do not get ideas only in those two hours, you get ideas any time. So, that is the difference between designers and engineers" (Interview with Kiaan, 29–02-20). Producing a novel idea sometimes feels to the designers like it is beyond their control:

> "The main thing is the creative part. Sometimes you don't get the ideas, something like a brain freeze happens. You might get some ideas instantly, within a minute, to create. Suppose a client wants a design for Valentine's Day. You might get the same ideas which is already available in all the platforms. So, even if you keep on thinking, it does not work at all. And sometimes, when you are not thinking about it, you are just walking on the street and you get an idea, 'I can put a design in this way', and you can immediately start. So, that is how it happens for me most of the time. As soon as I get an idea, when I am thinking about some project, I note it on in my notes and then I can implement that when I am designing it" (Interview with Moksh, 10-03-20).

What Moksh and Kiaan say about creativity and time adds another essential element to aligning relations that distinguishes design from many other jobs. At least in Kiaan's case, there is tension between his need for flexibility and the small window that remains for him to discuss ideas with his clients. Sometimes he cannot provide an idea in just the time the client needs or steer his mind towards an idea, as maybe an engineer could. Moreover, this underlines how closely creating designs and making connections with one's environment are interwoven: if designers tried to only focus on designing and shut out all outside influences as distractions, they would miss out on the inspiration that comes with not sitting at one's desk.

In short, freelancers are indeed rather flexible when it comes to creating designs. They can make their own schedules within the framework of deadlines. For some of them, time arbitrage enables them to take turns with their clients in feedback loops for bigger projects. However, they are also not completely free in timing their work. Clients may request more changes than expected or change the deadline for a project, and they also cannot always anticipate when inspiration hits. Thus, even for this part of their work, they must regularly deal with spontaneous schedule changes to synchronise their schedules with those of others. Moreover, looking at a broader time horizon, how much time they can allocate for a design also depends on their highly dynamic workload. In addition to how the work for a single job unfolds, platform workers also experience irregular rhythms regarding their overall workload. Freelancers cannot plan easily and encounter phases of high activity, where they must finish a lot of work with tight deadlines, on the one hand, and phases of low activity, where they cannot find work, on the other hand. The contingency of applying for briefs or taking part in design contests means that if every proposal works out, they may have more work than they can handle. All this plays into how flexible freelancers are able and required to be when it comes to aligning this part of their work with further elements of their lives.

Freelancers' flexible schedules also mean that they have to work on creating and negotiating them – a task that I categorise as an assembling practice here. Working as freelancers, their schedules are less fixed. Creating a schedule can be a big challenge for platform workers, as their work environment is highly dynamic. In this chapter, I will add to this the notion of aligning different, sometimes conflicting, time logics. Like the value of their work, schedules are also subject to negotiations between freelancers, clients, and platforms. Moreover, their work schedules impact and are impacted by the different elements of their lives, which I have outlined in the first part of this chapter. When gig workers create a schedule for themselves, they must consider all these different elements, and they must flexibly react to changes. It is therefore important not to mistake flexibility for complete freedom here: like in the previous chapters, flexibility also requires continuous work to make and sustain connections. In this chapter, this implies assembling one's time to make space for work and other responsibilities. In the highly volatile context of platform work, freelancers cannot create a fixed schedule that will accommodate everything, but they must continuously negotiate their schedule. This flexibility is not good or bad in itself: it holds opportunities to combine different responsibilities, but it can also make it harder to combine them and create the pressure of always being on call.

Moreover, freelancers usually have different projects at the same time. Accordingly, they must manage different projects and prioritise some over others. The freelancers in this study use different strategies to manage the projects they have. Suveer, for example, asks clients to communicate to him clearly if a project is urgent so that he can prioritise it accordingly: "I am also writing my clients: If they have multiple projects, then set their priority.

And if you have an urgent problem, then writing 'urgent' in the post. I can manage all the projects and all the jobs according to them" (Interview with Suveer 27-02-21). Krishnam tries to prioritise higher-value projects. Freelancers can come up with a structure or routine themselves to some extent, but this routine regularly changes. Their prioritisation is not a solid structure but can be disrupted by urgent client requests, for example.

To stay on top of their different jobs, freelancers also make use of different technological tools. Krishnam, for example, usually starts his workday by checking various apps for new messages from his clients:

> "I will start my workday typically with opening up my phone and see if there's a new project available for me. I am connected with my clients through various apps the first thing I'll do is to check them. Also, sometimes i will just resume any previous work if paused and get to my projects folder in my PC for completion" (Krishnam's photo diary, day 2).

Janbir, too, uses different tools to stay in touch with his clients, and keeps an overview of his different tasks via tools provided by Upwork:

> "I plan my workday in advance. I used to maintain Task management software, but now I Marking emails, Whatsapp/ skype messages, and Upwork job board is my main tool to make a to-do list. I always work on a priority basis. Also, I try to serve them during their Business hours" (Janbir's photo diary, day 2).

Connecting these different media of communication and different technological tools also presents challenges: as Vertesi (2014) argues, heterogeneous technological infrastructures present different standards and interactional possibilities. They produce "seamful spaces" (ibid.), requiring those who use them to create fleeting moments of alignment to make them work together.

Unlike creating designs, coordinating with clients is usually a synchronous task: freelancers communicate with clients in video or audio calls, for example, to discuss ideas and potential trajectories. Serving overseas clients during their business hours for synchronous cooperation comes with challenges, however. Jiya, who works asynchronously with her clients most of the time, still needs to do part of her work synchronously. To be able to create a design according to her clients' ideas, she usually schedules audio or video calls with them, for example via Skype. When she works on larger projects, she additionally coordinates her work with further designers, who contribute different elements to the project. These designers are often located yet in other countries, such as the Philippines. These instances of coordination make it necessary for her to adapt to others' schedules and to their time zones. That is, she cannot plan her days completely freely and she cannot always predict how her schedule will unfold. Moreover, she does not always have clients from the US, but also from Australia, for example, and must adapt her schedule accordingly. While she can coordinate with US clients in the afternoon, she must adapt her schedule to work early in the morning for Australian clients, for instance.

Suveer also works predominantly through Upwork and regularly connects to clients in various time zones. This means that he cannot simply shift his rhythm to fit US business hours, as that would mean not being available for his Australian clients. This is how he describes his work rhythm:

"I am working east to west, almost all the clients in between, although in a middle part. And then, I can manage my time according to my clients. Australian clients, I am working in the early morning, my early morning, because of five to six hour difference. If I am working in 8 or 9 am, then there it's 2 pm or 1 pm accordingly. They are in a half day. I am matching my time according to them. If I am working a US client, then my night-time is their daytime. Definitely, clients want working in their time, according to their time. [...] In my real life, I have to sleep 3 am or 2 am daily, almost 1 am or 2 am daily in the night, my night. And I get up in the morning 8 am. If I am tired and I get up 7 or 8 am, because my son is starting the class, then I manage the time accordingly" (Interview with Suveer, 27–02-21).

He orients his work schedule to when his clients need him, respectively. At the same time, he also has obligations like getting his son ready for school and, as he stresses, working out regularly to stay fit.

Like in BPO call centres, remote platform workers' jobs make it necessary for them to communicate with their overseas clients in real-time, albeit only for some elements of their work. Both types of work, then, require them to adapt to different time zones. However, while BPO workers' rhythms of work and life are disconnected from their immediate surroundings in terms of their days and nights and by working on weekends or holidays, their schedule has its own regularity. For a lot of the freelance workers in my study, by contrast, their rhythm is not so much shifted as it is spread across their days and nights. Advik has a rather fixed schedule, which is spread across all his waking hours and shifted towards US business hours, while Suveer works with clients from a variety of different time zones and adjusts his schedule accordingly, and Jiya generally keeps a fixed schedule, which she departs from if her present client's time zone requires it. Similarly, Shevchuk et al. (2021) find that especially freelancers who work in different time zones than their clients work a high proportion of non-standard hours. They argue that being fast to reply to job offers is crucial for platform workers to secure a job and that freelance workers feel compelled to be awake during prospective clients' business hours as a result.

So far, I have established that the translocality of work relations, the freelance character of work, and the creativity that is needed for it, all affect how gig workers can align platform work with further elements of their lives. In the following part of the chapter, I will outline how the characteristics of platform work add to this.

7.2.3 Platform mechanisms

As I have outlined above, practices of assembling and practices of creating designs come with different temporalities and spatialities. I will focus here on practices of assembling, which regularly require designers to interact with the platform as they find and apply for jobs, make and sustain connections with clients, and manage their online reputation.

Freelancers on an online platform deal with a great deal of competition – as Arnav puts it: "Like every day is a new beginning, A freelancer has to compete with millions everyday" (Arnav's photo diary, day 2). I want to stress two elements of this statement: every day is a new beginning for freelancers as they do not have a structure to fall back on. This points to the dynamic and flexible character of platform work. Connected to this, having to compete with millions everyday points to a combination of flexibility and volatility. While part of this is like other freelance work as well, the scope of the competition is much greater with platform work. Accordingly, standing out and convincing clients to hire them takes significant effort. As I have described in Chapter 5.2, this requires them to continuously work on their online reputation and reviews. Moreover, even compared to other forms of freelance work, platform work is often connected to very strong fluctuations in how much work the freelancers have, partly due to the systems of being rated by clients (cf. Wood & Lehdonvirta, 2021b). As Moksh describes:

"I am into freelance designing. I catch clients online to Upwork and various other platforms. It looks easy but it is really tough. At times, you don't have work for months to do. And at times you have work which you alone can't manage" (Interview with Moksh, 10–03–20).

On the one hand, these fluctuations make it hard for gig workers to count on an income from platform work to support themselves and others who depend on them. On the other hand, they depend more on others to support them with their work or financially. This leaves freelancers in an ambiguous situation: On the one hand, their work is not regular or predictable, and they cannot rely on a stable income or a certain number of jobs every month. On the other hand, they must stay active and make platform work a priority, as they need to put in constant work to keep up their reputation.

When they are connecting to clients, freelancers are also required to reply to messages fast and reliably. As I have described in Chapter 6.2, being responsive is key to forming relationships of trust with clients. Leaving a good impression on one's client not only contributes to the success of a single job, but may also lead a client to hire the same freelancer again for the next job. However, being fast to reply to messages is also important when interacting with the platform. Upwork, for example, monitors how fast freelancers reply to clients' messages and shows it on their profiles. Both the global competition and the monitoring mechanisms put in place by the platform create conditions that make it hard to just leave work to fixed timings and to switch off notifications.

The different elements of freelance work in this setting reinforce each other: the competition with other freelancers for jobs is exacerbated by the global reach of the platform. The need to manage client relations is spread to different time zones by just this global reach, and with the platform on their smartphone and reputation systems putting pressure on them, this means that freelancers are on call – anytime and anywhere.

7.3 Synthesis: Ambiguous alignment

To sum up, I have argued in this chapter that how freelancers connect to a global assemblage of platform work is interwoven with other forms of connections they make. To start with, I have pointed out how they combine platform work with other forms of paid and unpaid work. How they do this affects how they experience their work on the platform, how flexibly they can dedicate time to platform work, and to what extent they depend on an income from the platform. Workers are connected with others in relationships of mutual care and responsibility: On the one hand, this means that they dedicate part of their time to caring for others, or that there are often several people who depend on a platform worker's income. On the other hand, freelancers also count on the support of others to buffer a high workload or to support them financially in phases of low activity. To understand designers' work on the platform, then, it is necessary to also look at how it relates to other elements of their lives. The practices of assembling that I have characterised as the foundation of the global assemblage of platform work also include practices of aligning the relations of platform work with further elements of everyday life. Based on this notion, in the second part of the chapter, I have outlined the challenges and opportunities that platform work poses for aligning it with other elements of the life-work continuum. These challenges and opportunities are expressed temporally and spatially in ambiguous ways.

Practices of assembling are interwoven with practices of creating designs: as Repenning (2022) argues for the case of fashion designers using Instagram in various parts of their work processes, "platforms co-constitute work practices, spaces, and places in the field of creative work" (p. 221). To carve out their specific spatialities and temporalities, I will disentangle them analytically here. Creating designs is mostly stationary work, as freelancers need heavy hardware and software for detailed designs. Moreover, this part of their work is rather solitary and requires them to stay focused and keep distractions at bay for an extended time. As most of them work from home, this can be a challenge and requires them to set boundaries and to find ways of 'being at work' inside their homes, and often around other family members. In this part of their work, freelancers depend on others' time requirements only indirectly: they must finish their work by deadlines that are set by or negotiated with their clients. Within these timeframes, they can make their own schedule, although they must be prepared to adjust to spontaneous client requests. For creating designs, time differences do not have an adverse effect, as they can work asynchronously with their clients. Being in different time zones can even be an advantage, as it allows freelancers to incorporate feedback when it is night-time for their clients and to have it ready by the time their clients' business hours start. This part of freelance work allows them quite a high degree of flexibility to integrate it with other elements of their lives. However, there are also elements beyond their control: First, some of the freelancers explain that inspiration often hits them at unexpected times. Second, the fluctuation in their workload is something they cannot plan for. As I have described above, sometimes gig workers cannot find work, and other times they have more work than they can handle on their own. Accordingly, they must flexibly adjust to changes they cannot predict, and often also depend on others' flexibility to make it work.

Practices of assembling, by contrast, are based on making and sustaining connections. They necessitate connecting to clients on several levels. This includes, first, writing a proposal and convincing the client to pick them for a job. When the mode of allocating work is based on design contests, this overlaps with practices of creating designs. Especially if the freelancers rely on platform work to a large extent, reacting to design briefs is time sensitive: if another convincing designer is quicker, the chance is gone. Second, practices of assembling are necessary on different levels during the process of working with a client. A lot of clients and freelancers prefer discussing modifications of designs synchronously, for example via audio or video calls. As the freelancers are usually the ones to adapt to their clients' respective time zone and their clients are often spread across different time zones, their working times, too, are spread. Moreover, they depend on agreements with their clients, so they cannot flexibly fit these appointments into their schedules. This becomes even harder to plan if clients ask them for last-minute changes. In addition to their clients' different time zones, freelancers may have to coordinate with others contributing to the same project, who are often in yet another time zone. Differently from creating designs, much of the practices of assembling can also be done in a very mobile way. Messaging clients and checking new design briefs is often done via smartphone, making it possible for this part of work to seep into times and places beyond fixed working hours and their fixed workplace. This is exacerbated as the global competition and platform mechanisms require them to be constantly 'on call'. What is more, the practices of negotiating value and establishing trust, which I have described in Chapters 5 and 6, require continuous work. These practices are not bound to fixed working times but make it necessary for freelancers to be flexible and adjust to ever-changing conditions.

While the flexibility of creating designs may help with aligning different elements of life, practices of assembling in the context of translocality and platform mechanisms involve continuous work and flexible adjustment to the needs of others. Consequently, this aspect of platform work often cannot be adjusted to the time requirements of other elements of life but, by contrast, different elements of life may need to be flexibly shuffled around to accommodate the many moving parts of platform work. Aligning different elements of life in a global assemblage of platform work, then, means continuously working on creating fleeting moments of alignment. Based on this observation, I argue that the characteristics of platform work that I have described above create 'seamful spaces' (Vertesi, 2014). Vertesi originally introduced this concept to better grasp work contexts that include several different infrastructures, which work according to distinct logics or ontologies. She contends that in everyday practice, using different technologies is far from a seamless experience: there is a possibility for action, but it requires actors to continuously work on creating copresence through heterogeneous infrastructures, creating a seamful interactional space. Within this space, there is no stable balance but only fleeting moments of alignment (Vertesi, 2014, p. 268). Connecting heterogeneous technical infrastructures in the way Vertesi (2014) refers to is part of freelancers' work practices, for example, when they communicate with clients via different communication tools, or when they use task management software to manage their projects on one or several platforms. Beyond the technological understanding of seamful spaces that Vertesi puts forward, the different relationships that make up freelancers' work and lives can also be understood as seamful spaces. They continuously work on temporarily aligning not just technologies, but also different responsibilities and different relationships, as well as different time zones and spaces of work and non-work. Designers align their work on the platform with their lives beyond the platform, and as the examples have shown, they are not separated with clear boundaries but rather patched together to create temporary seams or messy overlaps (cf. Vertesi, 2014, p. 266). As a result, time and space are atomised into many moving parts, requiring freelancers to work on aligning them without being able to create a stable structure.

Within this dynamic environment, flexibility is connected to diverse degrees of agency. As I have described above, flexibility can have quite different implications, depending on the situation. Whether flexibility is a challenge or an opportunity is connected with power relations or actors' capacity to assemble (McFarlane, 2009, pp. 566–567). In relations between workers, clients, and platforms, workers are often required to flexibly adapt to clients' time demands: They work at night to adapt to their business hours, they adjust their schedules to clients' requests for alterations in their work, and they often feel obliged to cater to spontaneous deadline changes. Platforms provide a framework for these relations and their ranking and reputation systems contribute to the freelancers' need to go to great lengths when it comes to adapting to clients. At the same time, not all freelancers have the same capacity to assemble: Those who do not rely completely on platform work can rather afford to only accept work that fits into their schedule.

8. Synthesis: Negotiating Relations – Assembling Global Platform Work

The purpose of this study was to explore and theorise remote gig workers' everyday work practices of making and sustaining global connections mediated by online platforms. I have established in the beginning that remote work in the gig economy entails practices of assembling, that is, navigating a complex, opaque, and volatile work environment. In the analysis section, I have compiled elements of an assemblage of global platform work: negotiating value, managing emotions, and aligning relations. In this chapter, I explore the connections between these practices to create a clearer picture of what is new about this work and how it can be conceptualised. In the first part of the chapter, I briefly summarise my findings against the backdrop of the research questions posed in the beginning. In the second part, I synthesise these findings into four characteristic practices of assembling against the backdrop of the conceptual framework of the study. Finally, I set these practices in the context of features of the platform-mediated work environment.

8.1 Summary of findings and answers to research questions

In Chapter 5, I explored the question of how value emerges from relations between freelancers, clients, and platforms. The value of freelancers' work is interwoven with remuneration, but it also has an affective dimension. Freelancers and clients not only often disagree about the value of a service, but they may even disagree about what constitutes value in the first place. While the value of freelancers' work is often mainly associated with the designs that they create, practices of assembling, too, create value, albeit in a more subtle and volatile way. In Chapter 6, I explored how gig workers manage their own and their clients' emotions and how platforms mediate emotional connections. The chapter builds on the argument from *negotiating value* that the freelancers produce an image of themselves that is supposed to appeal to clients. In Chapter 7, I explored how freelancers' relations extend beyond platform work. In this chapter, I described how the assemblage of platform work is interconnected with practices of assembling beyond platform work. In line with my observations from the previous chapters, freelancers are continuously working on making and sustaining connections – with clients, but also with other actors around them. Moreover, I complemented this with how freelancers are supported by others who sustain relations of mutual care with them. Throughout the three chapters, I have related the practices to three key features of the platform-mediated work environment, reflected in the three guiding research questions.

The first research question was: *how do gig workers navigate the volatility of work relations?* Both the literature on the gig economy and the material I gathered throughout the research process suggest that platform work is characterised by loose and short-term work connections. My goal was to explore how platform workers' everyday work practices reflect this, how they organise their work in this context, and what strategies they develop to deal with the volatility of their work environment. I found that practices of assembling entail continuous negotiations over the basic terms of work. The two main findings from Chapter 5 are, first, that value is negotiated in a contingent, "heterarchical" (Girard & Stark, 2005) process, and, second, that the process of negotiating value is closely connected to the process of producing the worker as a "subject of value" (van Doorn, 2014). This process of negotiation takes place on small and big scales. On a small scale, freelancers negotiate their position in a working relationship through communication with clients, for example. On a bigger scale, they invest in future relationships, sometimes accepting losses in the short run, in the hope of being rewarded by a higher market value. A central take-away from this chapter is, then, that practices of assembling do not result in a stable product, but that the freelancers must continuously work on relationships with their present clients, partially to invest in relationships with future clients.

In Chapter 6, I found that the uncertainty of gig work has an emotional impact, as the lack of planning security causes stress and anxiety for workers. Moreover, through ranking and reputation systems, working on an image of themselves is deeply entangled with working on relationships with clients for gig workers. Managing emotional connections is one aspect of how freelancers negotiate their value and scoring high on the respective reputation metrics of the platform they use invokes trust with their clients. However, having a good reputation does not mean that the freelancers can get complacent: their value is continuously re-negotiated, and one bad review can drastically reduce their capacity to assemble (cf. Wood & Lehdonvirta, 2021b). Platform workers spend considerable time and effort trying to establish trust with clients and thus motivate them to start or keep working together; the freelancers in this study often lead clients returning for follow-up projects back to the elusive impression of getting along well or 'just clicking'. Gig workers' dependence on clients' emotional reactions to what they do further underscores the contingency of their work, as they can only try to anticipate clients' expectations but not predict them. Long-term connections between freelancers and clients do happen, but they are an exception rather than an inbuilt part of the system.

In Chapter 7, I connected the uncertainty of the loose work connections to the work of continuously aligning platform work with freelancers' lives beyond platform work. As in the other chapters, there is a process of negotiation, especially concerning the freelancers' schedules. I describe platform work and the other elements of their lives as "seamful spaces" (Vertesi, 2014) – they are not bounded but rather floating around and the freelancers must continuously work on aligning them. The loose and short-term work connections of gig work require constant changes in workers' routines. That is, gig workers often do not have a set routine that they adapt if changes arise but make up temporary routines and align different elements of their lives momentarily. The chapter also shows that there is great variation between freelancers' experiences: their lives beyond platform work have a significant impact on how they can align different elements.

The second research question was: *how do online platforms mediate work practices?* This question is directed at how gig workers interact with online platforms, and how platforms frame and structure interaction. My goal was, again, to explore how workers negotiate connections with and mediated by online platforms, framed as actors in the assemblage of platform work. By relating work practices to the framework set up by the platform, I also explored workers' agency beyond categories of employment. This question is connected to the first one, as the organisation of work connections is influenced by platforms. The logic by which a platform allocates gigs, such as through design contests or by applications as a response to design briefs, plays a key role in how stable or volatile work connections are. Online platforms shape relations by technological means, by setting up terms of use, and by acting as mediators in conflicts between freelancers and clients.

By setting up a framework for interaction, online platforms play a powerful role in the assemblage. The different online platforms used by the workers in this study allocate gigs according to different logics, such as through design contests or by applications as a response to design briefs. These variations are reflected in different work practices and experiences. Moreover, platforms provide a range of possible uses to workers when it comes to curating their profiles, communicating with clients, or negotiating the rate for their service. Platforms also frame negotiations about value, for example by stratifying the pool of registered freelancers into hierarchies. What is more, the various reputation mechanisms that online platforms provide commensurate value: they condense the impressions that the freelancers have left with previous clients into a measure of how the chances are that they will perform well. Value, here, is also connected to power in the sense of "capacity to assemble" (McFarlane, 2009, pp. 566). That is, online platforms contribute to structuring the field by establishing hierarchies and categories and sorting workers into them. The mechanisms of sorting often remain opaque to the workers.

In addition to providing a framework for interaction, online platforms also mediate connections. Concerning value, this happens for example when there is a conflict between clients and freelancers about whether a job was successfully completed. How freelancers establish trust and form emotional connections with their clients is also closely associated with the reputation mechanisms set up by online platforms. At the same time, the restricted time and forms of communication can make it challenging for workers to connect with clients on an emotional level. As I have found in Chapter 6, trust is put in the online platform by both workers and clients rather than established between workers and clients. Workers rely on the platform to make sure they are paid for their service, and clients rely on the platform to make sure they must only pay if a service is performed. Online platforms may reduce uncertainty by verifying profile information, for example, but even in this case, it is the platform that is the bearer of trust. Thus, online platforms are indispensable actors in the work relationships described in this study. However, the control over the situation exerted by online platforms has its limits, and workers do exert agency in how they navigate the framework set up by the platforms. They shared accounts of moving away from the platform for follow-up projects, for example, or of working around the platforms' control mechanisms. Platforms do not exercise complete control but are part of negotiations. Agency, then, does not lie solely with online platforms but is continuously negotiated. This reflects the non-linear causality of an assemblage, which "is located not in a pre-given sovereign agent, but in interactive processes of assembly through which causality operates as a non-linear process" (B. Anderson et al., 2012, p. 180).

The third research question was: *how do remote freelancers align global work relations with local, situated practices?* This question focused on the tension between the global dispersion of work enabled by online platforms and its unequal distribution and valuation. Again, I used a lens of everyday work practices of assembling to approach the question, focusing on workers' experiences and challenges. Notions of global and local were layered in the workers' experiences: they were not only affected by their actual geographical location but also by their discursive location in categories like 'low-income country'. In Chapters 5 and 6, workers' locations were predominantly relevant on a discursive level. Research participants reasoned that clients from Europe or the US perceived them as "cheap labour" (Interview with Sarabjit, 09-03-20) and that their motivation for hiring them rather than someone from their local labour market was saving money through arbitrage. Moreover, freelancers found that the knowledge of certain cultural codes, for example in their use of the English language, affected the value attributed to them and their work. Cultural familiarity also seemed to play a significant role in workers' endeavours to establish emotional closeness with clients.

However, the analysis also showed that the designers who participated in this study do not simply fit into categories like 'Global South' or 'low-income country'. Instead, their roles and positions are ambivalent and always negotiated with others. While they experience prejudice against South Asians and are well aware that they earn less on average than fellow gig workers in other countries, the platform workers also found that they could often still earn more money through platform work than with local projects. Some workers also outsource jobs via online platforms, for example. In the position of the client, they often choose workers from other countries, such as Pakistan, Vietnam, or the Philippines, whom they find to do the job at a lower rate than locally. Moreover, they experience their own and their clients' locations as just one of many factors that influence their work relationship and pay more importance to how experienced they are, for example.

In Chapter 7, the tension between local life worlds and globally spread work connections played a central role. I found that "temporal disjunctures"

(Mankekar & Gupta, 2017) between workers' locally grounded relationships and their globally spread work relationships mediated by online platforms posed challenges that go beyond the "social death" that Aneesh (2015) has found business process outsourcing (BPO) call centre workers in India to experience. This is due to the spread of clients' locations across various time zones, because of which work times, too, are often spread across various times of day and night. Moreover, the fluctuation of workload and unpredictability of jobs, which I have described above, further contribute to the challenges of aligning global work relations with various further elements of workers' lives. Thus, gig workers' physical locations influence their work experiences despite the technological connection through online platforms.

Workers navigated these lines of tension in diverse ways. Regarding the valuation of their work based on their location, they often used local rates as a point of reference to assess whether a job was worth their time. Moreover, they tried to distance themselves from stereotypes they experienced by focusing on reviews they had received from international clients, for example. Regarding the alignment of work spread across time zones, workers often try to establish at least a rough routine for themselves. Importantly, they often do not navigate the challenges of alignment alone: many mobilise a support system of family and friends to buffer the challenges of aligning the timing of clients' globally spread business hours with their further responsibilities.

In the following subchapter, I synthesise the findings from the previous chapters into four characteristic practices of assembling. The subchapter will elucidate the connecting threads between the practices and point to the characteristics of platform work that these practices reflect.

8.2 Practices of assembling

I have focused on practices of assembling in this study to shed light on an unpaid and often unrecognised aspect of remote freelancers' work. The broad perspective on work that I employed was informed by the premise that the category of work is socially constructed and depends on power relations (cf. Star & Strauss, 1999). Starting from this assumption, I drew on feminist perspectives that have challenged the idea of work as an essential category. These frameworks, first, expand the range of practices counted as work: They foreground invisible background work in handling technology (Star & Strauss, 1999; Vertesi, 2014), as well as emotional and affective dimensions of paid work (Hardt, 1999; Hochschild, [1983] 2012; Mankekar & Gupta, 2016). Moreover, Marxian-inspired authors have explored the "free labour" (Terranova, 2000) that keeps the digital economy going – practices that blur the boundaries of work and play. Second, the conceptual approaches that I build on stress the interdependence of different forms of work. The notion of reproductive labour (Mackenzie & Rose, 1983) sheds light on the unpaid domestic work often done by women, without which capitalist production could not be kept up. Subsequent approaches have built on and expanded this to go beyond a binary of productive and reproductive spheres: Ivancheva and Keating (2020), for example, propose to study work and life, or productive and reproductive spheres, as a continuum, and to consider economic actors' entanglement in interdependent relationships.

I have constructed the field of research as a global assemblage, first, to account for the dynamic and volatile connections that make up platform work and, second, to grasp the tension of digitally mediated translocal work connections. By framing practices of assembling as making and sustaining connections, I have aimed to incorporate a variety of practices irrespective of their direct economic productivity. The four characteristic practices of assembling reflect the volatility of work connections, the mediation by online platforms, and the translocality of work relationships.

8.2.1 "It's like shooting in the dark": Guessing and anticipating

"Shooting in the dark", as Ankit, one of my research participants has called it (Interview with Ankit, 01–03-20), is a practice that cuts across what I have described in the previous chapters: practices of assembling include working on reaching a goal without knowing the path towards it. As I have elucidated above, the platform-mediated work environment is complex and opaque. With the potential to connect to thousands of clients all over the world through online platforms, freelancers face a lot of decisions. Complexity and opacity are entangled: the sheer number of options, that is, the complexity of the environment, make it hard for gig workers to grasp what is worth spending their time and energy on. Moreover, online platforms add a layer of opacity through their mediation of visibility, value, and trust according to logics that often remain hidden from the freelancers. Negotiations between freelancers, clients, and platforms are contingent and thus hard to anticipate, making it hard for them to plan for a certain outcome. In the following paragraphs, I will explicate *guessing and anticipating* as an element of practices of assembling and point out what sets it apart from existing conceptions of work.

In Chapter 5, I have described how elusive value is in the freelancers' practices of assembling. Practices of assembling, rather than creating a product, can be understood as an investment with an uncertain outcome. When freelancers apply for a job through one of the online platforms that I have described in Chapter 4.3, they perform a considerable amount of unpaid work without knowing whether it will pay off eventually. Depending on what platform they use, there are different stakes: if freelancers do not hit the mark on a platform that operates mainly through design contests, such as 99designs, they create a complete design based on the information provided in a design brief but will only be paid for their work if their design is chosen from a usually large number of contest entries. While workers only start creating a design after closing a contract on a platform like Upwork, the fierce competition and restricted communication on the platform also mean that they must usually answer a lot of briefs to land one job. Similarly, once they have closed a contract or won a design contest, freelance designers perform a considerable amount of unpaid work producing designs that they have to redo entirely because they did not meet their client's expectations.

Gig workers often have little information on what the client wants, as they have little time for each project and the platform-mediated process reduces communication with clients. On the level of negotiating short-term value, then, shooting in the dark means that the freelancers invest time and effort into something without knowing if it is really what is needed – what Ankit has called "an educated guess" (Interview with Ankit, 01–03–20). The same practice of shooting in the dark is also present in freelance designers' attempts to improve their status on a platform. This is illustrated by Ankit's account of how he tries to be featured on 99designs' 'inspiration' page. Being featured there helps designers to be more visible to clients and to be directly invited to work together instead of having to go through the contest stage. As Ankit told me, the staff of 99designs handpicks designs according to what they find unique or creative. So, in the hopes of being featured, he tries to post in the community forum of the platform regularly to catch the staff members' attention in addition to catching their eye by winning contests. But in the end, it is still up to the platform to decide which design is creative and unique.

For freelancers who are new to platform work, *guessing and anticipating* mainly happens in the form of trial and error: within a context of uncertainty, they spend quite a lot of time writing unsuccessful proposals, for example. Their isolation from other platform workers exacerbates this – unlike in an office environment, for example, platform workers cannot rely on mentors or more experienced colleagues to teach them. As they gain experience, freelancers invent strategies to introduce some structure and predictability: to generate a continuous and sustainable income from their work on the platform, designers must weigh risks and rewards. In platforms with various levels, this means that they calculate if they should enter a contest for a higher paying design, thereby risking not being chosen and having worked in vain, or enter a contest for a lower paying design, where their chances are higher to succeed. While increased "gig literacies" (Sutherland et al., 2020) thus reduce the necessity to 'shoot in the dark', it is a continuous aspect of practices of assembling, and freelancers cannot foresee the outcomes of the complex negotiations of relationships between themselves, platforms, and clients. Just like the things that the freelancers plan for do not always happen, sometimes things happen as an indirect result of what they do on an individual level: even though the freelancers act in isolation from each other, their choices have an impact on other freelancers, whom clients and platforms will assess with reference to them.

As I have carved out in Chapter 6, establishing work relationships in a platform-mediated environment is also based on managing others' emotions and establishing a relationship of trust with them. Connecting in mostly written form with clients from various backgrounds on an emotional level, too, involves guessing and trying to anticipate reactions. Establishing trust can be a challenge for both sides in this context. At the same time, the impact of emotional connections on work relations creates additional contingency: again, designers can build on their experiences with previous clients to some extent, but they can never clearly predict their reactions. For graphic designers working through an online platform, this means that they invest in the market value of their personal brand without really being able to tell what a successful strategy looks like. With a lot of platforms, designers are sorted into several categories that affect what jobs are accessible to them. However, they often do not know what exactly they need to do to increase their position in the hierarchy. Furthermore, they try to increase their visibility by posting in online forums or by changing their profile information, for example. However, the algorithm that the platform deploys affects freelancers' visibility in ways they cannot oversee, and it continually changes. What van Doorn (2014) has called 'affective ambiguities', then, is expressed in trying to master a game the rules of which are both obfuscated and changing all the time. Freelancers are confronted with an ambiguous situation that suggests agency while also bringing a lot of uncertainty.

To sum up, shooting in the dark consists of trial and error and of trying to anticipate short-term and long-term outcomes of practices. These practices reflect the opacity, complexity, and contingency of the platform-mediated work environment. Other types of work also include practices of shooting in the dark: designers who do not use online platforms, too, may participate in design contests and potentially create a design in vain, for example. Job applicants may write a lot of applications before being invited to a job interview and pitching an idea to others usually involves uncertainty about how they will react. However, for practices of assembling, shooting in the dark is much more prevalent. With the mass of potential jobs and the enormous competition, freelancers spend a lot of time and effort trying to get an overview and doing work that potentially amounts to nothing. Remote freelancers' work includes a high proportion of reaching out to clients whom they do not know yet, leaving them in a steady state of trial and error, whereas other jobs have a higher proportion of stabilised relationships. Moreover, as the examples of freelancers who also do local jobs have shown, these are often initiated via recommendations by friends, for example. While online platforms can provide a sense of security to some extent through rating systems or acting as an escrow for payments, on the interpersonal level, the work relationships on online platforms are much more a leap of faith.

With practices of assembling, workers cannot directly aim at producing a certain outcome. While reproductive labour or invisible background work also refer to forms of work that are unpaid and often overlooked, what sets practices of assembling apart is their irregularity. There is a constant need for workers to perform these practices, but their results vary greatly. Uncertainty about the outcomes of one's practices remains part of practices of assembling, and it is harder to direct one's practices to a desired outcome. As B. Anderson et al. (2012) point out: "The implication of assemblage thinking is that causality is located not in a pre-given sovereign agent, but in interactive processes of assembly through which causality operates as a non-linear process" (p. 180). Freelancers contribute to shaping the relationships in this assemblage, but the outcome of their practices depends on the decisions made by multiple other actors, too.

8.2.2 "Every day is a new beginning": Adapting to constant change

The second aspect of practices of assembling that has emerged from the analysis is *adapting to constant change*. It relates to *guessing and anticipating*: as I have argued above, uncertainty regarding the outcomes of one's practices is a part of platform work even for experienced freelancers. The platform-mediated work environment is characterised by constant change and loose relationships – as Arnav has put it, "every day is a new beginning" (Arnav's photo diary, day 2). In this section, I will elucidate how freelancers deal with the volatility of their work environment along three axes of volatility: loose work connections, the volatility of status, and the dynamic development of the platforms. Moreover, I will point out how practices of *adapting to constant change* differ from other forms of work.

First, gig workers' practices of assembling are informed by the notion that they can be replaced in an instant by someone from the global 'crowd'. Loose and short-term work connections are characteristic of the gig economy – against the background of the oversupply of labour on gig work platforms, workers are considered easily replaceable. Therefore, adapting to new clients and their needs is a constant necessity for them. While some of the freelancers in this study have built long-term work relationships with clients that may last several years, this does not coincide with a high degree of stability in a platform-mediated work environment. There is less work of adapting to new clients for them, but they must continuously keep up the relationship or risk their clients moving on to someone else. Introducing some stability into their work relationships thus implies continuously managing their clients' emotions.

Loose work connections also have an impact on freelancers' work rhythms, which are often unstable and hard to predict. As freelancers, they produce their own structures, but they must remain open to changes and there is no stable foundation to fall back on. Both their workload and their income, thus, vary greatly: there are phases when there is no paid work at all and other phases when the workload is high, sometimes even overwhelming. The freelancers develop different strategies to buffer this volatility: they need to make sure that they only take as much work as they can manage and that they can meet their expenses in phases when they cannot find work. As I have described in Chapter 7, gig workers often combine various sources of income. Connecting this to the broader context of interdependent relationships of care and responsibility, volatility and fluctuation also make it especially necessary for freelancers to activate their support system; their family members, for example, alleviate some of the uncertainties of platform work financially or by helping in phases of high activity. Not being able to rely on a stable income, but continuously having to try to find work takes a heavy toll on many of the designers to whom I have talked.

Second, gig workers must continuously work on their online status to avoid it deteriorating. As I have described in Chapter 5, freelancers' capacity to assemble increases with their reputation on the platform or platforms they use. However, their online reputation, too, is very volatile. If the freelancers do nothing for some time, their reputation will automatically deteriorate. Moreover, a single negative review by a client can severely decrease their rating (cf. Wood & Lehdonvirta, 2021b). Consequently, freelancers must work continuously on keeping their status up. In addition to preparing for potential changes, then, *adapting to constant change* implies keeping up a fragile equilibrium through continuous work.

Third, gig workers need to regularly adapt their strategies to changes in their work environment. The mechanisms with which platforms operate are not only opaque, as I have outlined regarding *guessing and anticipating*, but also dynamic. Therefore, freelancers cannot simply stick with a strategy that has been successful in the past but need to adapt their strategies regularly to an environment that keeps changing. I have described this concerning options like payment per hour or milestone or fixed price offers in Chapter 5.1, for example. This adds to the continuity of trial and error, as they need to find new strategies and regularly adapt to an environment that is new to them. Beyond the changing terms and conditions, the dynamic platform landscape also implies that the freelancers may have to adjust to an overall new platform occasionally, for example, when platforms merge, as in the case of Elance and oDesk.

To sum up, the need to continuously start over is characteristic of practices of assembling and sets it apart from other forms of work. Structures of organizing work have partially dissolved, and workers must continuously adapt their practices to changing situations. While work relationships in freelance work, in general, are often volatile and dynamic, platform work adds volatility as the work environment itself is highly dynamic and the reputation systems put in place by the platforms require continuous activity from the freelancers. Moreover, the global dimension of competition adds to the impression that workers are disposable and easily replaced. While continuous work is necessary to make new connections and to sustain existing ones, what this work looks like exactly changes and strategies need to be adapted. This sets *adapting to constant change* apart from routine background work or reproductive labour. The constellations in the assemblage change dynamically and are hard to predict, as they depend on decisions by multiple actors. This underscores that flexibility, for the platform workers, often implies reacting to dynamic developments and adapting other elements of their lives rather than spontaneously changing their work schedules according to their own wishes.

8.2.3 "Freelancers must be able to put up with all types of clients": Producing relatable selves

To compete with other people who are offering their services via online platforms, freelancers need to try and stand out to clients as well as aim to gain their attention and trust. Therefore, another part of practices of assembling is *producing relatable selves*. The image that freelancers present is always produced in relation to others and connected to the emotional labour of anticipating what others may expect or want from them. In this section, I will outline how the affective dimension of practices of assembling connects to how freelancers manage the value of their work in relation to other actors in the assemblage and how their subjectivities emerge from these practices.

First, as I have described in Chapters 5 and 6, freelancers' chances of success reflect their capacity to assemble, that is, their agency depends on how well they can make connections with others. How they can present themselves and what counts as a measure of their employability does not lie completely with them but also depends on other actors in the assemblage. Negotiating emotional connections and negotiating the value of their work are entangled for these freelancers. On the level of specific everyday practices, writing personalised cover letters is an example of how gig workers establish trust with their clients and at the same time increase the perceived value of what they can provide. The emotional labour that they put into empathising with their clients is also an investment in the hopes of a financial reward. The service that they provide to their clients has an emotional component and being nice to work with plays into the freelancers' reputation and, by extension, their capacity to assemble.

Second, online platforms mediate freelancers' work on producing relatable selves. The range of possible uses that the platform provides affects the image that they can present to the world. Producing relatable selves contains elements of self-branding (cf. Gandini & Pais, 2020): freelancers continuously work on their online image and try to anticipate their clients' needs. As I have noted in the section above, in the volatile environment of platform work there is a constant need for freelancers to perform their hireability. As freelancers negotiate their positions with clients and platforms, they cannot foresee whether the image they produce will prompt the reaction that they hope for. Moreover, as I have elucidated in Chapter 5, online platforms commensurate freelancers' relatability through different reputation mechanisms. Thus, how workers can present themselves is mediated by the online platforms they use. Richardson (2017) argues that "the worker is both creator and created through relationships with machines" (p. 254), that is, workers are simultaneously influenced by the platform they use and their practices have an effect on the assemblage of platform work. As they work on creating relatable selves, workers' subjectivities take shape in relation to other actors in the assemblage.

Third, the selves that freelancers produce reflect the multitude and volatility of the work connections that they make. Online personas are not simply a role that freelancers play online, but the affective labour (Hardt, 1999) of relating to clients and platforms contributes to the production of their subjectivities as workers. As Ibert and Schmidt (2014) have argued for musical actors, remote freelancers are required to produce "prismatic identities" (pp. 12–14), that is, they show different aspects of themselves according to what they anticipate their respective clients to be looking for. With remote freelance work this is exacerbated by different cultural contexts: studying BPO workers in India, Mankekar and Gupta (2016) have contended that producing culturally appropriate affect by nuances of speaking in just the right tone or using language that 'feels right', for example, becomes part of their subjectivity as workers (pp. 26–27). This is true for practices of assembling, too, but it is extended by the need to produce flexible selves. Freelancers have the task to hit the mark in communicating with clients from all over the world, following different feeling rules (Hochschild, [1983] 2012; cf. also Koch, 2013) and cultural codes (Mankekar & Gupta, 2016). Unlike workers overseas who operate from within a stable structure, remote freelancers' connections are loose and spread out in a constellation of relationships across different scales.

As they connect with people from various countries outside of the framework of an institutionalised office setting, freelancers must also adapt their ways of connecting on an affective level in several ways – as Krishnam expresses it: "freelancers must be able to put up with all types of clients" (Krishnam's photo diary, day 4). As I have elucidated above, gig workers are confronted with different people from diverse backgrounds regularly. Thus, practices of assembling produce flexible selves. Producing a "self that works" (Gandini & Pais, 2020, p. 232), then, is not enough for remote freelancers, as their selves only work with some of their clients. Moreover, how others perceive them is not completely in the freelancers' control. The country in which freelancers are based also affects clients' reactions to them, as I have shown in Chapter 5.2. However, not all freelancers reported differences in how they deal with clients from different countries. Instead, how they get along with a client is often affected by clients' previous experiences with design, for example.

To sum up, freelancers do not approach the assemblage of platform work as static or bounded entities, but their subjectivities as workers are dynamic and subject to negotiation. Their practices partially reflect what has been discussed as self-branding (Flisfeder, 2015; Gandini & Pais, 2020; Hearn, 2010; van Doorn, 2014), but also go beyond it in some respects. Within the space of assemblage, the image that freelancers present to clients is subject to negotiations between freelancers, clients, and platforms. In a context where clients come from various backgrounds and have diverse implicit expectations, rather than simply playing a role, freelancers produce highly flexible and dynamic selves.

8.2.4 "It looks easy, but it is really tough": Creating temporary alignment

In the previous three sections, I have characterised practices of assembling as acting in a context of uncertainty and volatility and pointed out how freelancers' subjectivities develop in dynamic negotiations in the assemblage. In this section, I will build on these observations to focus on freelancers' practices of *creating temporary alignment*. While the previous practices referred to single or sequential relationships, this one focuses on the coordination of constellations, including but also going beyond how freelancers interact with and via gig work platforms. I argue that practices of assembling include creating – and frequently adapting – structures and routines, aligning their overlapping roles, and reducing uncertainty for other actors in the assemblage.

First, freelancers create momentary alignment in how they organise their everyday work. As I have outlined for *adapting to constant change*, there is a lot of fluctuation between phases of high and low activity for freelancers, and it is hard to predict what even their next workday will look like. When they come up with a structure for their days and weeks, they must account for these potential changes, trying to balance the time they invest and the chances of rewards. Moksh explains: "It looks easy, but it is really tough. At times, you don't have work for months to do. And at times you have work which you alone can't manage." (Interview with Moksh, 10-03-20). Freelancers' routines, in other words, must often be adapted and allow for spontaneous changes. On a small scale, this includes making sure to assemble different platform-mediated tasks: this is similar to other jobs, where part of the daily work often consists of prioritising tasks. However, the volatility of tasks exacerbates this challenge. Moreover, as platform workers connect to clients in different time zones, "temporal disjunctures" (Mankekar & Gupta, 2017) between local contexts and clients' business hours leave their schedules potentially spread across all hours of the day and night.

The friction becomes even more apparent when the focus shifts beyond just platform work: as I have demonstrated in Chapter 7, freelancers combine their work on the platform with various other responsibilities in their lives, such as different forms of paid work, or family and care responsibilities. The setup of these different elements varies between different freelancers – how central the role of their income from platform work is in this setup affects to what extent they face the challenge of adapting the rhythm of other responsibilities to the fluctuating rhythms of platform work. Their lives beyond the platform do not just pose challenges for alignment, but can also alleviate friction, for example when family members help freelancers out in phases of high activity. As freelancers flexibly adapt their rhythms to the moving elements of platform work, they continuously work on creating "fleeting moments of alignment" (Vertesi, 2014, p. 268). They temporarily align not just technologies but also different responsibilities and relationships, as well as different time zones and spaces of work and non-work. Even if they find alignment, it is only temporary, and the constellation may disintegrate anytime. It is thus necessary to work on either keeping it up or finding new constellations. As their work is globally spread and divided into small chunks, creating alignment becomes more difficult and fragile for designers in this context.

Second, regarding the production of flexible selves in practices of assembling, *creating temporary alignment* includes dealing with the tension between different versions of themselves that the freelancers put forward in their different work relationships. As I have outlined in *producing relatable selves*, freelancers integrate what they expect different clients to want from them into how they carry themselves. As they frequently deal with different clients in parallel, they establish different strategies for presenting themselves and establishing and emotional connection. At the same time, both workplace and working hours blur into times and places outside of work. As they manage these different relationships, freelancers also produce various images or selves in parallel. This can produce friction when they face different expectations. When freelancers combine local projects with remote work, for example, they switch between different expectations of their service and different temporalities; at the same time, while they usually earn more via online platforms than they do locally, they sometimes find themselves confronted with ideas that delineate them as 'cheap labour' in the global system of platform work. Continuously assembling their different tasks, then, also leaves them continuously assembling their subjectivities.

Third, while freelancers continuously work on creating moments of alignment for themselves, they additionally work on alleviating uncertainty for their clients. The freelancers do so, for example, by adapting to their clients' business hours, or by explicating their thought process and thus reducing opacity for their clients. They are simultaneously expected to be very flexible and gain trust by being fast in their reactions and dependable in their predictions. *Creating temporary alignment*, then, also extends to producing stability for others. Freelancers are required to make the tough job of aligning their different responsibilities look easy. This points to the distinct positions in the global assemblage of platform work: while the connections are loose for everyone, freelancers also work on making the experience smooth for other actors.

To sum up, to understand freelancers' practices and experiences in the assemblage of platform work, it is important to also relate them to further elements of their lives. Practices of assembling, then, also include coordinating constellations and continuously adapting and re-arranging relationships. Coordinating different elements of life is not a challenge reserved for platform workers – the feminist perspective on studies of work that I am taking on in this thesis uses the multitude of interdependent responsibilities as a basic premise. However, the volatility and unpredictability of gig work, in connection with the spread of work across different time zones and the home as a predominant place of work, make the work of creating alignment a constant need. At the same time, especially designers who do not depend on their income from platform work can adapt the rhythm of gig work to their needs, moving gigs around flexibly to fit their schedules. Below, I connect the practices of assembling back to the features of a platform-mediated work environment.

8.3 Work in a volatile, complex, and opaque environment

The observations on remote freelance work in this thesis hold insights for the broader context of studying platform work: practices of assembling reflect the volatility, opacity, and complexity of the platform-mediated work environment. In this context of uncertainty, platform workers continuously work on trying to predict outcomes, adapting to constant change, presenting themselves in various ways and creating momentary alignment between different elements of their lives. While uncertainty is part of most work settings in some way, I argue that the mediation by online platforms, the organisation of work as gigs, and the global spread of work relationships, all contribute to making uncertainty especially prevalent in gig work. This study has shown that workers find strategies to deal with this uncertainty, but also that this has an emotional impact on them and requires continuous effort. Relating practices of assembling back to the wider context of the global assemblage of platform work, the uncertainty in this work context is not simply a feature of digital work but also resembles platform workers' vulnerable position. Their uncertainty is connected to not being in control or, in the image of the assemblage, a limited capacity to assemble. In many situations, the platform workers are the ones being chosen and not the ones choosing, and they bear most of the risks and uncertainty. For most freelancers, being flexible is something that they must do rather than have the freedom to do. Flexibility rather entails adaptability than freedom to them, as they are required to react to constantly changing situations. What is more, freelancers also carry the burden of reducing uncertainty for others in the assemblage.

Rather than a simple transaction of selling their time to someone else, work in this context entails continuous negotiations. Thus, framing work as making and sustaining connections goes beyond adding unpaid practices to the equation – it entails calling into question the equation itself. The negotiations that I have described involve trying to anticipate the value of one's work, both in specific situations and as it is anticipated to evolve. Moreover, freelancers do not simply put in time and get out money: they grapple with their work relations on an emotional level, both by managing their own and others' emotions. In this process, workers' subjectivities are dynamically negotiated. What is more, the relations in question have more than two sides: Platforms commensurate value and structure the terms for negotiation. In addition, workers draw on support from others, so that the time that they put in is interwoven with the need to make and sustain connections with others beyond their paid work, as well as others' efforts to make and sustain connections with them. While these practices reflect the characteristics of a platform-mediated work environment, they also provide clues for how the concept of work should be adapted to changing work constellations. In the final chapter, I will point out how this perspective can contribute to closing the gaps that I have proposed at the beginning of this study.

9. Conclusion

The purpose of this study was to explore and theorise remote gig workers' everyday work practices of making and sustaining global connections mediated by online platforms. Starting from the observation that online platforms are transforming the world of work, leading to a complex, volatile, and dynamic work environment, I have argued that novel work practices are emerging that existing concepts of work cannot fully grasp. To address this, I have focused on everyday practices by freelance designers based in India, who connect to overseas clients via online platforms, guided by the central research question of the study: *how can platform work be conceptualised through the lens of making and sustaining connections?* I established at the beginning of the study that the category of work is socially constructed and thus also depends on power relations. Based on this premise, I explored a range of practices directed at navigating the platform-mediated work environment to build up a notion of work as practices of assembling. With online observations, in-depth semi-structured interviews, and digital photo diaries, I iteratively compiled elements of a global assemblage of platform work and related them to each other. From this kaleidoscope of practices, I distilled four characteristic features of practices of assembling: guessing and anticipating, adapting to constant change, producing relatable selves, and creating temporary alignment. These features reflect how freelancers interact with the platform-mediated work environment by continuously negotiating uncertain relations.

In this chapter, I first outline the contributions to the literature. Second, I reflect on the significance of the study beyond the specific field of research in which it is embedded. I conclude by pointing out some limitations and unfinished thoughts, as well as potential directions for further research.

9.1 Main contributions

Overall, this study responds to the call to bring together anthropological approaches to work cultures and digitalisation in everyday life by exploring how digital media are incorporated into and shape work practices (cf. Eckhardt et al., 2020, p. 3). I aim to contribute to debates on the transformation of work in digitally mediated environments from a feminist perspective, expanding the notion of work to incorporate relationships and their various dimensions. Constructing the field of research as a global assemblage (Collier & Ong, 2005), I have focused especially on unpaid practices of navigating the uncertainty of the platform-mediated work environment. Against this backdrop, I will outline the main contributions of this thesis on a methodological, empirical, and conceptual level below.

First, I have combined different methods of gathering material, which have jointly served to carve out the interplay of online platforms and workers, contributing to "non-digital-centric approach[es] to the digital" (cf. Pink et al., 2016, p. 7) in the field of digital ethnography. The use of digital photo diaries has prompted research participants to reflect on the more subtle aspects of their working lives and to transcend preconceptions about what counts as work. In combination with semi-structured interviews, I have given space to research participants to share their reflections and interpretations. Moreover, presenting preliminary results in follow-up interviews supported the relational negotiations over meaning in the research process. By incorporating and making transparent the research process, as well as foregrounding ambiguities, I contribute to feminist methodologies that stress the situatedness of knowledge production (cf. Haraway, 2006). Overall, the combination of ethnographic methods put forward in this study elucidates the heterogeneity and ambiguities in workers' experiences.

Second, on an empirical level, I have contributed to knowledge on platform work by addressing some of the blind spots in the existing literature. I have added empirical insights on aspects of platform work that have received little scholarly attention so far, thereby expanding the range of different practices and experiences covered. By now, research on platform work has especially focused on location-based work, such as delivery riders, and microtasks, such as Amazon Mechanical Turk (cf. Oechslen, 2020). By focusing on remote freelancers performing complex tasks, I have carved out challenges that are specific to this field, such as standing out to clients and striving to make emotional connections via limited communication options. Moreover, so far, platform work has predominantly been studied through a Western lens, focusing on and generalising from workers located in Europe or the US. By exploring the work experiences of platform workers in India, I contribute to the emerging literature on platform work beyond the Global North (cf. e.g. Graham & Anwar, 2019; Qadri, 2021; Shevchuk et al., 2021; Wallis, 2021; Wood et al., 2019a). In terms of translocal work relations, I have found the connections to be more diverse and fluid than is often assumed, with platform workers switching roles and negotiating their positions according to different situations. Thus, I added insights on how freelance workers negotiate their roles between the narrative of a global labour market and being categorised as 'cheap labour', for example.

Furthermore, by foregrounding the unpaid work of navigating the uncertainty of platform work and the emotional toll that this takes, this study contributes to a more nuanced and complete picture of working conditions in the gig economy (cf. e.g. Ravenelle, 2019; Sutherland et al., 2020; Wood et al., 2019a). Based on freelancers' need to produce a sense of stability for clients while being required to flexibly adapt to constant change themselves, I have argued that freelancers are generally in a relatively vulnerable position. At the same time, I have shown that the volatility of gig work has diverse implications for different freelancers, depending on their support system and their further responsibilities. While some freelancers enjoy the flexibility of working at irregular hours or manage to arrange their work schedules according to their requirements, especially those who depend on their income from platform work must often try to adapt all other responsibilities to its fluctuating requirements. Through the notion of "capacity to assemble" (McFarlane, 2009, p. 567), power relations are reflected in a relational instead of an absolute way: freelancers' capacities to assemble are not static but negotiated with other actors in the assemblage, and they may differ depending on the specific situation. Thus, the study contributes to a more nuanced understanding of working conditions that goes beyond a dichotomy between stability and precarity.

Third, on a conceptual level, I have developed the framework of practices of assembling, that is, a relational understanding of work, bringing together assemblage theory and feminist critique of work. By doing so, this study departs from standard employment as a main reference and thus contributes to a broader understanding of work, including its anthropological dimensions. This framework can be put to use to better grasp the heterogeneous and ambivalent implications of a platform-mediated work environment and highly flexible work contexts more broadly. The image of assemblage reflects the volatility of gig work and the need to continuously work on a fleeting balance that comes with it.

Through the lens of negotiating connections, I contribute to the literature on agency and control in platform work (cf. e.g. Jarrahi et al., 2020; Rosenblat & Stark, 2016; Shapiro, 2018). This perspective on the dynamic negotiations of platform work contributes to transcending established categories. I find that as they negotiate relations with clients and platforms, freelance workers do have agency, on the one hand: they can choose between different platforms or leave platform work altogether, and their practices affect the larger relations of the assemblage. On the other hand, freelancers have little control over the outcomes of their decisions, as information is unequally distributed. I have proposed to study work as the continuous effort of making and sustaining connections. Workers' effort of making and sustaining connections extends to both human and nonhuman actors in the assemblage. Thus, the interaction between workers and the platforms that they use can be grasped as a dynamic process of negotiation, integrating platforms as both actors and mediators of connections.

Framing work as making and sustaining connections makes it possible to integrate multiple spatial imaginaries (cf. McFarlane, 2009, p. 566) and thus incorporate the translocal social relations of globalised work. The tension inherent in the global assemblage reflects the ambivalences of unevenly dispersed global work relationships. The study of freelancers based in India has shown that workers' location implies different things to different actors and their roles in specific situations. Their location is entangled with negotiations over the value of their work and the emotional connections that they form with clients. Thus, the perspective on platform work as a global assemblage can also contribute to debates on the globalisation of work (cf. e.g. Graham & Anwar, 2019). In addition to the entanglement of global and local scales, the assemblage perspective also reflects the entanglement of physical and virtual elements in workers' practices. By applying a perspective focused on the everyday practices of using digital media, I have aimed to transcend binary understandings of virtual or physical spaces as bounded entities.

Moreover, this framework foregrounds the interdependence of different dimensions of work. To grasp the scope of unpaid work done by gig workers to navigate the uncertain work environment of the platform, concepts of work are necessary that extend beyond the job descriptions on the platform, also taking relationships beyond paid work into account (cf. Jarrahi et al., 2020). Through the notion of making and sustaining connections, I have integrated paid and unpaid tasks into a shared framework. Thus, work is detached from economic productivity, making space for a more nuanced classification of what platform work entails. In doing so, I build on existing notions of invisible work or unpaid labour (cf. e.g. Star & Strauss, 1999; Terranova, 2000) and extend them with a notion of volatility and contingency to make them more compatible with platform workers' experiences. Throughout the thesis, I have described how practices of assembling are connected with and prepare the ground for practices of creating designs. Additionally, I have elucidated how workers are integrated into interdependent relationships of mutual care and responsibility. This focus contributes to feminist perspectives that seek to bring to light the interconnectedness of paid and unpaid work, responding to the need to embed economic actors within relationships beyond paid work by including care in studies on precarious working conditions (cf. Ivancheva & Keating, 2020).

To sum up, this study aims to contribute a conceptual framework grounded in practices of making and sustaining connections to grasp the heterogeneous and ambivalent implications of a platform-mediated work environment. Its focus on relational practices allows for an exploration of platform work beyond a dichotomy between flexibility and stability, incorporating affective relationships within and beyond platform work, entangled physical and virtual elements of practices, as well as multiple spatial scales. The empirical insights gained in this study reflect this framework by outlining characteristic practices of assembling in the context of platform work. Below, I will reflect on how the results of this study can inform research and practice beyond the specific focus on remote platform work.

9.2 Significance and implications

While the continuous work of making and sustaining connections as I have described it in this study reflects the volatility of platform work, the conceptual framework that I have used can inform the study of work cultures more broadly. As work is becoming increasingly flexible, with entrepreneurial and project-based elements in a wide range of professions, the framework of practices of assembling points beyond the context of platform-mediated work. Understanding work through a relational and practice-based lens can help to better grasp the affective elements of work: it is not only platform workers who continuously make and sustain connections, but this is also part of teachers', carpenters', or office clerks' jobs, for example. As the assemblage framework includes human as well as nonhuman actors, technological or other tools can be included in analyses. Teachers may connect to students, parents, and co-workers, for instance, by sharing the space of the classroom or using video calling software. Differently from platform workers, they may have more fixed routines and be able to establish more stable connections, so the rhythms of their work are possibly more regular. With a focus on making and sustaining connections, important aspects of the teaching job, such as establishing a community in the classroom and making students feel safe to speak up, could be explored, for example. What is more, the assemblage perspective can integrate interdependent relationships beyond the classroom, such as more experienced teachers mentoring new colleagues or teachers with care responsibilities aligning grading papers with their own children's sleeping schedule. Thus, this framework can provide insights in a broad range of fields, bridging analytical gaps between paid and unpaid work, and foregrounding the embeddedness of workers in interdependent relationships.

Moreover, by amplifying stories of everyday work experiences in the gig economy, I have elucidated unpaid and largely invisible aspects of gig work. Beyond the realm of academic research, this can contribute to the articulation of demands for fair working conditions. On an empirical level, my observations have supported the argument that platform work usually comes with a lot of unpaid extra work. Additionally, I have shown that there is an imbalance between workers and clients in terms of uncertainty, with workers usually being more vulnerable and less protected by the conditions set up by online platforms. These insights into remote freelancers' everyday work can be used by gig workers, workers' initiatives and unions, platform operators, as well as policy makers seeking to adjust regulatory frameworks to changing work environments. On a more general level, I also hope that understanding the everyday negotiations of gig workers' lives may "begin a longer conversation about the better workplaces we might imagine for the future" (Gregg, 2011, p. 18). Taking this idea of continuing the conversation as a starting point, I will reflect on some issues that this study has left open and new questions that it has raised in the final subchapter and point to how future research may contribute to answering them.

9.3 Limitations and directions for further research

First, as I have pointed out in Chapter 4, how I have constructed the field by relating to different actors has necessarily produced a partial account. I have not aimed to generate all-encompassing universal knowledge but situated engagement with the knowledge shared by research participants (cf. Haraway, 2006). Perspectives by other researchers, thus, could add to the account by forming different relations – both with research participants and analytically. Moreover, while I have touched upon the role of power in the assemblage of platform work, further studies could delve deeper into how social categories of difference are negotiated in the everyday practices of platform workers and thus develop the material and relational qualities of race, gender, or sexuality further in this context (cf. Kinkaid, 2020, p. 460).

Second, the larger context of the assemblage of platform work could be elaborated more by adding further entry points. The empirical case of graphic designers based in India has pointed to specific practices of assembling, which could be complemented by in-depth studies of further local contexts and fields of platform work. Moreover, different actors in the assemblage, such as platforms or clients, could be the focus of further studies. What is more, while I have traced translocal work connections based on research participants' accounts, these connections could also be followed further, thus incorporating further situated accounts. These expansions could add more layers of interdependence between actors and between different dimensions of work. I have shown how practices of creating designs depend on practices of assembling, and how designers depend on their families, for example. Building on this, further studies could elucidate interdependent relationships in the larger context of the assemblage: This could include elaborating how gig workers' practices of assembling prepare the ground for the platform economy on a larger scale, as well as adding the role of the data that they provide in the process, for example.

Third, while I have expanded the notion of work to unpaid practices, I still focused my analyses on unpaid practices that are directly connected to and support paid work. However, "life's work" (Mitchell et al., 2004) encompasses a much wider range of practices: eating, sleeping, or taking a shower could all be integrated there. This restriction was partly due to the limited possibilities for participating in research participants' everyday lives. Thus, I could only catch glimpses of how the practices that I observed were integrated into a larger context. The range of interdependent relationships that

I have subsumed under the category 'beyond platform work' could be differentiated and elaborated more by future studies, building on more extensive participant observation, for example. The approach of understanding work as an assemblage thus provides various loose threads for future studies to take up and make further connections.

List of Figures

Figure 1 Arnav's daughter 142
Figure 2 Krishnam's workspace 148

Works Cited

Agrawal, Ajay, Nicola Lacetera, and Elizabeth Lyons (2016). Does standardized information in online markets disproportionately benefit job applicants from less developed countries? *Journal of International Economics*, 103, 1–12.
Altenried, Moritz (2017). Die Plattform als Fabrik. *PROKLA. Zeitschrift für kritische Sozialwissenschaft*, 47, 175–92.
Altenried, Moritz (2021a). Mobile workers, contingent labour: Migration, the gig economy and the multiplication of labour. *Environment and Planning A: Economy and Space*, online first.
Altenried, Moritz (2021b). Was ist eine Plattform?: Politische Ökonomie und Arbeit im Plattformkapitalismus. In Moritz Altenried, Julia Dück and Mira Wallis (eds.). *Plattformkapitalismus und die Krise der sozialen Reproduktion*, 50–69. Münster: Westfälisches Dampfboot.
Altenried, Moritz (2022). *The digital factory: The human labor of automation*. Chicago: University of Chicago Press.
Altenried, Moritz, Manuela Bojadžijev, and Mira Wallis (2020). Körper, Daten, Arbeitskraft – Ein Gespräch zu Migration und Arbeit unter digitalen Bedingungen. In Dennis Eckhardt, Sarah May, Martina Röthl and Roman Tischberger (eds.). *Digitale Arbeitskulturen: Rahmungen, Effekte, Herausforderungen*, 43–53. Berlin: Humboldt-Universität zu Berlin.
Amrute, Sareeta B. (2016). *Encoding race, encoding class: Indian IT workers in Berlin*. Durham, NC: Duke University Press.
Anderson, Ben, Matthew Kearnes, Colin McFarlane, and Dan Swanton (2012). On assemblages and geography. *Dialogues in Human Geography*, 2, 171–89.
Aneesh, Aneesh (2006). *Virtual migration: The programming of globalization*. Durham, NC: Duke University Press.
Aneesh, Aneesh (2009). Global labor: Algocratic modes of organization. *Sociological Theory*, 27, 347–70.
Aneesh, Aneesh (2015). *Neutral accent: How language, labor, and life become global*. Durham, NC: Duke University Press.

Anwar, Mohammad A., and Mark Graham (2021). Between a rock and a hard place: Freedom, flexibility, precarity and vulnerability in the gig economy in Africa. *Competition & Change*, 25, 237–58.

Ardévol, Elisenda, and Edgar Gómez-Cruz (2014). Digital ethnography and media practices. In Fabienne Darling-Wolf (ed.). *The international encyclopedia of media studies: Research methods in media studies*, 1–21. Malden, MA/Oxford/Chichester: Wiley Blackwell.

Arendt, Hannah (1969). *The human condition*. Chicago: The University of Chicago Press.

Ash, James, Ben Anderson, Rachel Gordon, and Paul Langley (2018). Digital interface design and power: Friction, threshold, transition. *Environment and Planning D: Society and Space*, 36, 1136–1153.

Barratt, Tom, Caleb Goods, and Alex Veen (2020). 'I'm my own boss...': Active intermediation and 'entrepreneurial' worker agency in the Australian gig-economy. *Environment and Planning A: Economy and Space*, 52, 1643–61.

Beerepoot, Niels, and Bart Lambregts (2015). Competition in online job marketplaces: Towards a global labour market for outsourcing services? *Global Networks*, 15, 236–55.

Buchanan, Ian (2021). *Assemblage theory and method*. London: Bloomsbury Academic.

Bucher, Eliane, and Christian Fieseler (2017). The flow of digital labor. *New Media & Society*, 19, 1868–86.

Cameron, Jenny, and J. K. Gibson-Graham (2003). Feminising the economy: Metaphors, strategies, politics. *Gender, Place & Culture*, 10, 145–57.

Cant, Callum (2020). *Riding for Deliveroo: Resistance in the new economy*. Cambridge, UK/Medford, MA: Polity Press.

Casilli, Antonio (2017). Digital labor studies go global: Toward a digital decolonial turn. *International Journal of Communication*, 11, 3934–54.

Caza, Brianna B., Erin M. Reid, Susan J. Ashford, and Steve Granger (2022). Working on my own: Measuring the challenges of gig work. *Human Relations*, 75, 2122–59.

Chan, Ngai K. (2019). "Becoming an expert in driving for Uber": Uber driver/bloggers' performance of expertise and self-presentation on YouTube. *New Media & Society*, 21, 2048–67.

Cirucci, Angela M. (2017). Normative interfaces: Affordances, gender, and race in Facebook. *Social Media + Society*, 3, 1–10.

Clark, Marianne (2021). Signs, beaches and bodies in pandemic times. *Media International Australia*, 178, 8–15.

Clifford, James, and George E. Marcus (eds.). (1984). *Writing culture: The poetics and politics of ethnography*. Berkeley/Los Angeles/London: University of California Press.

Collier, Stephen J. (2016). Global assemblages. *Theory, Culture & Society*, 23, 399–401.

Collier, Stephen J., and Aihwa Ong (2005). Global assemblages, anthropological problems. In Aihwa Ong and Stephen J. Collier (eds.). *Global assemblages: Technology, politics, and ethics as anthropological problems*, 3–21. Malden, MA: Blackwell Publishing.

Cooper, Adam, Sharlene Swartz, and Molemo Ramphalile (2021). Youth of the global south and why they are worth studying. In Sharlene Swartz, Adam Cooper, Clarence M. Batan and Laura Kropff (eds.). *The Oxford handbook of global south youth studies*, 32–54. New York: Oxford University Press.

D'Cruz, Premilla, and Ernesto Noronha (2016). Positives outweighing negatives: The experiences of Indian crowdsourced workers. *Work Organisation, Labour & Globalisation*, 10, 44–63.

DeLanda, Manuel (2016). *Assemblage theory*. Edinburgh: Edinburgh University Press.

Deleuze, Gilles, and Félix Guattari (1993). *A thousand plateaus: Capitalism and schizophrenia*. Minneapolis: University of Minnesota Press.

Demirel, Pelin, Ekaterina Nemkova, and Rebecca Taylor (2021). Reproducing global inequalities in the online labour market: Valuing capital in the design field. *Work, Employment and Society*, 35, 914–930.

Dunn, Michael (2020). Making gigs work: Digital platforms, job quality and worker motivations. *New Technology, Work and Employment*, 35, 232–49.

Eckhardt, Dennis, Sarah May, Martina Röthl, and Roman Tischberger (2020). Digitale Arbeitskulturen: Transformation erforschen. In Dennis Eckhardt, Sarah May, Martina Röthl and Roman Tischberger (eds.). *Digitale Arbeitskulturen: Rahmungen, Effekte, Herausforderungen*, 3–15. Berlin: Humboldt-Universität zu Berlin.

Ettlinger, Nancy (2017). Paradoxes, problems and potentialities of online work platforms. *Work Organisation, Labour & Globalisation*, 11, 21–38.

Ettlinger, Nancy (2018). Algorithmic affordances for productive resistance. *Big Data & Society*, 5, 1–13.

Faust, Friederike (2019). *Fußball und Feminismus: Eine Ethnografie geschlechterpolitischer Interventionen*. Opladen/Berlin/Toronto: Budrich UniPress.

Federici, Silvia (1975). *Wages against housework*. Montpelier: Falling Wall Press.

Feher, Michel (2009). Self-Appreciation; or, the aspirations of human capital. *Public Culture*, 21, 21–41.

Flisfeder, Matthew (2015). The entrepreneurial subject and the objectivization of the self in social media. *South Atlantic Quarterly*, 114, 553–70.

Friedman, Gerald (2014). Workers without employers: Shadow corporations and the rise of the gig economy. *Review of Keynesian Economics*, 2, 171–88.

Gandini, Alessandro (2019). Labour process theory and the gig economy. *Human Relations*, 72, 1039–56.

Gandini, Alessandro, and Ivana Pais (2020). Reputation and personal branding in the platform economy. In Stephanie Taylor and Susan Luckman (eds.). *Pathways into creative working lives*, 231–48. Cham, Switzerland: Palgrave Macmillan.

Gandini, Alessandro, Ivana Pais, and Davide Beraldo (2016). Reputation and trust on online labour markets: The reputation economy of Elance. *Work Organisation, Labour & Globalisation*, 10, 27–43.

Gerber, Christine, and Martin Krzywdzinski (2019). Entgrenzung in der digitalen Onlinearbeit am Beispiel von Crowdwork. In Hans Hanau and Wenzel Matiaske (eds.). *Entgrenzung von Arbeitsverhältnissen*, 25–47. Baden-Baden: Nomos Verlagsgesellschaft.

Girard, Monique, and David Stark (2005). Heterarchies of value: Distributing intelligence and organizing diversity in a new media startup. In Aihwa Ong and Stephen J. Collier (eds.). *Global assemblages: Technology, politics, and ethics as anthropological problems*, 293–319. Malden, MA: Blackwell Publishing.

Goods, Caleb, Alex Veen, and Tom Barratt (2019). "Is your gig any good?" Analysing job quality in the Australian platform-based food-delivery sector. *Journal of Industrial Relations*, 61, 502–27.

Graham, Mark, and Mohammad A. Anwar (2019). The global gig economy: Towards a planetary labour market? *First Monday*, 24.

Graham, Mark, Isis Hjorth, and Vili Lehdonvirta (2017a). Digital labour and development: Impacts of global digital labour platforms and the gig economy on worker livelihoods. *Transfer: European Review of Labour and Research*, 23, 135–62.

Graham, Mark, Vili Lehdonvirta, Alex Wood, Helena Barnard, Isis Hjorth, and David P. Simon (2017b). *The risks and rewards of online gig work at the global margins*. Oxford: Oxford Internet Institute.

Gray, Mary L., and Siddharth Suri (2019). *Ghost work: How to stop Silicon Valley from building a new global underclass*. Boston/New York: Houghton Mifflin Harcourt.

Gregg, Melissa (2011). *Work's intimacy*. Cambridge, UK: Polity Press.

Griesbach, Kathleen, Adam Reich, Luke Elliott-Negri, and Ruth Milkman (2019). Algorithmic control in platform food delivery work. *Socius: Sociological Research for a Dynamic World*, 5, 1–15.

Haraway, Donna (1988). Situated knowledges: The science question in feminism and the privilege of partial perspective. *Feminist Studies*, 14, 575–99.

Haraway, Donna (2006). A cyborg manifesto: Science, technology, and socialist-feminism in the late 20th century. In Joel Weiss, Jeremy Hunsinger, Jason Nolan and Peter Trifonas (eds.). *The international handbook of virtual learning environments*, 117–58. Dordrecht: Springer.

Hardt, Michael (1999). Affective labor. *boundary 2*, 26, 89–100.

Hardt, Michael, and Antonio Negri (2000). *Empire*. Cambridge, MA: Harvard University Press.

Haug, Frigga (2008). *Die Vier-in-einem-Perspektive: Politik von Frauen für eine neue Linke*. Hamburg: Argument.

Hearn, Alison (2010). Structuring feeling: Web 2.0, online ranking and rating, and the digital 'reputation' economy. *ephemera*, 10, 421–38.

Heiland, Heiner (2021). Controlling space, controlling labour?: Contested space in food delivery gig work. *New Technology, Work and Employment*, 36, 1–16.

Hess, Sabine, and Maria Schwertl (2013). Vom "Feld" zur "Assemblage"?: Perspektiven europäisch-ethnologischer Methodenentwicklung – eine Hinleitung. In Sabine Hess, Johannes Moser and Maria Schwertl (eds.). *Europäisch-ethnologisches Forschen: Neue Methoden und Konzepte*, 13–37. Berlin: Reimer.

Hine, Christine (2015). *Ethnography for the internet: Embedded, embodied and everyday*. London/Oxford/New York/New Delhi/Sydney: Bloomsbury.

Hjorth, Larissa, and Ingrid Richardson (2020). *Ambient play*. Cambridge, MA/London: The MIT Press.

Hochschild, Arlie R. (1979). Emotion work, feeling rules, and social structure. *The American Journal of Sociology*, 85, 551–75.

Hochschild, Arlie R. ([1983] 2012). *The managed heart: Commercialization of human feeling*. Berkeley: University of California Press.

Howcroft, Debra, and Birgitta Bergvall-Kåreborn (2019). A typology of crowdwork platforms. *Work, Employment and Society*, 33, 21–38.

Huber, Birgit (2013). *Arbeiten in der Kreativindustrie: Eine multilokale Ethnografie der Entgrenzung von Arbeits- und Lebenswelt*. Frankfurt am Main: Campus Verlag.

Huws, Ursula (2016). Logged labour: A new paradigm of work organisation? *Work Organisation, Labour & Globalisation*, 10, 7–26.

Ibert, Oliver, Anna Oechslen, Alica Repenning, and Suntje Schmidt (2022). Platform ecology: A user-centric and relational conceptualization of online platforms. *Global Networks*, 22, 564–79

Ibert, Oliver, and Suntje Schmidt (2014). Once you are in you might need to get out: Adaptation and adaptability in volatile labor markets-the case of musical actors. *Social Sciences*, 3, 1–23.

Illich, Ivan (1981). Shadow work. *Social Alternatives*, 2, 37–47.

ILO (2016). Non-standard employment around the world. Geneva: International Labour Organization.

ILO (2021). World employment and social outlook. Geneva.

Irani, Lilly (2013). The cultural work of microwork. *New Media & Society*, 17, 720–39.

Irani, Lilly (2015). Difference and dependence among digital workers: The case of Amazon mechanical turk. *South Atlantic Quarterly*, 114, 225–34.

Ivancheva, Mariya, and Kathryn Keating (2020). Revisiting precarity, with care: Productive and reproductive labour in the era of flexible capitalism. *ephemera*, 20, 251–82.

Jarrahi, Mohammad H., Will Sutherland, Sarah B. Nelson, and Steve Sawyer (2020). Platformic management, boundary resources for gig work, and worker autonomy. *Computer Supported Cooperative Work*, 29, 153–89.

Jørgensen, Kristian M. (2016). The media go-along: Researching mobilities with media at hand. *MedieKultur: Journal of media and communication research*, 60, 32–49.

Joyce, Simon (2020). Rediscovering the cash nexus, again: Subsumption and the labour-capital relation in platform work. *Capital & Class*, 44, 541–52.

Kalleberg, Arne L. (2018). *Precarious lives: Job insecurity and well-being in rich democracies*. Cambridge, UK/Medford, MA: Polity Press.

Kalleberg, Arne L., and Steven P. Vallas (2018). Probing precarious work: Theory, research, and politics. In Arne L. Kalleberg and Steven P. Vallas (eds.). *Precarious work: Causes, characteristics, and consequences*, 1–30. Bingley: Emerald.

Katz, Cindi (2001). Vagabond capitalism and the necessity of social reproduction. *Antipode*, 33, 709–28.

Kenney, Martin, and John Zysman (2016). The rise of the platform economy. *Issues in Science and Technology*, Spring 2016, 61–69.

Kinkaid, Eden (2020). Can assemblage think difference? A feminist critique of assemblage geographies. *Progress in Human Geography*, 44. 457–72.

Knecht, Michi (2013). Nach Writing Culture, mit Actor-Network: Ethnografie/Praxeografie in der Wissenschafts-, Medizin- und Technikforschung. In Sabine Hess, Johannes

Moser and Maria Schwertl (eds.). *Europäisch-ethnologisches Forschen: Neue Methoden und Konzepte*, 79–106. Berlin: Reimer.

Koch, Gertraud (2013). Feeling rules: Unfound treasures for the study of work cultures. In Gertraud Koch and Stefanie E. Buchanan (eds.). *Pathways to empathy: New studies on commodification, emotional labor, and time binds*, 123–40. Frankfurt am Main: Campus Verlag.

Koch, Gertraud, and Stefanie E. Buchanan (2013). Introduction: Getting There: From impediments to pathways to empathy. In Gertraud Koch and Stefanie E. Buchanan (eds.). *Pathways to empathy: New studies on commodification, emotional labor, and time binds*, 9–15. Frankfurt am Main: Campus Verlag.

Kolko, Beth E., Lisa Nakamura, and Gilbert B. Rodman (eds.). (2000). *Race in cyberspace*. New York: Routledge.

Krohn, Judith (2013). *Subjektivierung in einer Bundesbehörde: Verwaltungsmodernisierung am Beispiel des Bundesministeriums für Arbeit und Soziales*. Frankfurt am Main: Campus Verlag.

Krzywdzinski, Martin, and Christine Gerber (2021). Between automation and gamification: Forms of labour control on crowdwork platforms. *Work in the Global Economy*, 1, 161–84.

Kuehn, Kathleen, and Thomas F. Corrigan (2013). Hope labor: The role of employment prospects in online social production. *The Political Economy of Communication*, 1, 9–25.

Langley, Paul, and Andrew Leyshon (2017). Platform capitalism: The intermediation and capitalization of digital economic circulation. *Finance and Society*, 3, 11–31.

Latour, Bruno (2008). *Reassembling the social: An introduction to actor-network-theory*. Oxford: Oxford University Press.

Lazzarato, Maurizio (1996). Immaterial labor. In Paolo Virno and Michael Hardt (eds.). *Radical thought in Italy: A potential politics*. Minneapolis: University of Minnesota Press.

Lehdonvirta, Vili (2018). Flexibility in the gig economy: Managing time on three online piecework platforms. *New Technology Work and Employment*, 33, 13–29.

Li, Tania M. (2007). Practices of assemblage and community forest management. *Economy and Society*, 36, 263–93.

Light, Ben, Jean Burgess, and Stefanie Duguay (2017). The walkthrough method: An approach to the study of apps. *New Media & Society*, 20, 881–900.

Mackenzie, Suzann, and Damaris Rose (1983). Industrial change, the domestic economy and home life. In James Anderson, Simon Duncan and Raymond Hudson (eds.). *Redundant spaces in cities and regions?: Studies in industrial decline and social change*, 157–76. London: Academic Press.

Mankekar, Purnima, and Akhil Gupta (2016). Intimate encounters: Affective labor in call centers. *positions*, 24, 17–43.

Mankekar, Purnima, and Akhil Gupta (2017). Future tense: Capital, labor, and technology in a service industry. *HAU: Journal of Ethnographic Theory*, 7, 67–87.

Mankekar, Purnima, and Akhil Gupta (2019). The missed period. *American Ethnologist*, 46, 417–28.

Marcus, George E. (1995). Ethnography in/of the world system: The emergence of multi-sited ethnography. *Annual Review of Anthropology*, 24, 95–117.

Marcus, George E., and Erkan Saka (2006). Assemblage. *Theory, Culture & Society*, 23, 101–06.

Massey, Doreen B. (1994). *Space, place, and gender*. Minneapolis: University of Minnesota Press.

Massey, Doreen B. (1995). *Spatial divisions of labour: Social structures and the geography of production*. Basingstoke: Macmillan.

Matamoros-Fernández, Ariadna (2017). Platformed racism: The mediation and circulation of an Australian race-based controversy on Twitter, Facebook and YouTube. *Information, Communication & Society*, 20, 930–46.

McDowell, Linda (1992). Doing gender: Feminism, feminists and research methods in human geography. *Transactions of the Institute of British Geographers*, 17, 399–416.

McFarlane, Colin (2009). Translocal assemblages: Space, power and social movements. *Geoforum*, 40, 561–67.

Mitchell, Katharyne, Sallie A. Marston, and Cindi Katz (2004). *Life's work*. Oxford: Blackwell.

Moore, Phoebe V. (2018). *The quantified self in precarity: Work, technology and what counts*. London/New York: Routledge.

Myhill, Katie, James Richards, and Kate Sang (2021). Job quality, fair work and gig work: The lived experience of gig workers. *The International Journal of Human Resource Management*, 32, 4110–35.

Nadeem, Shehzad (2009). The uses and abuses of time: Globalization and time arbitrage in India's outsourcing industries. *Global Networks*, 9, 20–40.

Nakamura, Lisa (2012). *Race after the internet*. New York: Routledge.

Neilson, Brett, and Ned Rossiter (2008). Precarity as a political concept, or, Fordism as exception. *Theory, Culture & Society*, 25, 51–72.

Noble, Safiya U., and Brendesha M. Tynes (eds.). (2016). *The intersectional internet: Race, sex, class, and culture online*. New York: Peter Lang Publishing.

Oechslen, Anna (2020). Grenzenlose Arbeit?: Eine Exploration der Arbeitskulturen von Crowdwork. In Dennis Eckhardt, Sarah May, Martina Röthl and Roman Tischberger (eds.), *Digitale Arbeitskulturen: Rahmungen, Effekte, Herausforderungen*, 83–94. Berlin: Humboldt-Universität zu Berlin.

Oksala, Johanna (2016). Affective labor and feminist politics. *Signs: Journal of Women in Culture and Society*, 41, 281–303.

Ong, Aihwa, and Stephen J. Collier (eds.). (2005). *Global assemblages: Technology, politics, and ethics as anthropological problems*. Malden, MA: Blackwell Publishing.

Ortner, Sherry B. (1996). *Making gender: The politics and erotics of culture*. Boston: Beacon Press.

Ouma, Stefan (2015). *Assembling export markets: The making and unmaking of global food connections in West Africa*. Oxford: Wiley Blackwell.

Petriglieri, Gianpiero, Susan J. Ashford, and Amy Wrzesniewski (2018). Agony and ecstasy in the gig economy: Cultivating holding environments for precarious and personalized work identities. *Administrative Science Quarterly*, 14, 124–170.

Pink, Sarah, Heather A. Horst, John Postill, Larissa Hjorth, Tania Lewis, and Jo Tacchi (2016). *Digital ethnography: Principles and practice*. Los Angeles/London/New Delhi/Singapore/Washington, DC: SAGE.

Prassl, Jeremias (2018). *Humans as a service: The promise and perils of work in the gig economy*. Oxford: Oxford University Press.

Qadri, Rida (2021). Platform workers as infrastructures of global technologies. *Interactions*, 28, 32–35.

Ravenelle, Alexandrea J. (2019). *Hustle and gig: Struggling and surviving in the sharing economy*. Oakland, CA: University of California Press.

Repenning, Alica (2022). Workspaces of mediation: How digital platforms shape practices, spaces and places of creative work. *Tijdschrift voor economische en sociale geografie*, 113, 211–224.

Rest, Jonas (2016, May 20). "Viele ernähren mit ihrer Arbeit ihre Familie". *Frankfurter Rundschau*. https://www.fr.de/wirtschaft/viele-ernaehren-ihrer-arbeit-ihre-familie-11122619.html, accessed on 08/07/2018

Richardson, Lizzie (2017). Feminist geographies of digital work. *Progress in Human Geography*, 42, 244–63.

Robertson, Jennifer (2002). Reflexivity redux: A pithy polemic on "positionality". *Anthropological Quarterly*, 75, 785–92.

Rochet, Jean-Charles, and Jean Tirole (2003). Platform competition in two-sided markets. *Journal of the European Economic Association*, 1, 990–1029.

Rose, Gillian (1997). Situating knowledges: Positionality, reflexivities and other tactics. *Progress in Human Geography*, 21, 305–20.

Rosenblat, Alex, and Luke Stark (2016). Algorithmic labor and information asymmetries: A case study of Uber's drivers. *International Journal of Communication*, 10, 3758–84.

Ruyter, Alex de, and Martyn D. Brown (2019). *The gig economy*. Newcastle upon Tyne: Agenda Publishing.

Schneider, Daniel, and Kristen Harknett (2019). Consequences of routine work-schedule instability for worker health and well-being. *American sociological review*, 84, 82–114.

Scholz, Trebor (2017). *Uberworked and underpaid: How workers are disrupting the digital economy*. Cambridge, UK/Malden, MA: Polity Press.

Schor, Juliet B., William Attwood-Charles, Mehmet Cansoy, Isak Ladegaard, and Robert Wengronowitz (2020). Dependence and precarity in the platform economy. *Theory and Society*, 833–61.

Shapiro, Aaron (2018). Between autonomy and control: Strategies of arbitrage in the "on-demand" economy. *New Media & Society*, 20, 2954–71.

Shevchuk, Andrey, Denis Strebkov, and Alexey Tyulyupo (2021). Always on across time zones: Invisible schedules in the online gig economy. *New Technology, Work and Employment*, 36, 94–113.

Srnicek, Nick (2017). *Platform capitalism*. Cambridge, UK/Malden, MA: Polity Press.

Star, Susan L. (1999). The ethnography of infrastructure. *American Behavioral Scientist*, 43, 377–91.

Star, Susan L., and Anselm L. Strauss (1999). Layers of silence, arenas of voice: The ecology of visible and invisible work. *Computer Supported Cooperative Work*, 8, 9–30.

Strauss, Anselm L. (1985). Work and the division of labor. *The Sociological Quarterly*, 26, 1–19.

Strauss, Anselm L., and Juliet M. Corbin (2003). *Basics of qualitative research: Techniques and procedures for developing grounded theory*. Thousand Oaks: SAGE.

Sultana, Farhana (2007). Reflexivity, positionality and participatory ethics: Negotiating fieldwork dilemmas in international research. *Acme*, 6, 374–85.

Sutherland, Will, Mohammad H. Jarrahi, Michael Dunn, and Sarah B. Nelson (2020). Work precarity and Gig Literacies in online freelancing. *Work, Employment and Society*, 34, 457–75.

Tassinari, Arianna, and Vincenzo Maccarrone (2020). Riders on the storm: Workplace solidarity among gig economy couriers in Italy and the UK. *Work, Employment and Society*, 34, 35–54.

Terranova, Tiziana (2000). Free labor: Producing culture for the digital economy. *Social Text*, 18, 33–58.

Ticona, Julia, Alexandra Mateescu, and Alex Rosenblat (2018). Beyond disruption. 02.03.2022 https://datasociety.net/output/.

Upadhya, Carol (2016). *Reengineering India*. Oxford: Oxford University Press.

Vailas, Steven, and Juliet B. Schor (2020). What do platforms do?: Understanding the gig economy. *Annual Review of Sociology*, 46, 273–94.

van Dijck, José (2013). *The culture of connectivity: A critical history of social media*. New York: Oxford University Press.

van Dijck, José, Thomas Poell, and Martijn d. Waal (2018). *The platform society: Public values in a connective world*. New York: Oxford University Press.

van Doorn, Niels (2014). The neoliberal subject of value: Measuring human capital in information economies. *Cultural Politics*, 10, 354–75.

van Doorn, Niels (2017). Platform labor: On the gendered and racialized exploitation of low-income service work in the 'on-demand' economy. *Information, Communication & Society*, 20, 898–914.

van Doorn, Niels, and Darsana Vijay (2021). Gig work as migrant work: The platformization of migration infrastructure. *Environment and Planning A: Economy and Space*, online first.

Veen, Alex, Tom Barratt, and Caleb Goods (2020). Platform-capital's 'app-etite' for control: A labour process analysis of food-delivery work in Australia. *Work, Employment and Society*, 34, 388–406.

Vertesi, Janet (2014). Seamful spaces: Heterogeneous infrastructures in interaction. *Science, Technology, & Human Values*, 39, 264–84.

Voß, G. Günter (1998). Die Entgrenzung von Arbeit und Arbeitskraft. *Mitteilungen aus der Arbeitsmarkt- und Berufsforschung*, 31, 473–87.

Wallis, Mira (2021). Digital labour and social reproduction: Crowdwork in Germany and Romania. *spheres – Journal for Digital Cultures*, 1–14.

Waring, Marilyn ([1988] 2016). *Counting for nothing: What men value and what women are worth*. Toronto/Buffalo: University of Toronto Press.

Warren, Tracey (2021). Work–life balance and gig work: 'Where are we now' and 'where to next' with the work-life balance agenda? *Journal of Industrial Relations*, 63, 522–45.

Weeks, Kathi (2007). Life within and against work: Affective labor, feminist critique, and post-fordist politics. *ephemera*, 7, 233–49.

Wells, Katie J., Kafui Attoh, and Declan Cullen (2021). "Just-in-place" labor: Driver organizing in the Uber workplace. *Environment and Planning A: Economy and Space*, 53, 315–31.

Wittel, Andreas (2004). Culture, labour and subjectivity: For a political economy from below. *Capital & Class*, 28, 11–30.

Wittel, Andreas (2017). The political economy of digital technologies: Outlining an emerging field of research. In Gertraud Koch (ed.). *Digitisation: Theories and concepts for empirical cultural research*, pp. 251–273. Abingdon, Oxon/New York: Routledge.

Wood, Alex J. (2018). Powerful times: Flexible discipline and schedule gifts at work. *Work, Employment and Society*, 32, 1061–77.

Wood, Alex J., Mark Graham, Vili Lehdonvirta, and Isis Hjorth (2019a). Good gig, bad gig: Autonomy and algorithmic control in the global gig economy. *Work, Employment and Society*, 15, 56–75.

Wood, Alex J., Mark Graham, Vili Lehdonvirta, and Isis Hjorth (2019b). Networked but commodified: The (dis)embeddedness of digital labour in the gig economy. *Sociology*, 53, 931–50.

Wood, Alex J., and Vili Lehdonvirta (2021a). Antagonism beyond employment: How the 'subordinated agency' of labour platforms generates conflict in the remote gig economy. *Socio-Economic Review*.

Wood, Alex J., and Vili Lehdonvirta (2021b). Platform precarity: Surviving algorithmic insecurity in the gig economy. *SSRN Electronic Journal*.

Woodcock, Jamie, and Mark Graham (2020). *The gig economy: A critical introduction*. Cambridge, UK/Medford, MA: Polity Press.

Zimmerman, Don H., and D. L. Wieder (1977). The diary: Diary-interview method. *Urban Life*, 5, 479–98.

Zwick, Austin (2018). Welcome to the gig economy: Neoliberal industrial relations and the case of Uber. *GeoJournal*, 83, 679–91.

Acknowledgements

This book deals with interdependent relationships, and it could not have been written without the dense web of support spun by those around me in many different forms. I wish to express my gratitude to the many people who have accompanied and supported me in various ways over the past years.

I would like to especially thank Gertraud Koch and Oliver Ibert for supervising my thesis with great openness and reassurance, for sharing their feedback, and for encouraging me when I needed it.

Furthermore, I would like to thank the designers who have participated in this study for their time, openness, and willingness to reflect on and share their stories with me. Without them, this project would not have been possible. In addition, Carol Upadhya at the National Institute for Advanced Studies in Bengaluru has helped me tremendously in preparing and kicking off my field stay there by sharing her knowledge and networks with me.

Moreover, I am deeply grateful to my colleagues at the Leibniz Institute for Research on Society and Space in Erkner for their constructive feedback and stimulating conversations. Sharing ideas with my project team in the research department and beyond has been both helpful and inspiring. Especially Jana Kleibert, Gala Nettelbladt, Alica Repenning, Suntje Schmidt, Marc Schulze, and Sune Stoustrup have helped me greatly in taking this thesis from early drafts to the state that it is in now with their insightful and constructive feedback.

At the University of Hamburg, I was lucky to be part of another kind, encouraging, and inspiring group of PhD candidates. I have benefited greatly from the feedback and the fruitful exchange during our colloquia, and many ideas in this thesis have emerged from or taken shape through discussions in the studio on digitalisation and mediatisation with Ann Christin Bakhos, Lina Franken, Samantha Lutz, and Angeliki Tzouganatou.

Finally, my heartfelt thanks to my friends and family for being there for me throughout the ups and downs of writing this thesis, for listening to my ideas and frustrations, encouraging me and cheering me on, for food, spell-checks, and all the other moments of support and community, big and small.